IMAGES *of America*

LEDYARD AND GALES FERRY

IMAGES
of America

LEDYARD AND GALES FERRY

Kit Foster
for the Ledyard Historical Society

ARCADIA
PUBLISHING

ISBN 978-0-7385-3559-3

Published by Arcadia Publishing
Charleston, South Carolina

Printed in the United States of America

Library of Congress Catalog Card Number: 2004101334

For all general information, contact Arcadia Publishing:
Telephone 843-853-2070
Fax 843-853-0044
E-mail sales@arcadiapublishing.com
For customer service and orders:
Toll-Free 1-888-313-2665

Visit us on the Internet at www.arcadiapublishing.com

On the cover: The railroad came to Gales Ferry in 1899, when the Norwich and Worcester line to Allyn's Point was extended south to Groton. Building a railroad was dirty, backbreaking work, so these gandy dancers enjoyed a brief respite to pose for the camera.

Contents

ACKNOWLEDGMENTS

The author is grateful for the help of Janice Wightman Bell, Ledyard's town historian, and Sheila Anyan Godino for assisting with the research for this volume. The assistance of Nancy Downie, archivist at Our Lady of Lourdes Parish, is also appreciated. Unless otherwise credited, all photographs are from the collections of the Ledyard Historical Society.

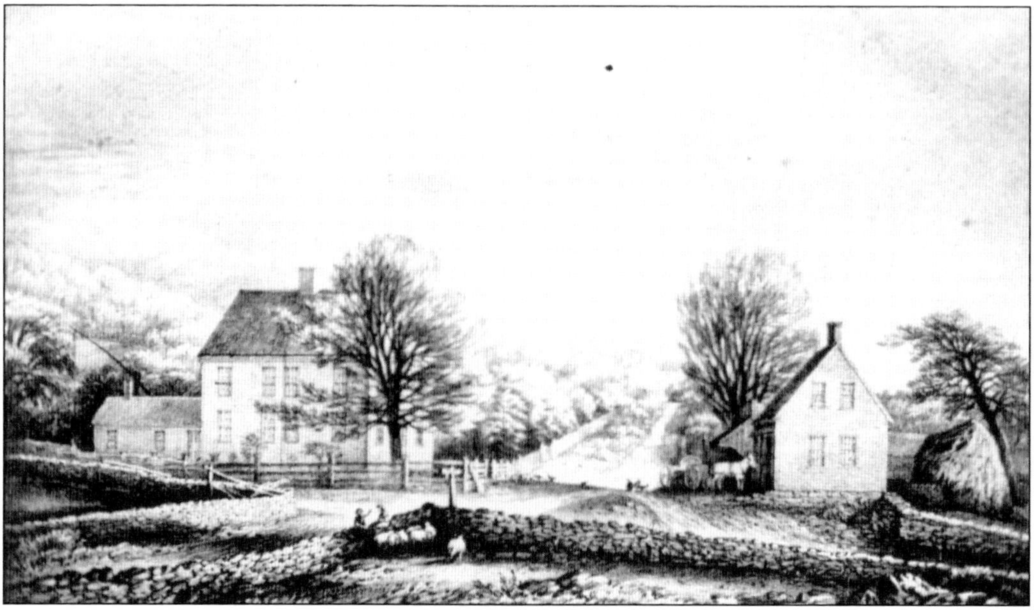

The earliest settlement in Ledyard was at "the Crossroads," where the Mohegan Trail (right to left) met the Preston–New London Road (into the distance). To the left in this early illustration is the Bill Homestead, and to the right is the Bill Store.

INTRODUCTION

Ledyard takes its name from Col. William Ledyard, commander of Colonial forces defending Fort Griswold in the American Revolution. On September 6, 1781, Ledyard commanded a brigade of 150 men protecting Fort Griswold in Groton Heights, overlooking New London Harbor. New London lay under siege by a British force led by Benedict Arnold, the American general who had defected to the enemy cause. A native of nearby Norwich, Arnold knew the area well and quickly overcame local resistance and burned the town. On the Groton side, Ledyard's men fought bravely but were overwhelmed by an advancing British force of 800. Ledyard ordered his men to lay down their arms. Local accounts hold that Ledyard offered his sword in surrender and was summarily run through with it. In any case, when the fighting ceased, more than half the defenders lay dead, and a majority of the survivors were severely wounded.

The name Ledyard has been linked to the southeastern Connecticut area since John Ledyard settled in Groton c. 1720. He and his wife, the former Deborah Youngs, had 10 children there. John and Youngs, the two oldest boys, became sea captains, and Nathaniel, the seventh child, a doctor. But it was William, sixth child and fourth son, whom fate chose to immortalize as local hero and inspiration for a town.

Until 1836, the present town of Ledyard was part of Groton, its neighbor to the south. A North or Second Ecclesiastical Society was established in Groton in 1725, in answer to the petition of 36 residents who claimed "extreme difficulties" in attending church because of their distance from the meetinghouse. A meetinghouse was constructed at the geographic center of this new territory, and in 1729, a "settled minister" was ordained. A community developed in the region of the meetinghouse that would, in time, be known as Ledyard Center.

Around the same time, settlements were forming some five miles to the west, along the banks of the Thames River. A trading post was established at Allyn's Point, site of the present Dow Chemical plant. In 1740, Ralph Stoddard and John Hurlbut established a ferry across the river, and around its terminus developed a village. Gales Ferry, as the village became known, took its name from Roger Gale, one of the ferry keepers. With its waterfront location, Gales Ferry was a transportation portal to the wider world and often attracted residents of a seafaring nature.

The division of 1836 was the culmination of a series of separatist sentiments extending back to 1813, when Ralph Hurlbutt petitioned for independence of the Second Society. Opposition was overwhelming at that time; in 1834, when the matter was considered again, sentiment was still negative but more narrowly so. At an October meeting that same year, by a vote of 123 to 93, the residents approved a petition for separation, which was accepted by the Connecticut General Assembly. "An Act to Incorporate the Town of Ledyard" was voted by the assembly on June 1, 1836, and 10 days later, the citizens of the new town met to elect their officials.

Addressing a need for a central place, the town meeting of 1844 voted to have all such assemblies in the basement under the meetinghouse, the Ecclesiastical Society having provided room when the group built a new church the previous year. For more than 100 years, the meetings were held there, until the construction of a consolidated school in 1949 provided a larger assembly room. In the early days, town meetings were all-day affairs, with a traditional sale of oysters at noon. Town government, in the traditional New England fashion, was headed by a board of selectmen until the adoption of a charter in 1971, which provided for an elected mayor and a nine-member town council.

The railroad reached Ledyard in 1844, when a line was extended south from Norwich to Allyn's Point. A coaling station for steamboats was established there, and it became a landing point, enabling boat passengers to debark for swifter completion of their journeys by rail. At the beginning of the 20th century, rail service came to Gales Ferry, as the rail line was extended to join existing tracks of the New York, New Haven and Hartford Railroad at Groton.

Commerce in early Ledyard consisted of shops and tradespeople in the villages. As transportation became easier and more convenient due to improved roads and the increasing availability of the automobile, village shops were less important, and in the early 20th century, both Ledyard Center and Gales Ferry lost some of their vitality as hubs of trade. Rapid population growth in Ledyard and the entire southeastern Connecticut region during the 1960s reversed this trend, but at a cost of some suburban sprawl along the major highways.

Industry was slow to come to Ledyard, arriving only in the 1950s, when Dow Chemical constructed a manufacturing facility at Allyn's Point. The site selection was, no doubt, based on the same factors that made Allyn's Point important a century earlier: the confluence of river, road, and rail access. Enlarged several times in the last half-century, the Dow plant remains Ledyard's sole major industry. A northern portion of the naval submarine base lies within the town's borders but, since it consists mainly of residences and a golf course, is not strictly industrial. The base, long a fixture in the region, arose from beginnings as a coaling station for naval ships in the 19th century.

In the early 21st century, Ledyard and Gales Ferry form a mature suburban community of nearly 15,000 people in a region undergoing social and economic transition. Long dominated by a defense industry concerned with building and operating submarines, the area is now home to two resort casinos, one of which, Foxwoods, is located in the northeast corner of the town of Ledyard. The ways in which this new leisure and service industry shapes the development of the town will become the next century's history.

One

The Crossroads

When the North Parish, later to become the town of Ledyard, was set off from Groton in 1725, its geographic center was selected as the site for a meetinghouse. Construction of a building began in 1727, but it was well into the 19th century before a village developed around it. More important to an agrarian economy was transportation, and the residential and commercial center of the 18th century arose at the intersection of the Mohegan Trail (now part of Colonel Ledyard Highway and Spicer Hill Road), with a road leading from New London to Preston (now Church Hill Road and a southerly portion of Colonel Ledyard Highway).

At this intersection were constructed nine houses, two stores, a tannery, and several shops, all between 1730 and 1800. The Crossroads also hosted a schoolhouse and, unusual for a Connecticut community, an Episcopal church. Eight of these buildings remain today.

The area of the Crossroads was home to some important people in American history, including Silas Dean (later Silas Deane), a member of the Continental Congress, and Samuel Seabury Jr., the first Episcopal bishop in America. Seabury, the son of a Congregational minister who converted to Anglicanism c. 1730, was educated at Yale and ordained in 1753. Following the American Revolution, it became impossible for the Episcopal Church, whose spiritual head was the king of England, to appoint bishops. Seabury, selected by his peers, traveled to Scotland to be consecrated by Scottish bishops, who did not recognize the authority of the monarchy.

Although it ceased to be a center of town activity by the mid-1800s, the Crossroads has retained the character of a small rural community. The old Bill Store stands at the northwest corner of Spicer Hill and Church Hill Roads, and directly opposite is the Bill Parsonage, built by John Smith c. 1792. Constructed on property owned by the Bill family intermittently since c. 1745, the house was given to the Congregational church by Henry Bill in 1874.

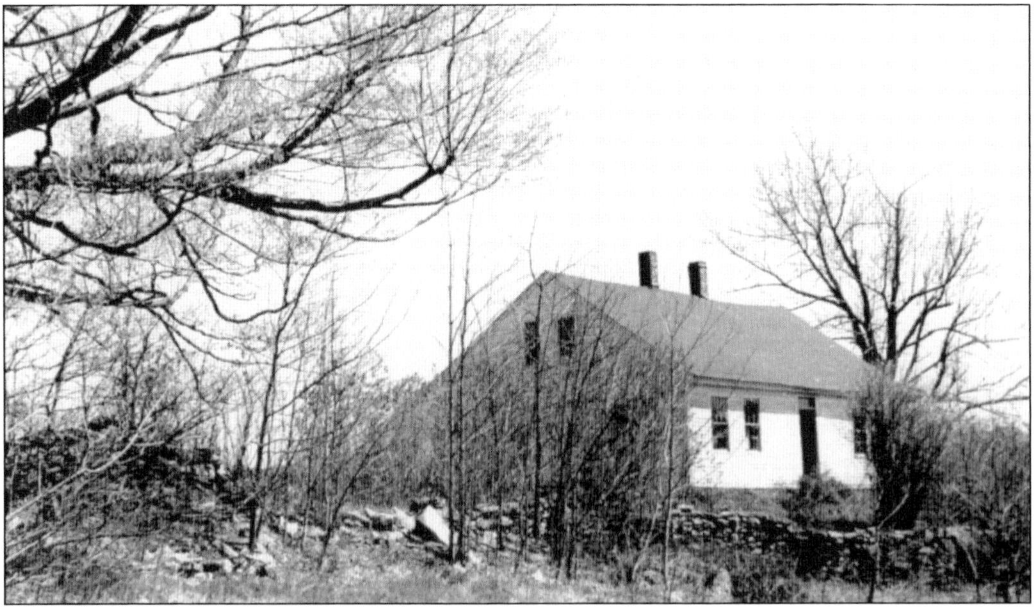

Nathaniel Brown of Norwich purchased land in 1722 and built this house on the Mohegan Trail, which the deed called the "Mistick Path," just north of the Crossroads. It is one of the eight remaining original buildings in the village. This photograph dates from 1948.

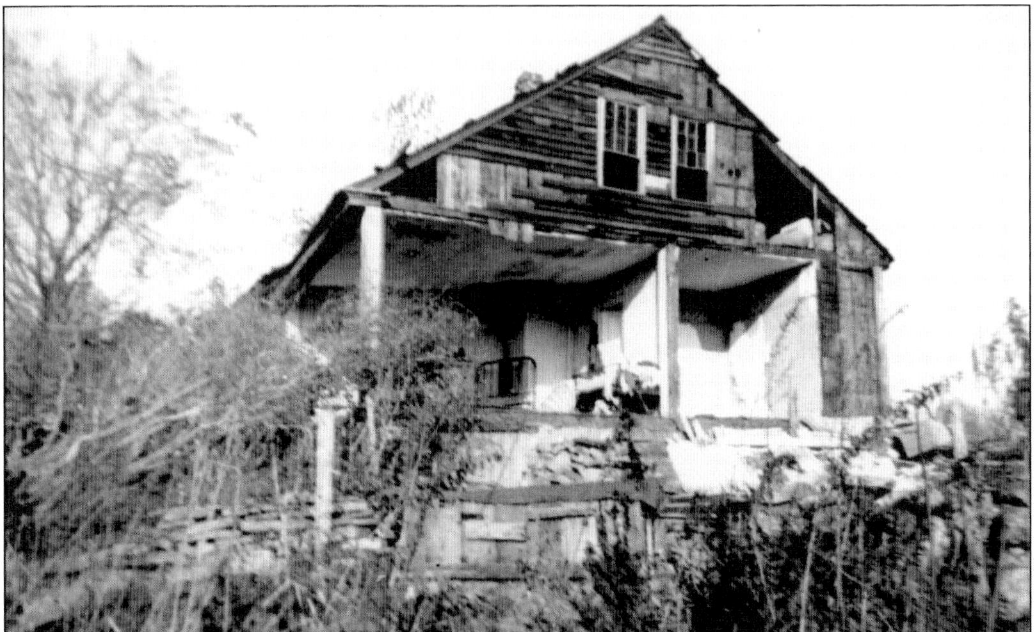

The Nathaniel Brown house was severely damaged in the hurricane of September 1938. Since repaired, it is now a residence fronting Colonel Ledyard Highway.

Israel Allyn (1822–1897) inherited the Nine Mile House from his father, Abel, in 1857. Active in town affairs, Israel served as a selectman, as a probate court judge, and as a representative to the Connecticut General Assembly.

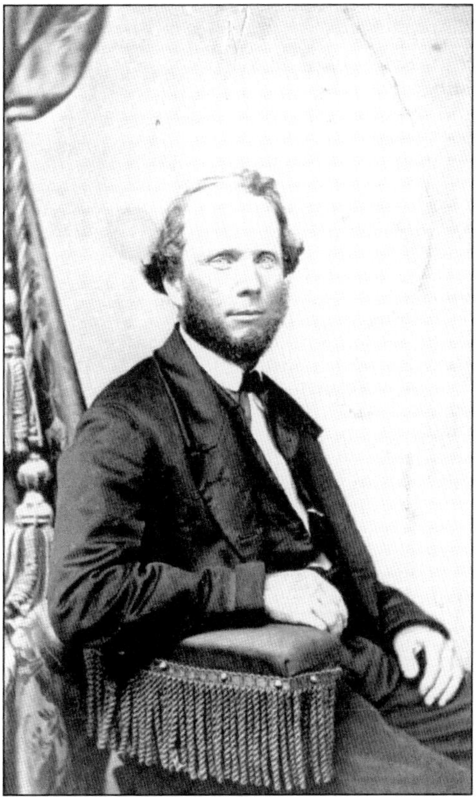

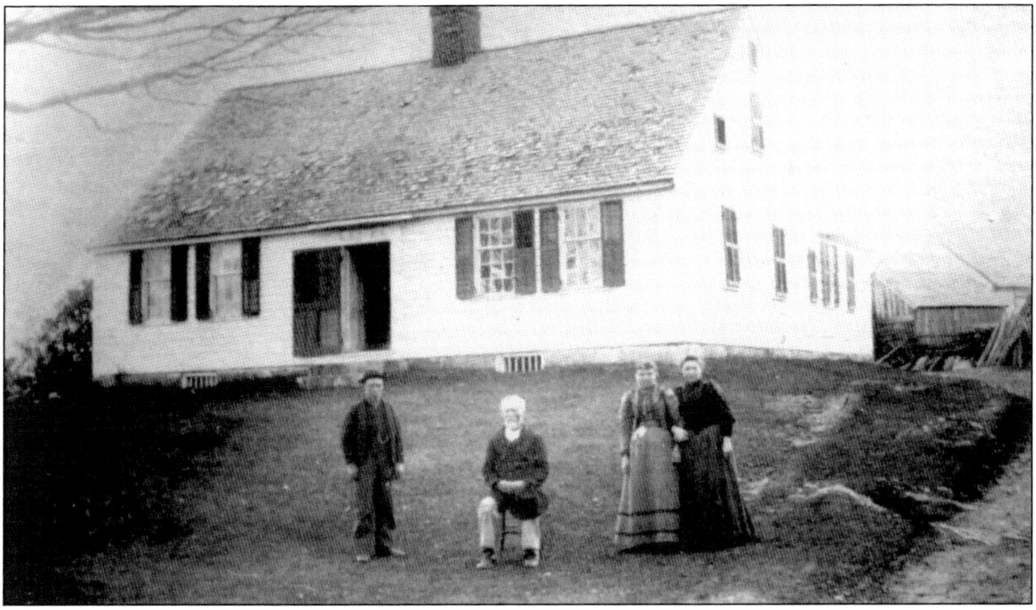

The Nine Mile House takes its colloquial name from the milestone behind which it stands. The stone's inscription reads, "9 MI to N L," which is believed to mean nine miles to Norwich Landing, although the stone has been transplanted to its current location. The house was built c. 1738 by John Wood Jr.

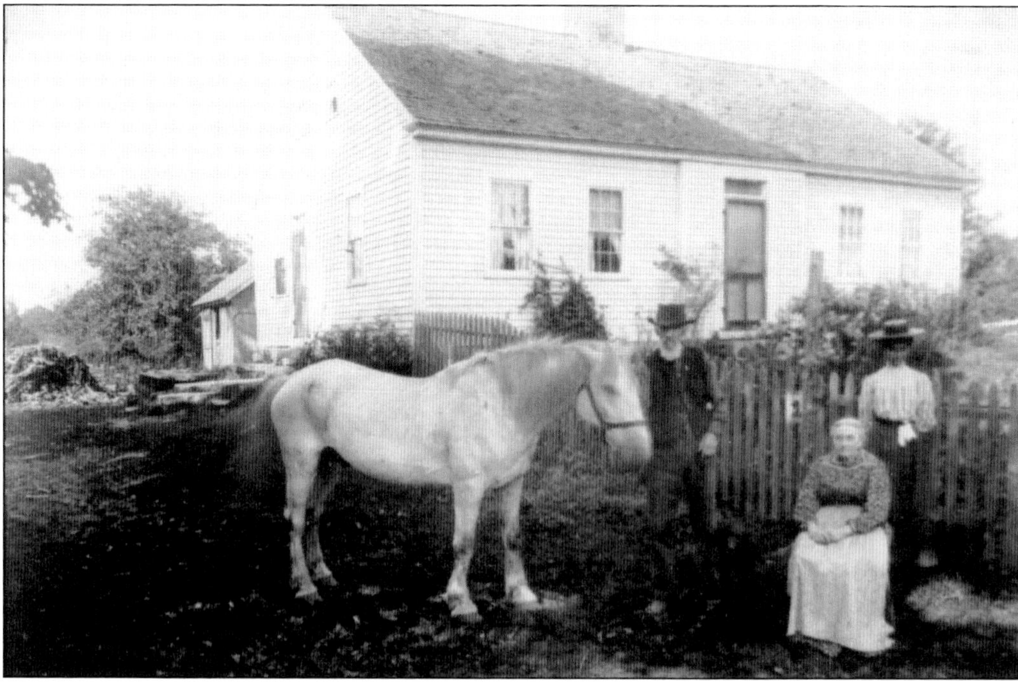

The Ebenezer Brown house stands on the present Spicer Hill Road just north of the Crossroads, slightly to the south of the Nathaniel Brown house. Built *c.* 1753, it was sold to James Allyn in 1796 and was eventually inherited by Allyn's granddaughter Mary Ann Caroline Hewitt. This photograph shows the Hewitts and their horse in front of the house, sometime before it passed out of the family in 1909.

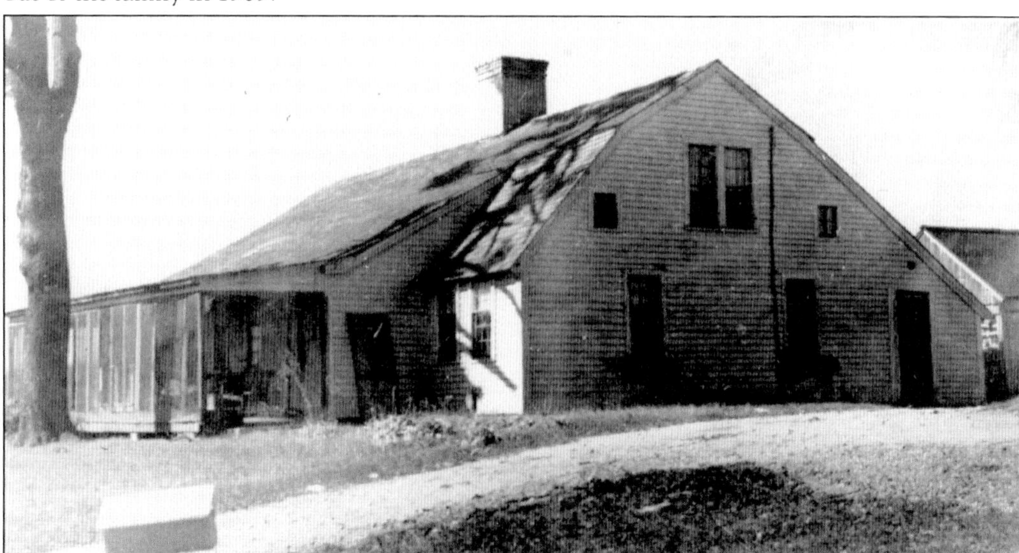

The Reynolds place dates from *c.* 1744, when it was built by Trustum Billing. It acquired the Reynolds name in 1840, when it was purchased by Henry Reynolds, and remained in the family for 76 years. This 1938 photograph shows porches and additions built over the years. Situated on the west side of the present Colonel Ledyard Highway, it was restored to its original configuration in the 1970s.

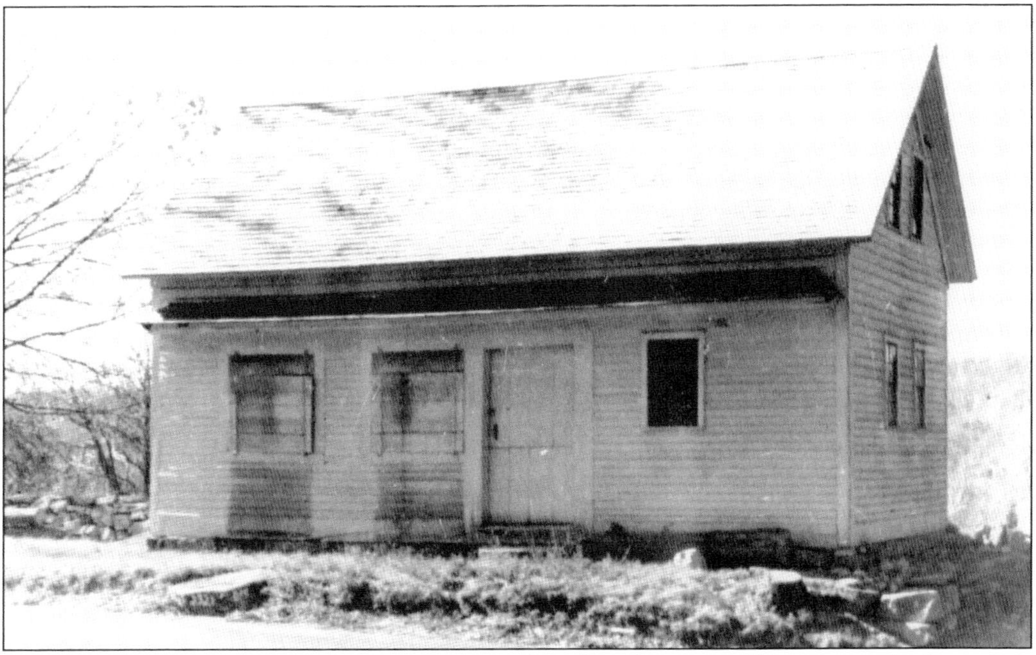

The Bill Store, on the northwest corner of Church Hill and Spicer Hill Roads, was built *c.* 1819. The record is unclear as to whether it was standing when the land was sold by Philip Gray to Gurdon Bill that year. Although there is no evidence that it ever served refreshment or provided lodging, it is sometimes called the Bill Tavern, and local tradition maintains that it was a way station for stagecoaches. This photograph dates from 1938.

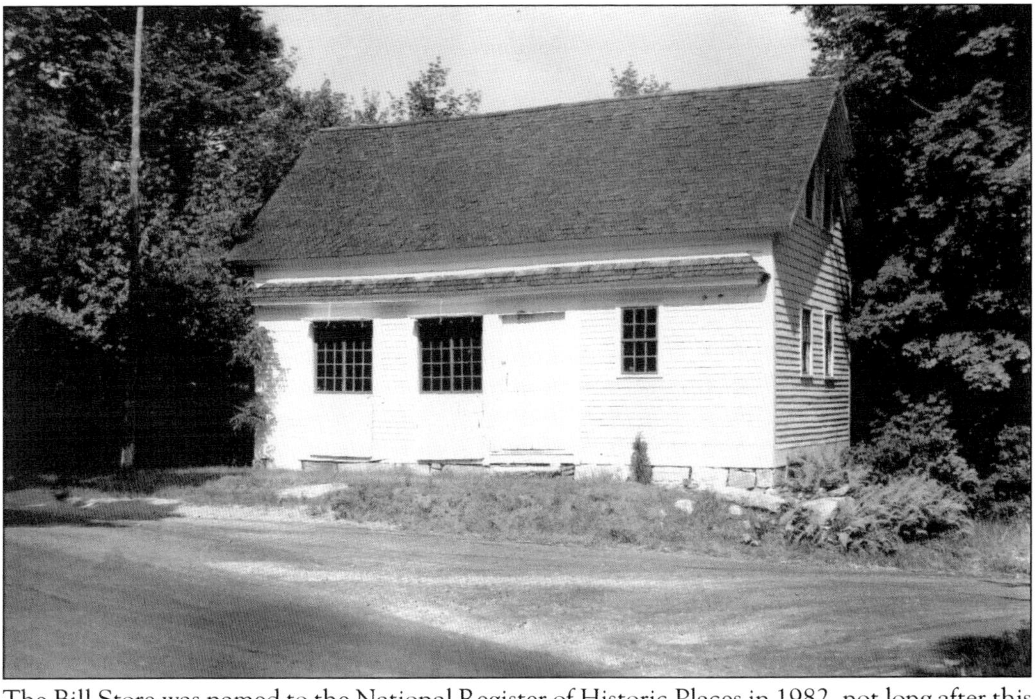

The Bill Store was named to the National Register of Historic Places in 1982, not long after this photograph was taken.

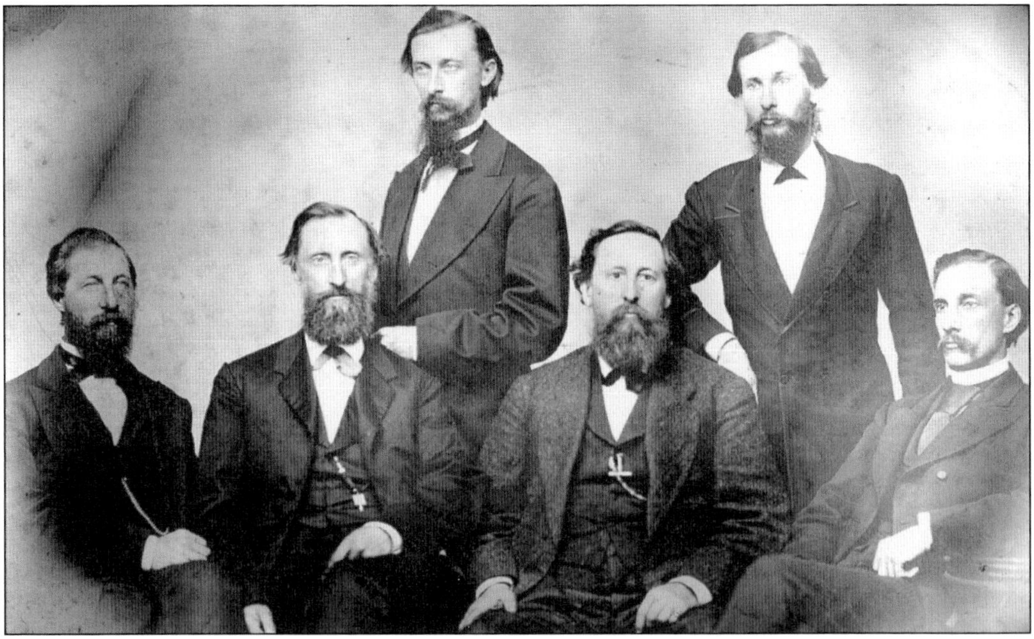

Six sons of Gurdon Bill (1784–1856) survived to adulthood. Pictured here are, from left to right, Frederic (1833–1865), Henry (1829–1891), Charles (1840–1897), Edward (1822–1867), Ledyard (1836–1867), and Gurdon Jr. (b. 1827). All but Edward were involved with their father's publishing business. Ledyard was the first-born child in the new town, which had separated that year from Groton.

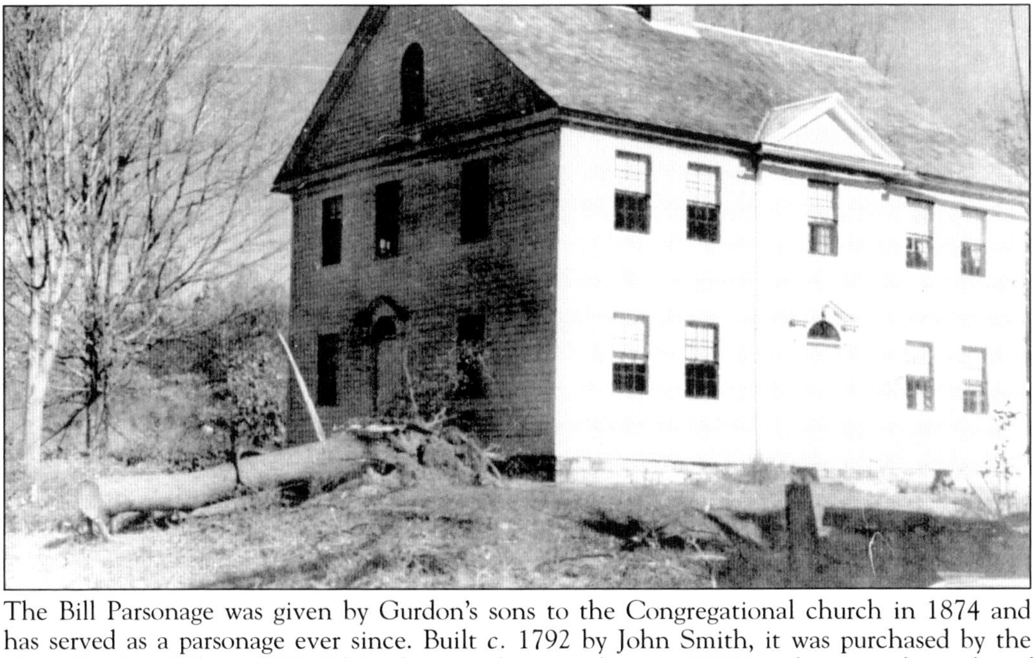

The Bill Parsonage was given by Gurdon's sons to the Congregational church in 1874 and has served as a parsonage ever since. Built c. 1792 by John Smith, it was purchased by the elder Gurdon Bill in 1819. This photograph was taken in 1938, perhaps in the wake of the September hurricane.

Gurdon Bill organized a Masonic lodge at his home in 1825, and it met there for 10 years. After his son Henry Bill endowed a library, a trustees' dinner was held following the annual meeting. For the first 26 years, the dinners were held on the second floor of the Bill Homestead.

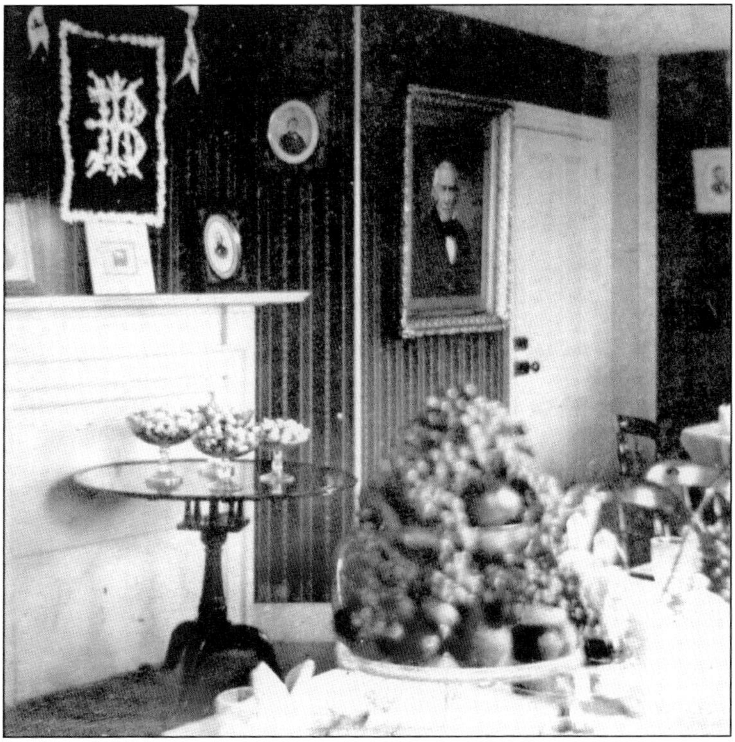

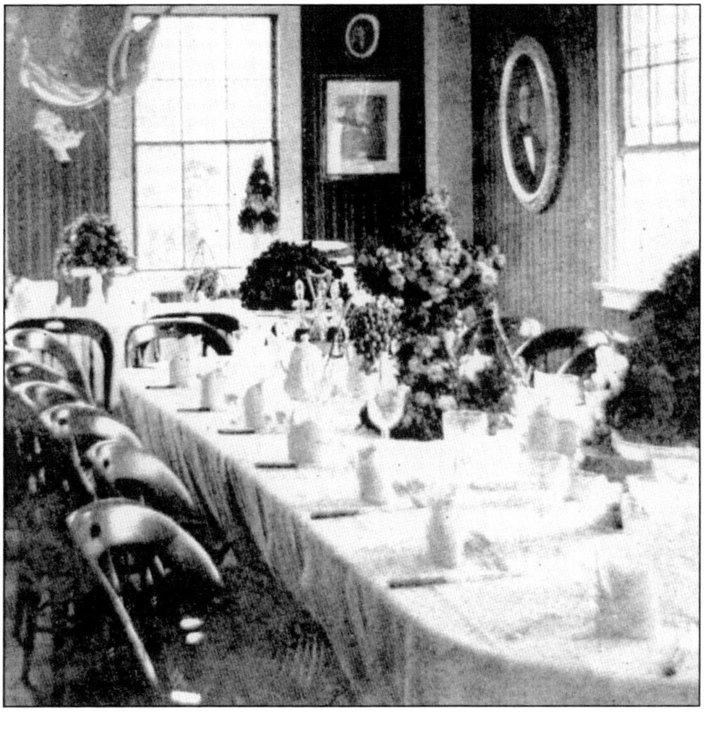

Elaborate affairs, the annual Bill Dinners were attended by the trustees and their wives. "The feast of fat things was sumptuous," reported a local newspaper. "Princely viands were served by young ladies of the parish."

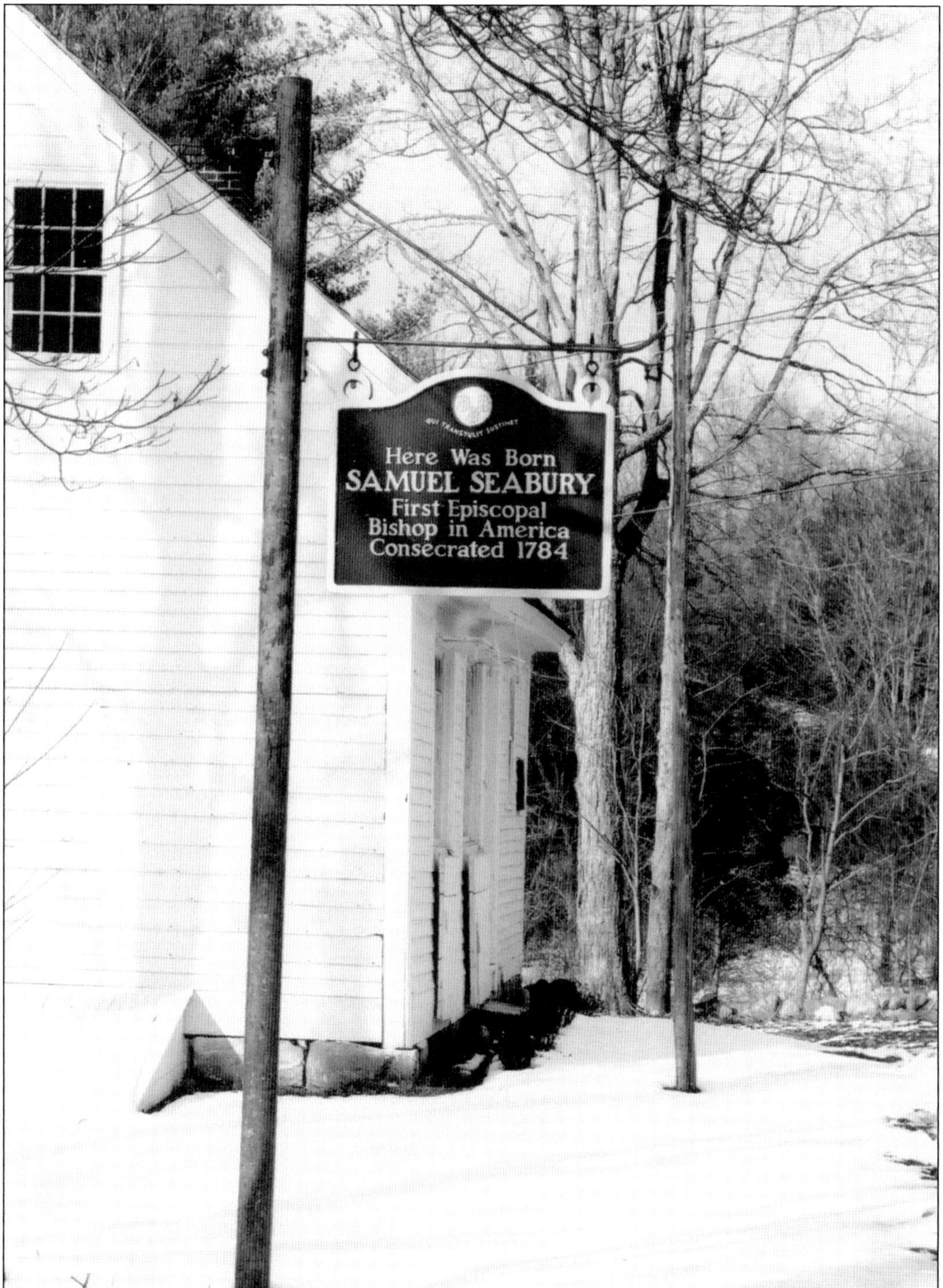

Samuel Seabury, the first Episcopal bishop in America, is remembered by a state historical marker next to the Bill Store identifying his birthplace. Seabury's birth at this site, however, has never been conclusively documented.

Two

THE CENTER

Transportation routes, no doubt, also influenced the development of land around the meetinghouse in the middle of the 19th century. By this time, the track from Stoddard's Wharf, on the Thames River north of Gales Ferry, was increasingly traveled. Soon the commercial center of the community, after its 1836 separation from Groton, moved from the Crossroads to what is now Ledyard Center. To natives it is often known simply as "the Center," for it is at the geographical center of the town.

The Center became not only the ecclesiastical and commercial focus, it was soon the governmental center as well. A notice board outside the meetinghouse kept the citizenry informed of meetings and local events, tax collections, and other important matters. A post office had existed in North Groton as early as 1828. On June 9, 1836, just nine days after the incorporation of the town of Ledyard, a post office was officially established. The early post offices were housed in stores, of which there were several from 1822 onwards. In 1876, according to *The Critic*, a Ledyard Center business directory, the village was home to a blacksmith, a printer, a cobbler, a carpenter, a wagon maker, a wheelwright, and a tavern.

Although it has been the center of town government since the incorporation of Ledyard in 1836, Ledyard Center did not have a town hall until the 1930s. Until that time, town meetings were held in the church, and town records were maintained by the town clerk in his home. The requisite municipal business was also done there. A modern administrative building, enlarged several times since, was built in 1956.

In fact, the Center was perhaps a more bustling place in the late 1800s than 50 years later. With improved roads and the coming of the automobile, local commerce became less imperative. In 1903, the Ledyard Center Post Office was closed, and mail delivery was instituted from Norwich. Although the Center has never lacked a store, specialty shops and tradespeople did not become commonplace until the 1950s.

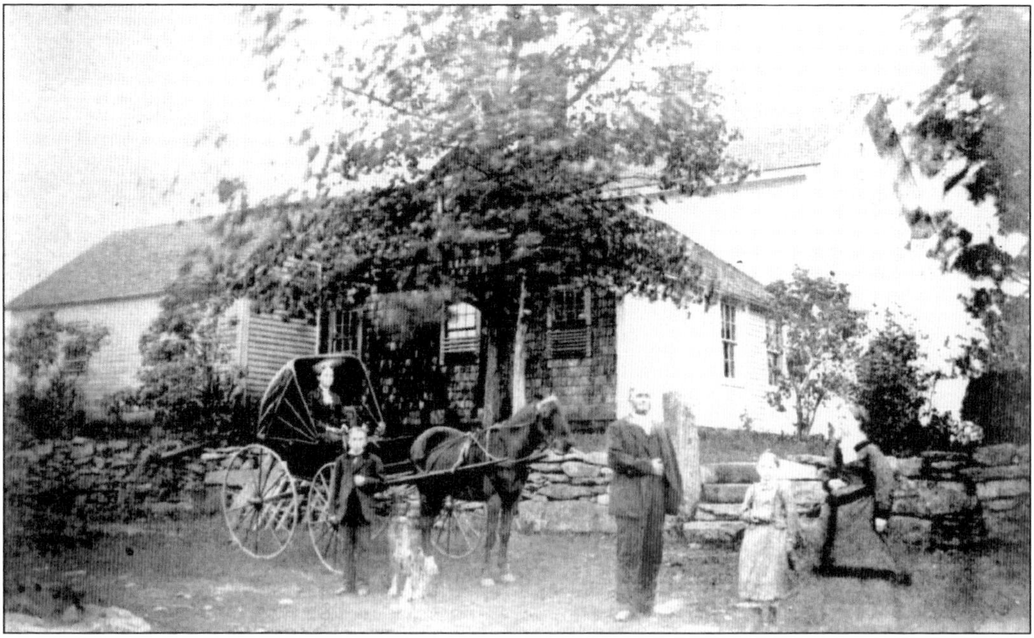

Until the early part of the 20th century, municipal business was conducted at the town officers' homes or businesses. Town clerk William I. Allyn, son of Israel Allyn of the Nine Mile House, did business from his home, located south of the Center on Colonel Ledyard Highway. Built c. 1852 by James A. Billings, the property is still in the Allyn family.

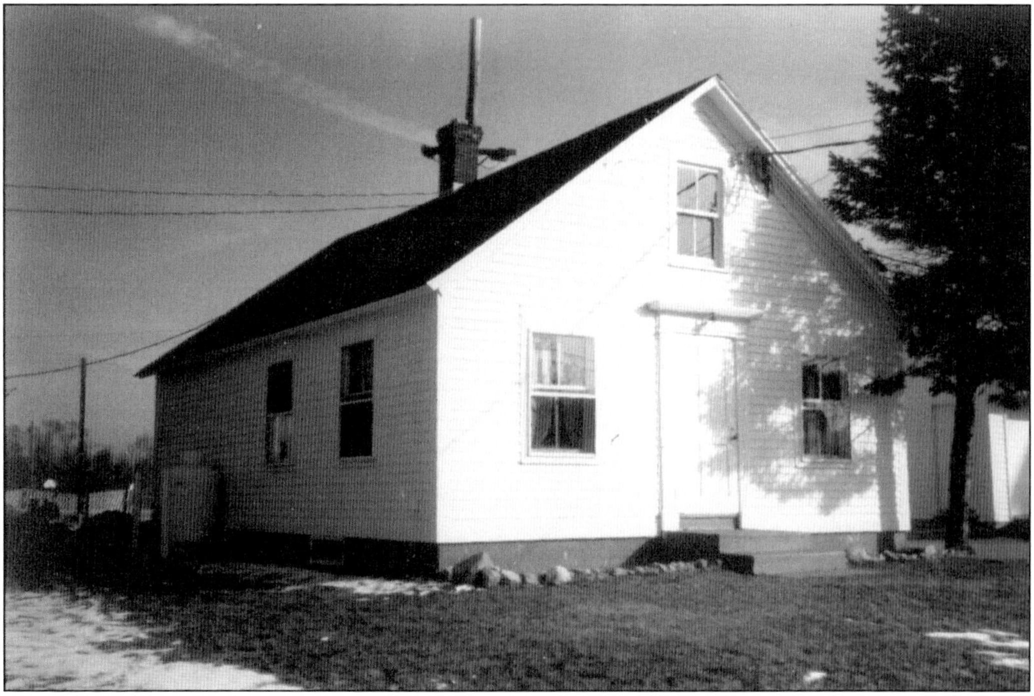

Ledyard's first town hall, built in the 1930s, resulted from a move to centralize operations and place records in a fireproof vault. It stands today, next to the Congregational church, and is used as an office by the Ledyard Fair.

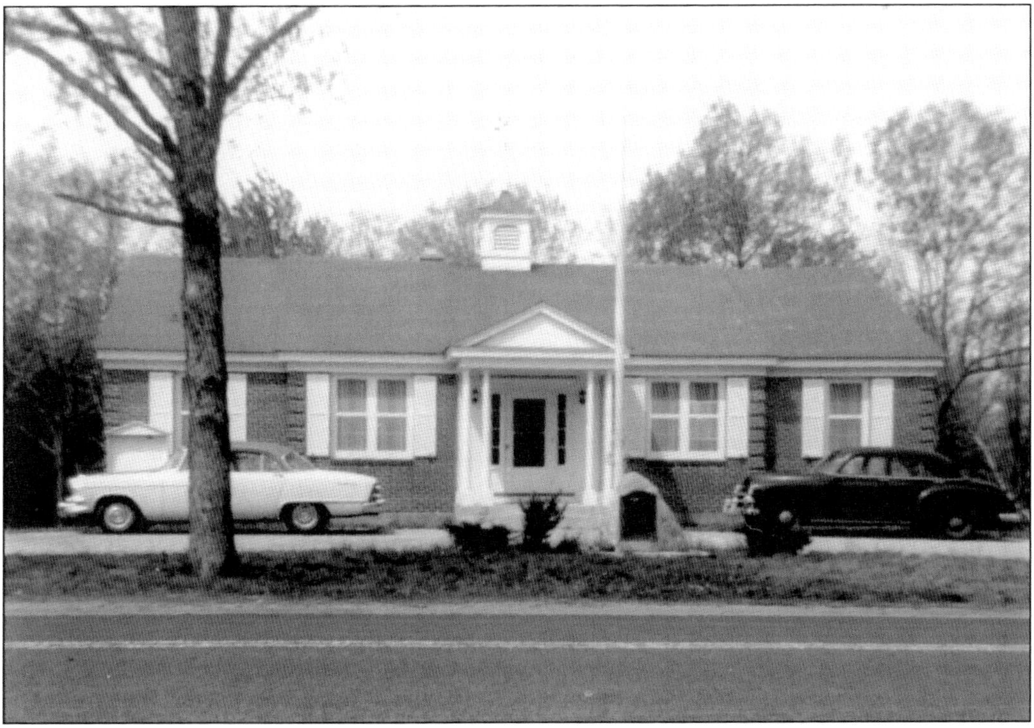

Ledyard's new town hall was built on the west side of Colonel Ledyard Highway in 1956. The increasing complexity and size of town government has required its expansion several times since, as well as the addition of several satellite offices in other parts of town.

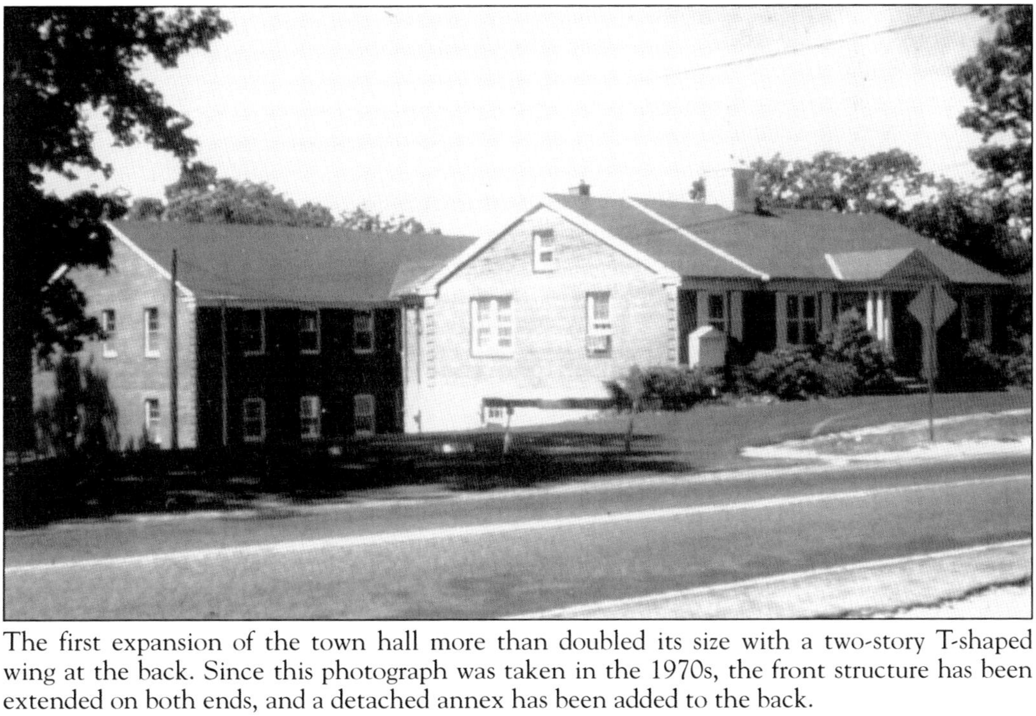

The first expansion of the town hall more than doubled its size with a two-story T-shaped wing at the back. Since this photograph was taken in the 1970s, the front structure has been extended on both ends, and a detached annex has been added to the back.

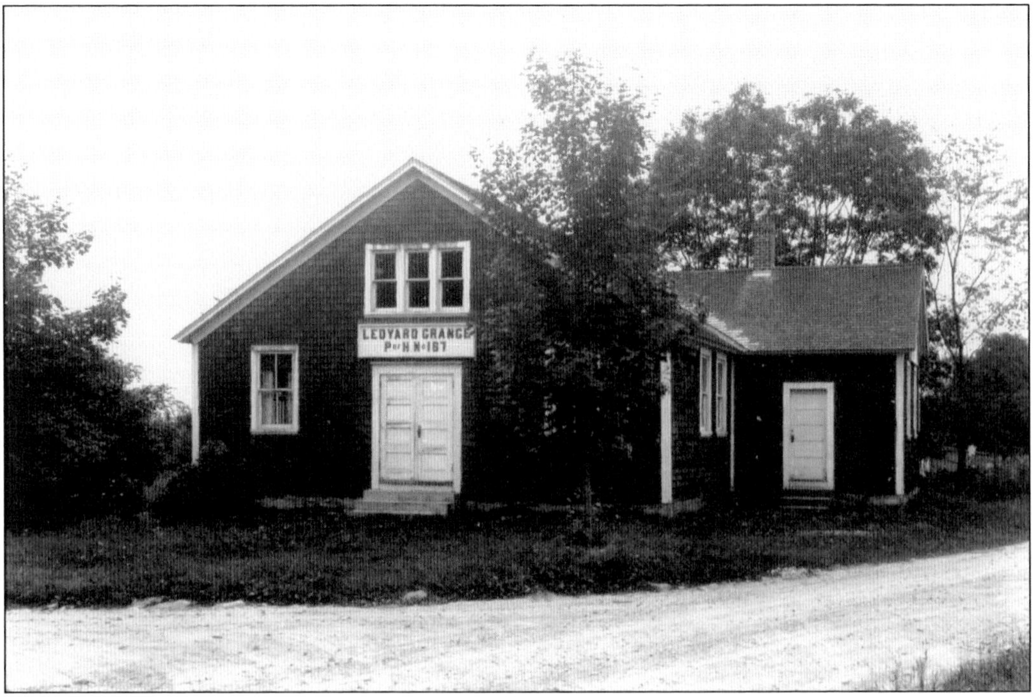

The National Grange of the Patrons of Husbandry, a fraternal organization devoted to sound agricultural practices and a rich social life, was founded by Oliver H. Kelley in 1867. In 1907, the Ledyard Grange was organized; members started the construction of this Grange Hall in 1922.

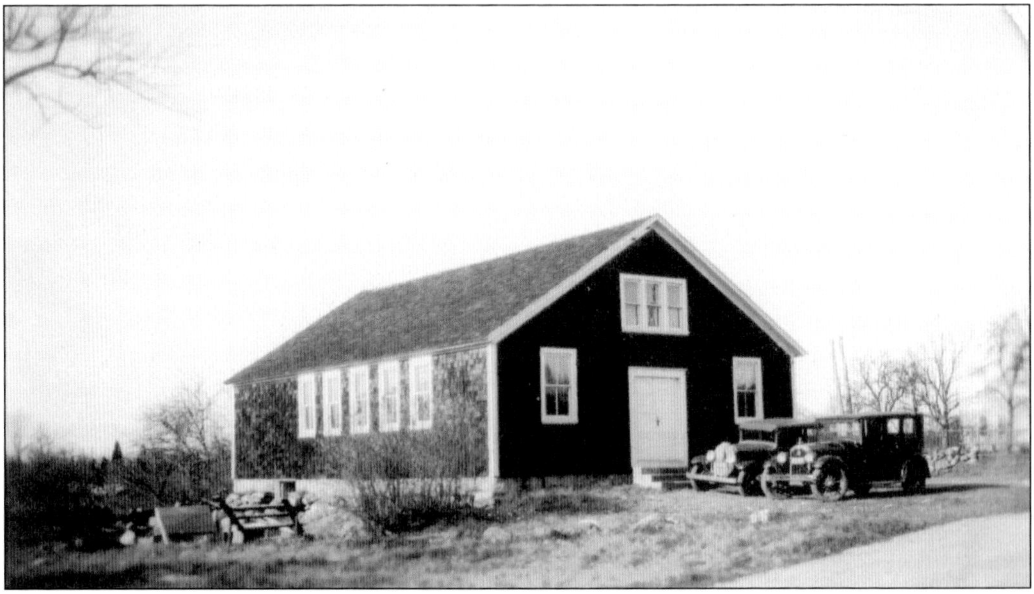

The Ledyard Grange was formed at a meeting in the basement of the Congregational church. The Grange Hall, located across Colonel Ledyard Highway from the church, was dedicated in 1929, the year before the photographs on this page were taken.

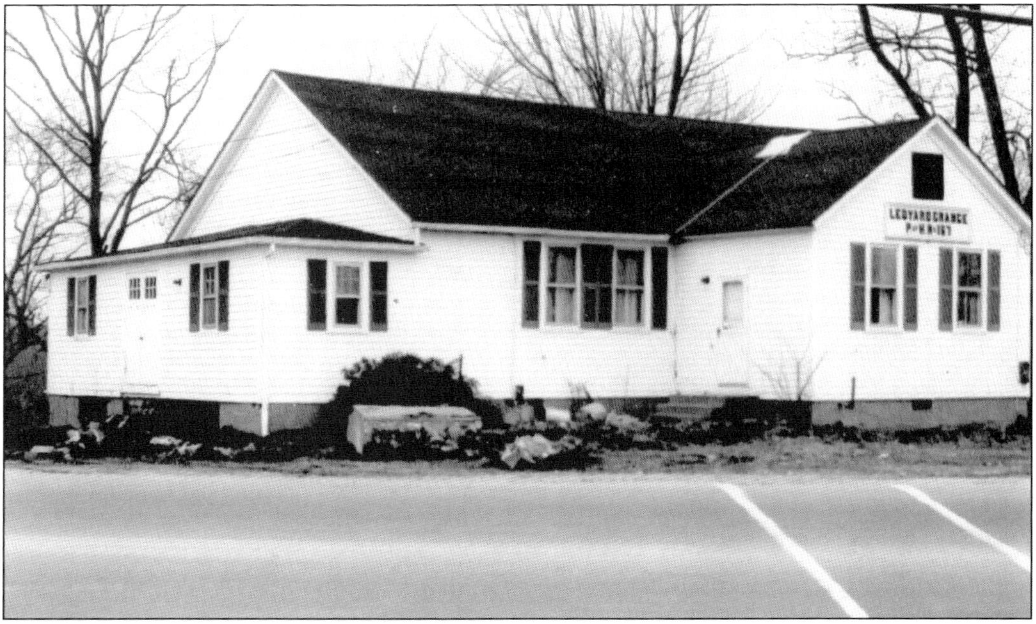

By 1986, the widened highway had already encroached on the Grange Hall. A planned realignment of Colonel Ledyard Highway at the intersection of Center Groton Road required the land on which it sat, so the hall was moved to a nearby site. When this photograph was taken, preliminary work for the move had opened the foundation.

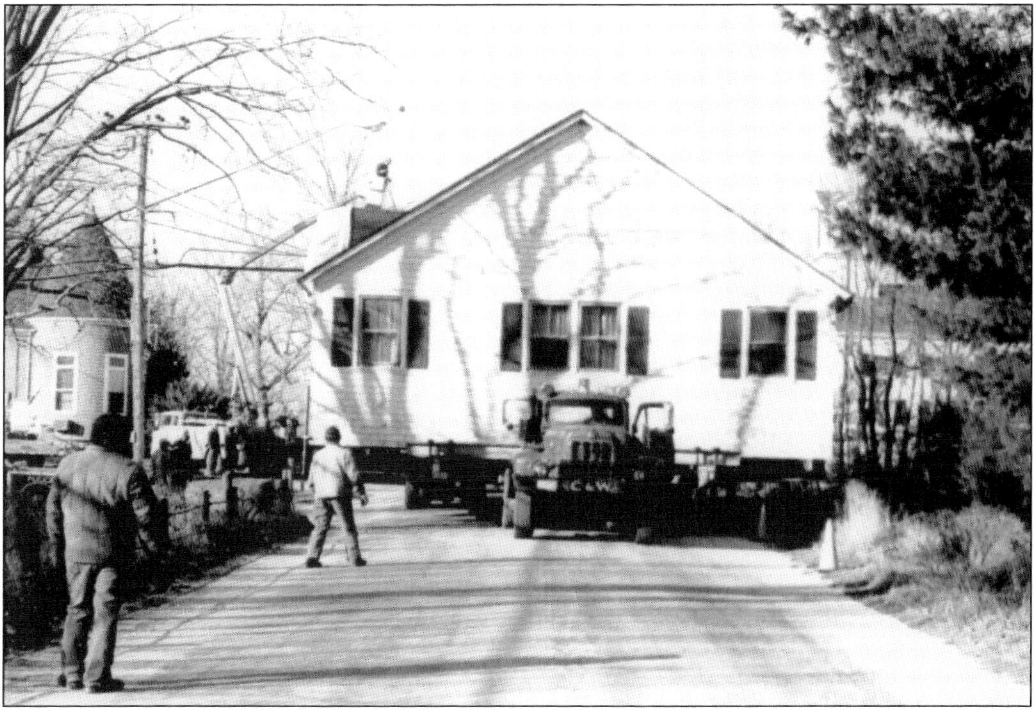

The Grange Hall, loaded on a huge flatbed trailer, was moved slowly to Fairway Drive, about a half-mile away. The Grange ceased operation in 2004. The building is now home to the Covenant Presbyterian Church.

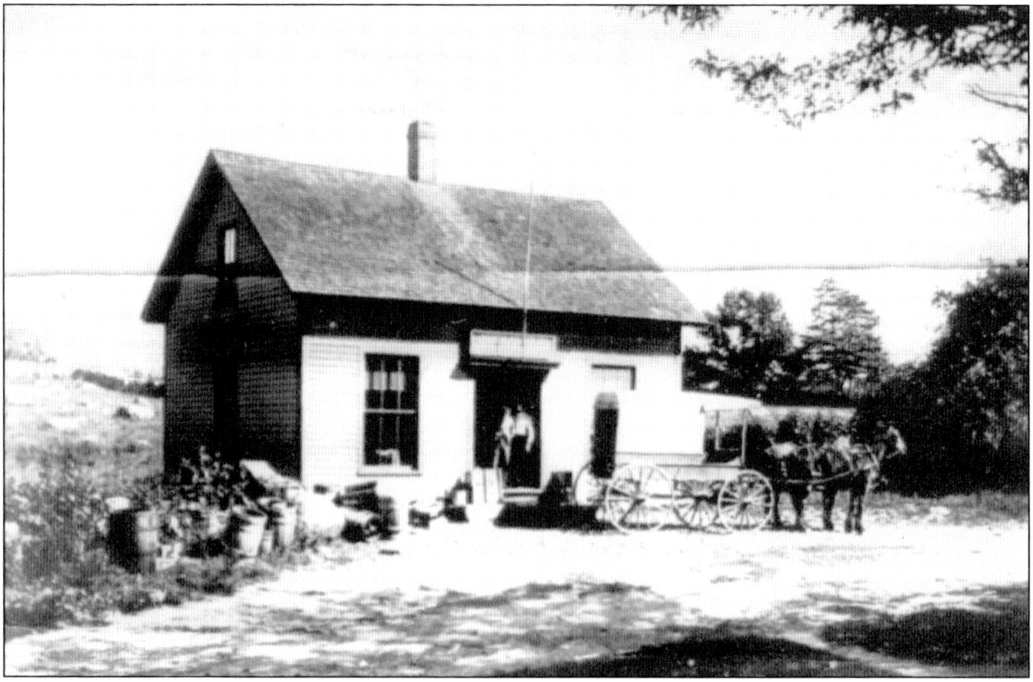

The John M. Gray Store, located on Colonel Ledyard Highway just south of the present post office, was built shortly before 1896. John Gray was the last postmaster of Ledyard for more than 50 years, as the post office was closed in 1903. When it was reestablished in 1959, it was a contract station. The building is now a private residence.

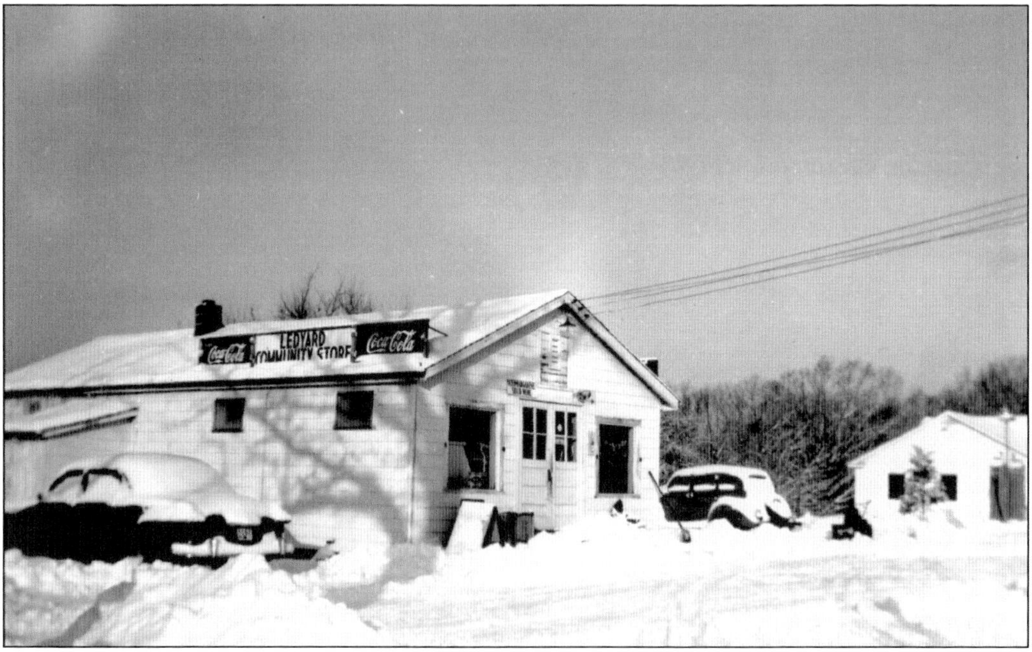

The first Ledyard Community Store (on the site of the present store, just south of the Ledyard Firehouse) was originally a small frame building. When this photograph was taken in the winter of 1954, it was run by the Gunuskey family.

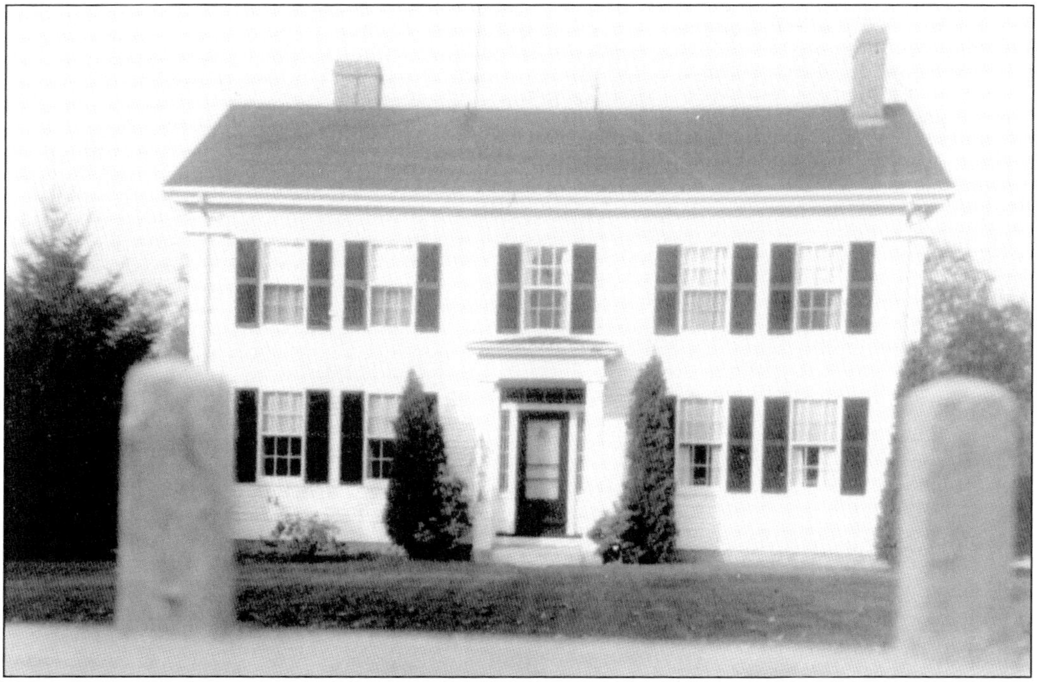

The Erastus Gallup house, built *c.* 1830, was originally located on the site of the Ledyard Center School. When its property was acquired by the town for the first consolidated school, it was moved to a site farther south on Colonel Ledyard Highway. This photograph was taken in 1963 at the house's new location.

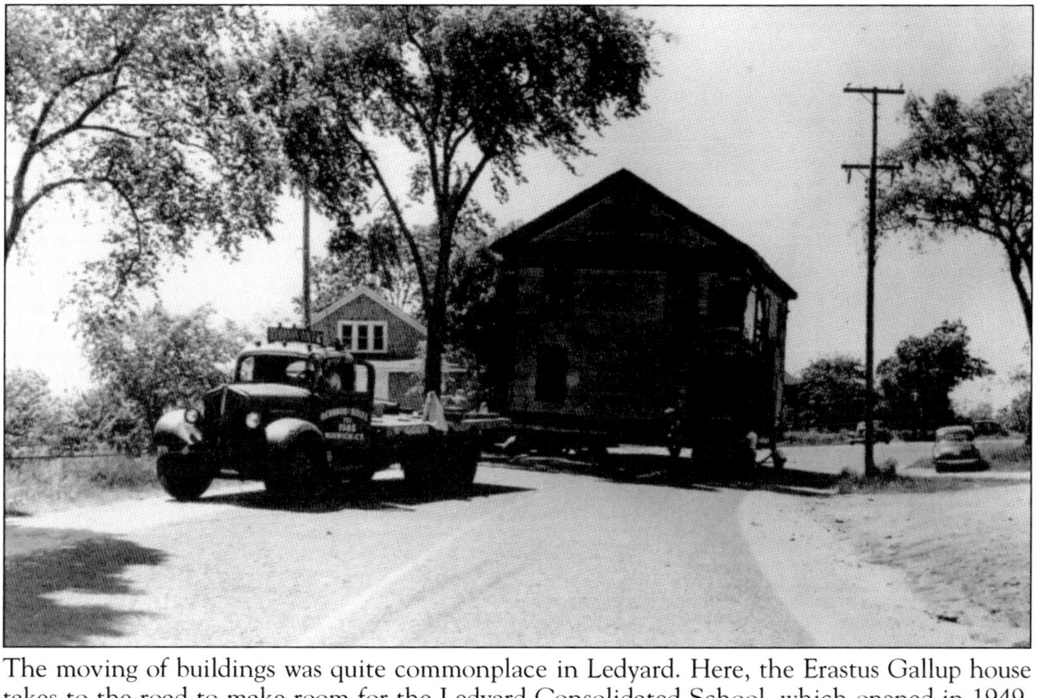

The moving of buildings was quite commonplace in Ledyard. Here, the Erastus Gallup house takes to the road to make room for the Ledyard Consolidated School, which opened in 1949. The Ledyard Grange, seen to the back, would itself follow the same road 40 years later.

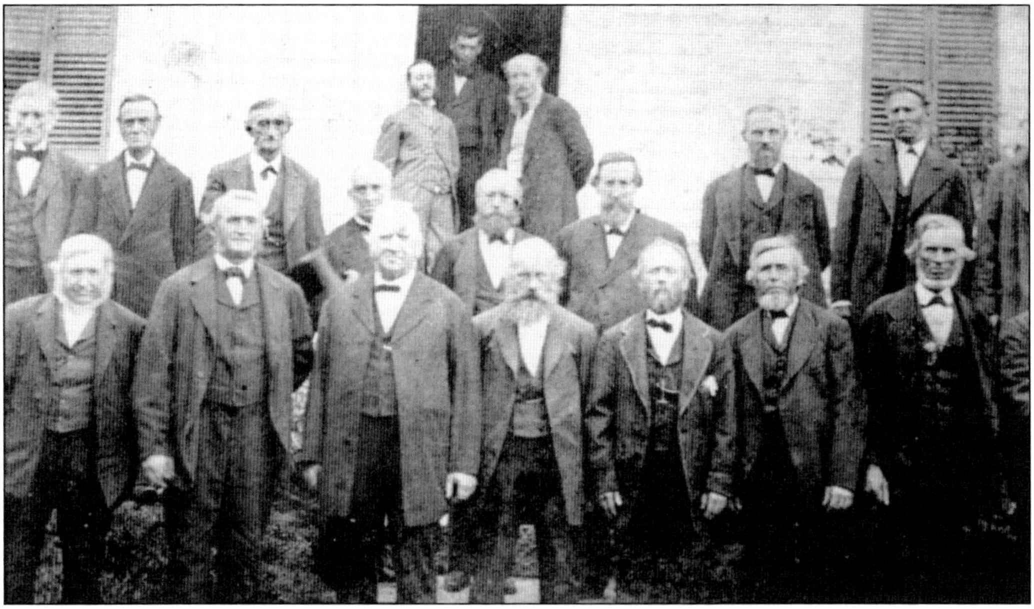

In 1867, Henry Bill gave $1,000 to purchase books for the use of Ledyard's townspeople. A board of trustees was formed, and the Bill Library was founded. The 1877 trustees are, from left to right, as follows: (first row) Palmer Allyn, Rufus Gallup, James Billings, Nathaniel Geer, Jacob Gallup, Israel Allyn, Sanford Billings, and Isaac Avery; (second row) Ralph Hurlbutt, Benjamin Lewis, Edmund Spicer, unidentified, Charles Cutting, Henry Bill, Nathan Sands, ? Gallup, Franklin Brewster, and Henry Larrabee. Standing in the doorway is Henry Ruggles; the men flanking him are unidentified.

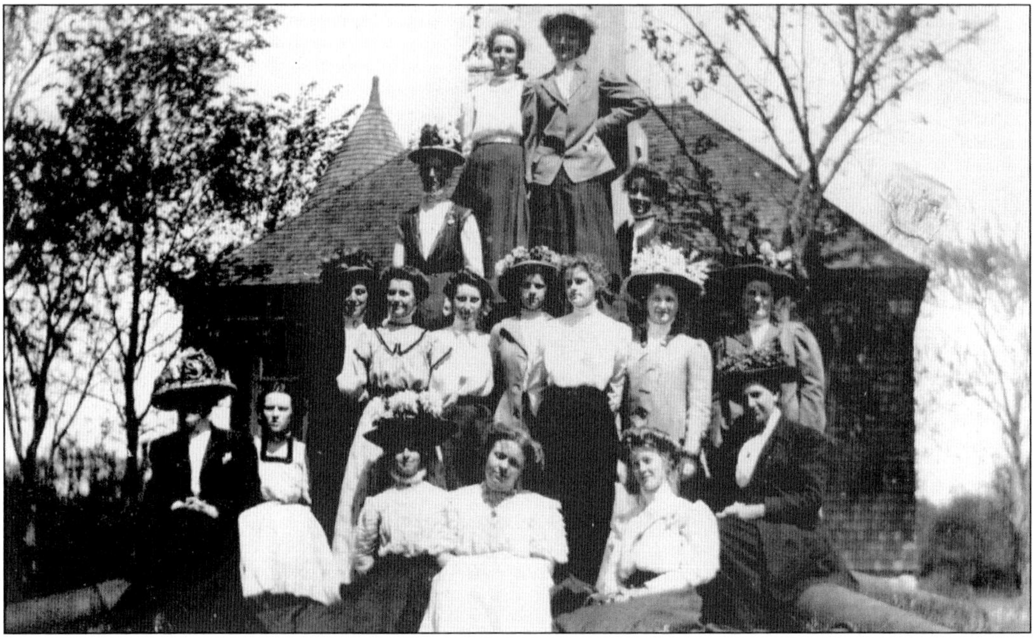

The Philathia Club poses in front of the Bill Library building *c.* 1895. The club's history and purpose seem to have gone unrecorded, but the organization was likely a counterpart of the Philathia Bible study groups found in churches today.

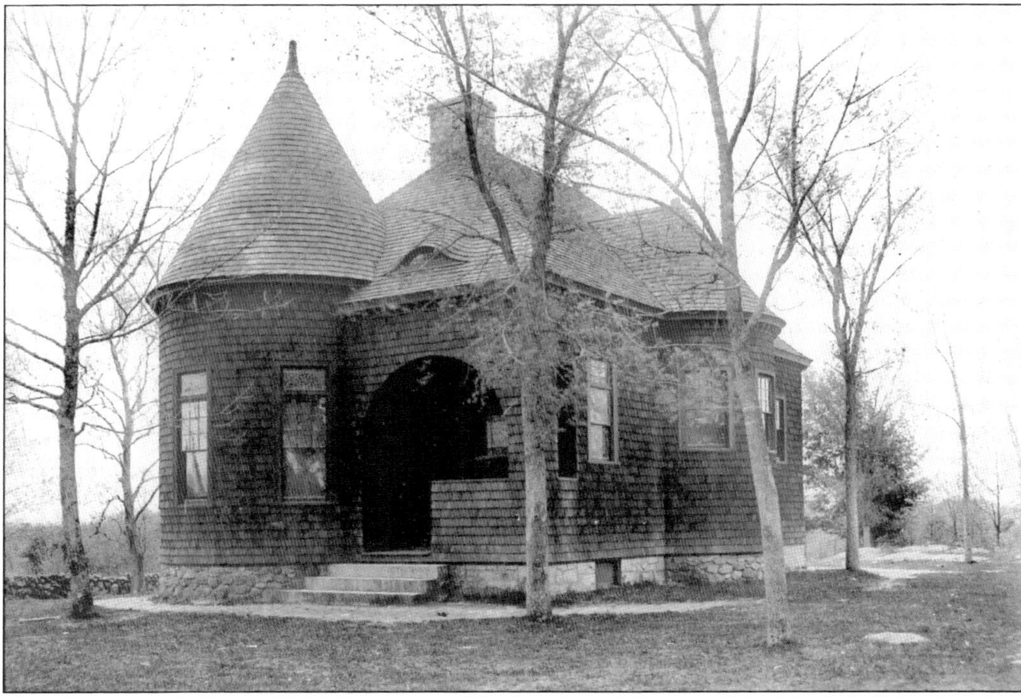

Initially, the library was housed in the gallery of the Congregational church. Its first building was completed in 1892, the year following Henry Bill's death. Located across from the church on Colonel Ledyard Highway, the Bill Library remained largely unchanged for more than 80 years.

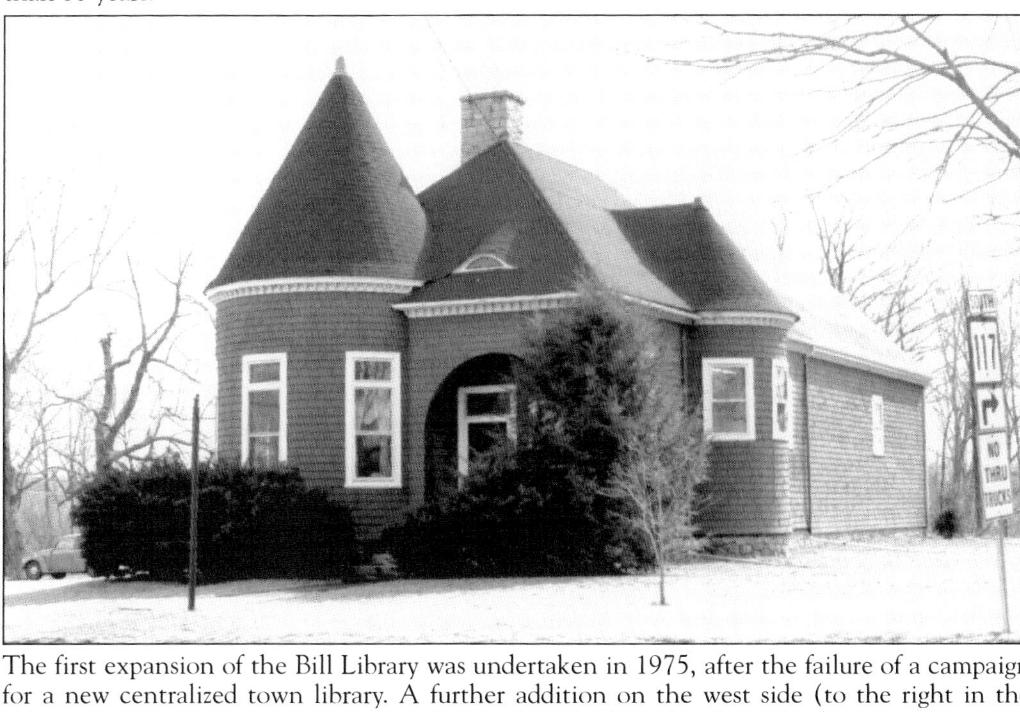

The first expansion of the Bill Library was undertaken in 1975, after the failure of a campaign for a new centralized town library. A further addition on the west side (to the right in the photograph) was completed in 1983 and more than doubled the size of the library.

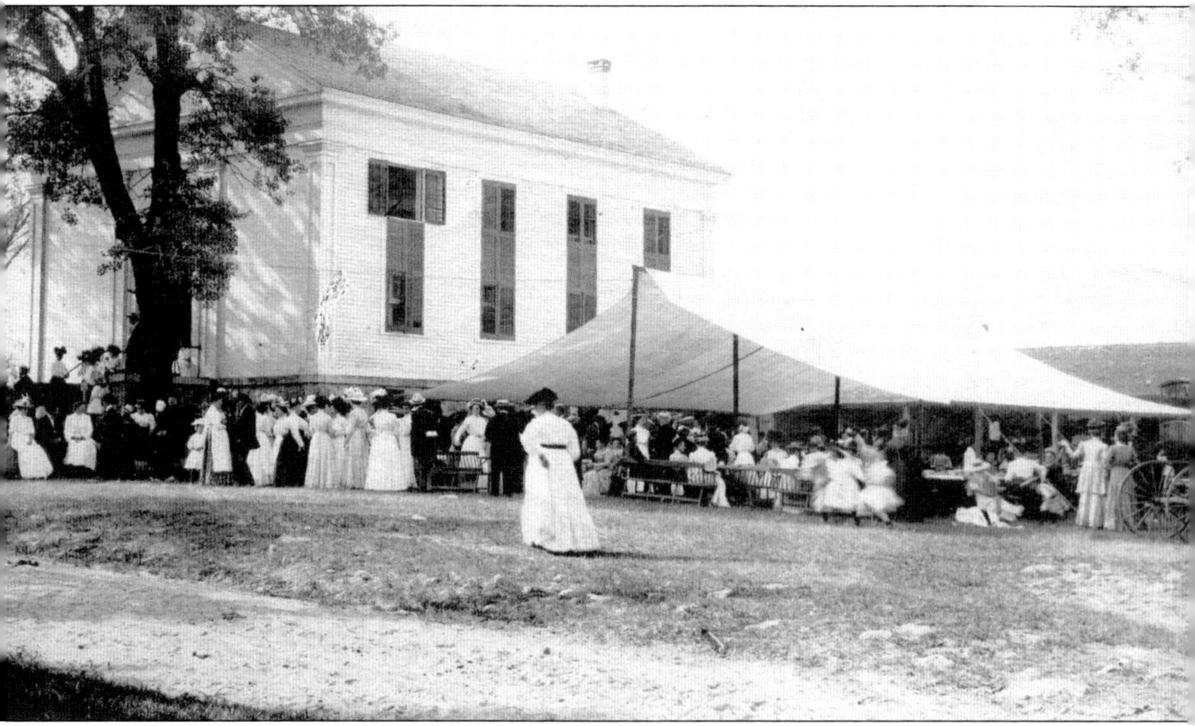

With the completion of the Bill Library building, the annual Bill Dinner was made a public affair, held under a tent on the lawn of the church. This photograph of the 1900 dinner shows that the outdoor venue had not resulted in casual dress.

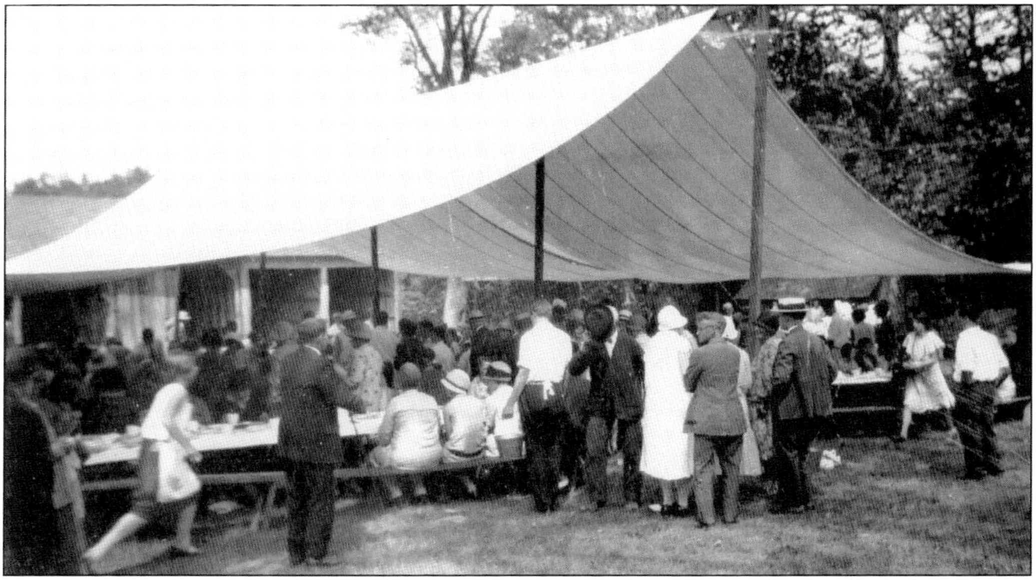

By 1930, the Bill Dinner had become a less formal affair. The Bills provided the use of a chowder house located behind the church, and two kettles of chowder were prepared—one with onions and one without. The Bill Library trustees still dine today, albeit as a private affair. The spirit of the public dinners is preserved by the chowder tent at the annual Ledyard Fair.

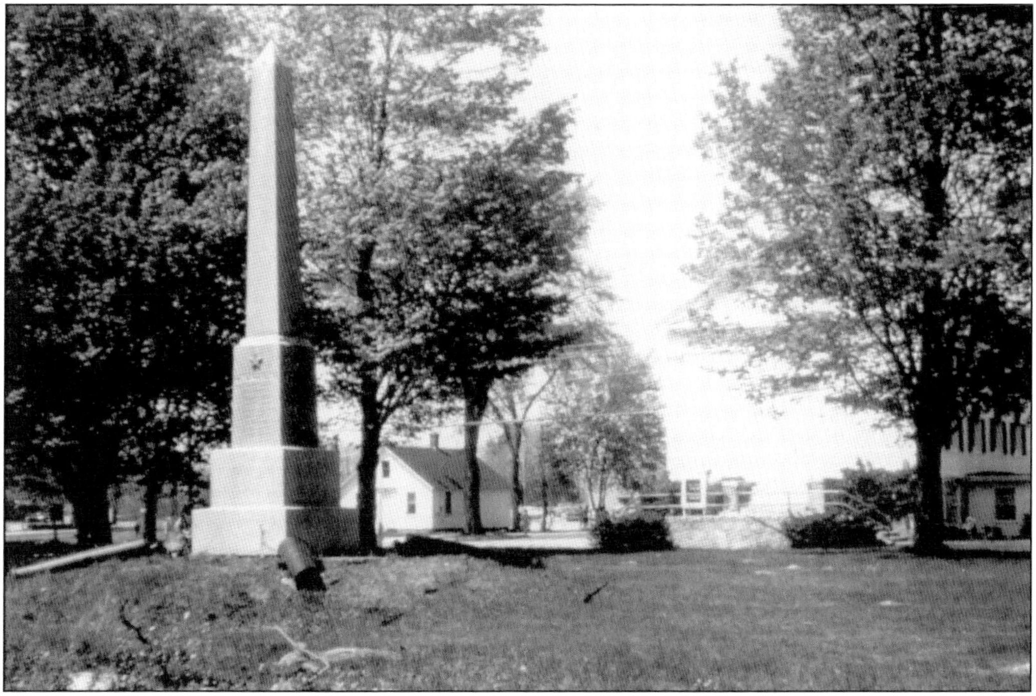

In March 1873, the Ecclesiastical Society deeded to Ledyard Bill (then living in Brooklyn, New York) a plot of land opposite the church "with the privilege to set a monument." That Independence Day, a Civil War monument was presented to the town by Ledyard Bill, in memory of the 29 men from the town who had given their lives. In recent years, separate monuments have been added to the site to memorialize those lost in subsequent wars.

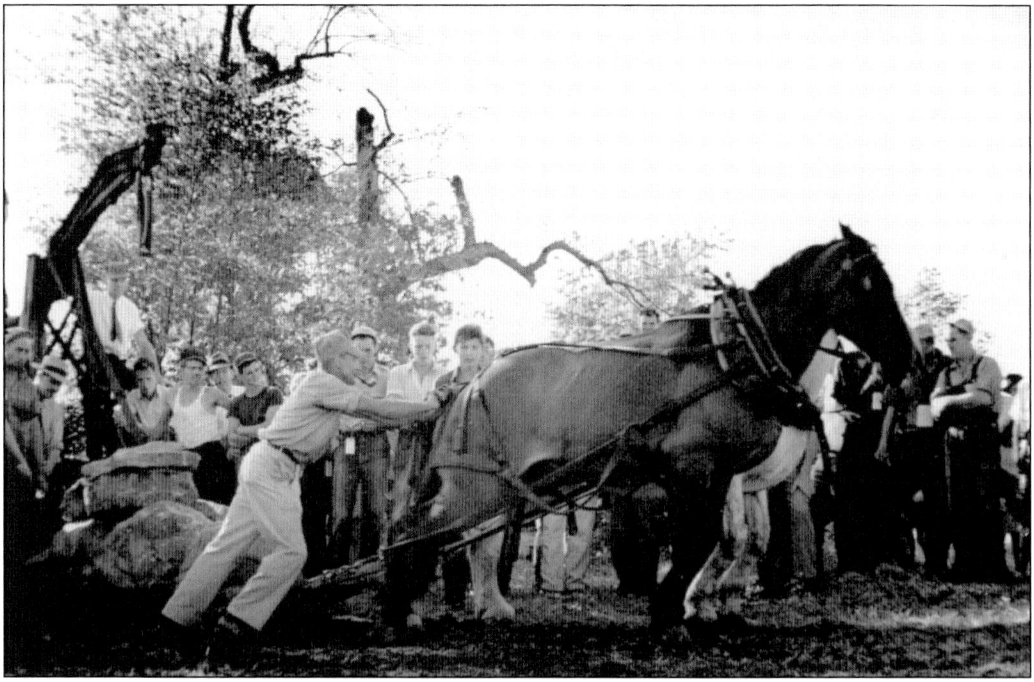

After World War II, the Ledyard Grange, the Ledyard Center Fire Company, and the Congregational church joined forces to hold an agricultural fair. The first one, in September 1946, featured traditional competitions, such as horse pulling.

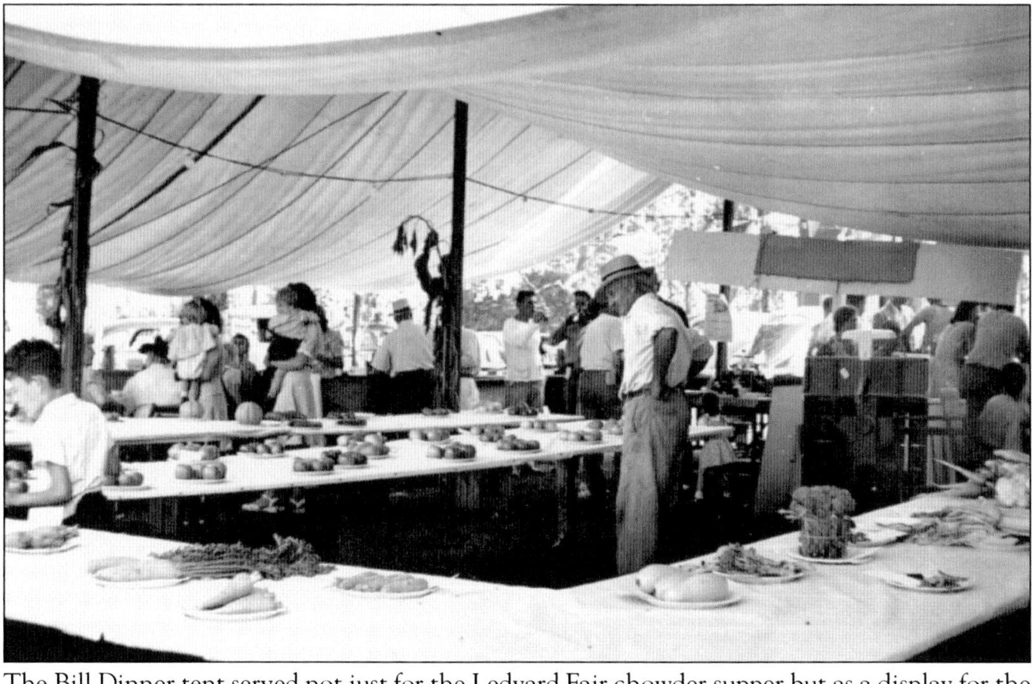

The Bill Dinner tent served not just for the Ledyard Fair chowder supper but as a display for the vegetable exhibit. Over the years, the expanded church and additional buildings have moved most fair exhibits indoors, but the country atmosphere survives.

The focal point for the Ledyard Fair has always been the church, but the grounds have been enlarged in recent years to include several pulling and show rings and a livestock barn.

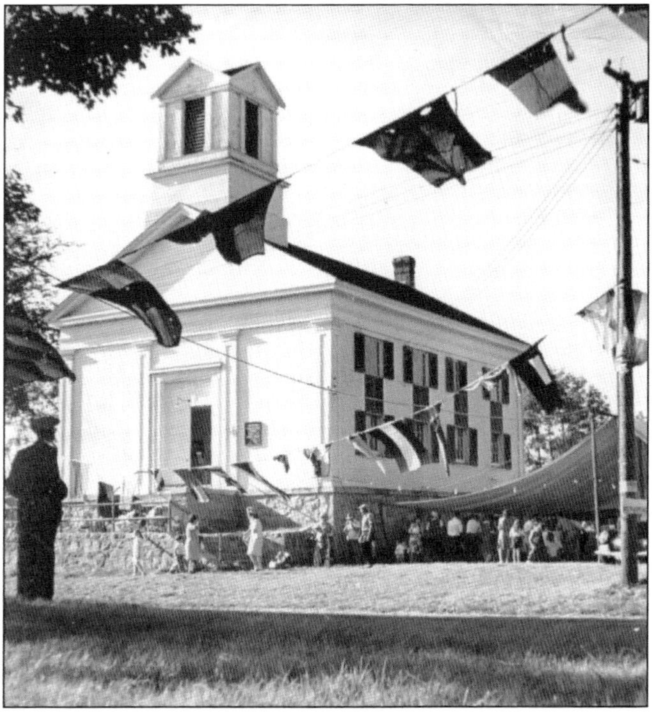

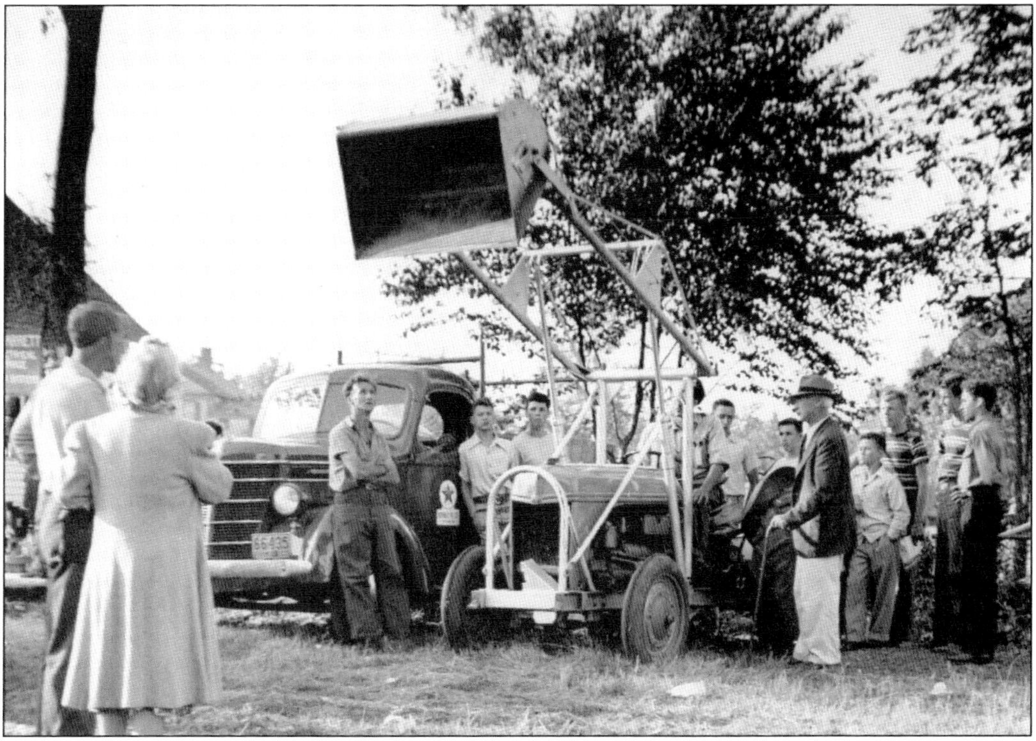

Farm machinery is always of interest to those attending an agricultural fair. The farmers at the inaugural 1946 fair were mesmerized by the hydraulic bucket loader, now commonplace but then a distinct novelty.

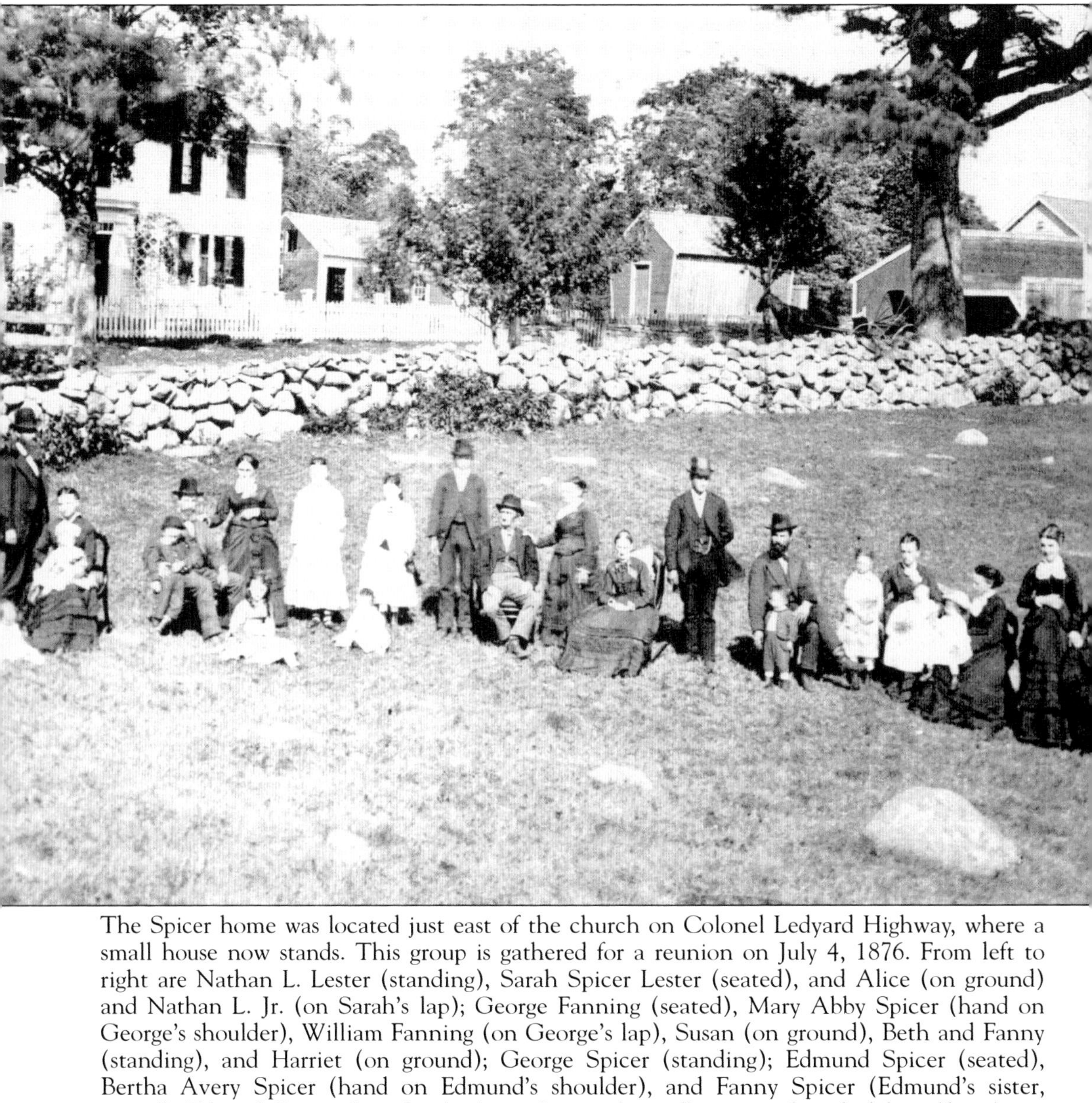

The Spicer home was located just east of the church on Colonel Ledyard Highway, where a small house now stands. This group is gathered for a reunion on July 4, 1876. From left to right are Nathan L. Lester (standing), Sarah Spicer Lester (seated), and Alice (on ground) and Nathan L. Jr. (on Sarah's lap); George Fanning (seated), Mary Abby Spicer (hand on George's shoulder), William Fanning (on George's lap), Susan (on ground), Beth and Fanny (standing), and Harriet (on ground); George Spicer (standing); Edmund Spicer (seated), Bertha Avery Spicer (hand on Edmund's shoulder), and Fanny Spicer (Edmund's sister, seated); Edward Spicer (standing); Amos Lester (seated), an unidentified boy (front), an unidentified girl, Carolyn (Carrie) Spicer (rear), and an unidentified girl (on Carrie's lap); Cecelia Spicer Lester (seated) and Ella Lester (on Cecelia's lap); and Anna Williams Spicer (standing), John Sands Spicer (seated), and John William Spicer (on John's lap).

Three

The Ferry

Ledyard's western village, Gales Ferry, developed at the terminus of a ferry crossing on the Thames River. In 1740, the Connecticut General Assembly granted to Ralph Stoddard Jr., John Hurlbut, and John Comstock the franchise to operate a ferry from "a point of land where a highway or road is laid out through ye farm of Mr. Ralph Stoddard . . . on the east to a point of land in Mr. John Comstock's field on ye west side." A settlement and center of commerce soon developed on that road. It is ironic that the village takes its name neither from Stoddard nor Hurlbut but from Roger Gale, whose tenure as ferryman, following Stoddard and Hurlbut's proprietorship, was a scant five years. Not much is known about Gale, who bought the ferry rights in 1759 and sold them to a New York concern in June 1964, leaving town. When last heard from, he was in the Bay of Honduras. Originally Gale's Ferry, the village name lost its possessive apostrophe at some forgotten point in history.

As the Gales Ferry settlement grew, the name was applied to larger and larger expanses, and now generally refers to the entire western section of Ledyard. To distinguish this original and largely unchanged section, the term "Gales Ferry Village" is usually employed, shortened by locals to "the Village," or, referring to the section closest to the river, "the Ferry." Following the extension of the railroad south through Gales Ferry at the beginning of the 20th century, a small summer community was developed on the riverside land just south of the Ferry. Named "the Bluff" for its situation high above the river, its properties were leased to railroad workers. The lots and cottages were later sold to private owners, and most are year-round homes today.

The business center of Gales Ferry was originally focused on the river, around the Lower and Upper Wharves. But it gradually moved east to settle in the present commercial complexes on Route 12.

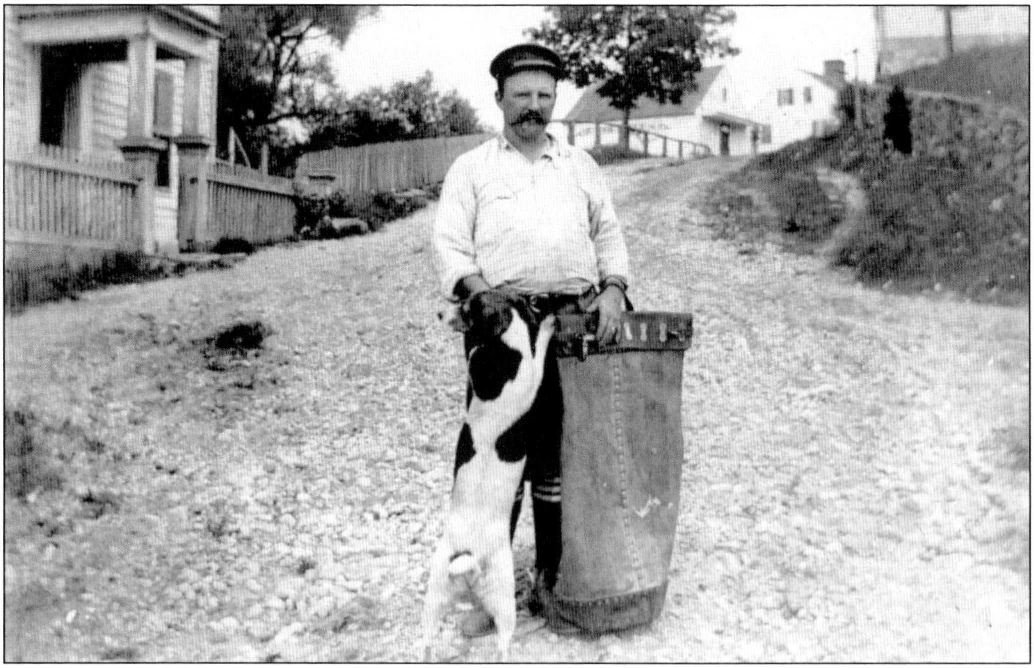

Jared Bolles was the first postal carrier in Gales Ferry, bringing the mail, which came by train to Montville, across the river by boat. The building to the left is the new house built by Roger Gale in 1763, since replaced by a succession of later buildings on the site. Behind Bolles is the post office and store, which later became a dwelling before being consumed by fire in 1955. The leather bag is the postal pouch; the name of the postal pooch is lost to history.

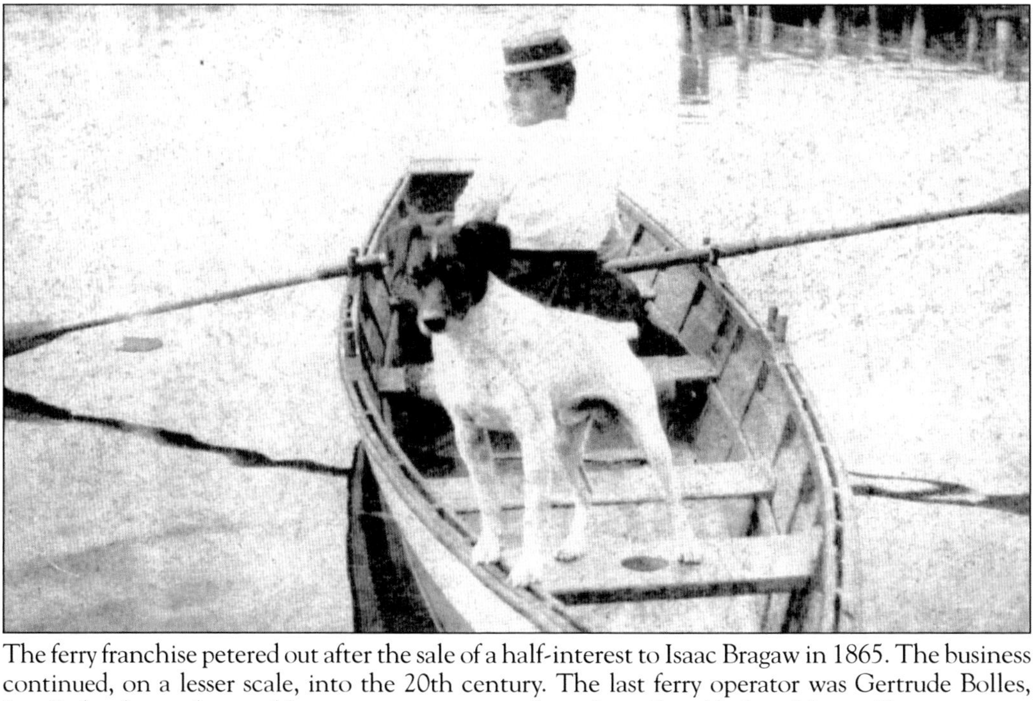

The ferry franchise petered out after the sale of a half-interest to Isaac Bragaw in 1865. The business continued, on a lesser scale, into the 20th century. The last ferry operator was Gertrude Bolles, Jared's daughter, who would row passengers across from the railroad halt at Uncasville.

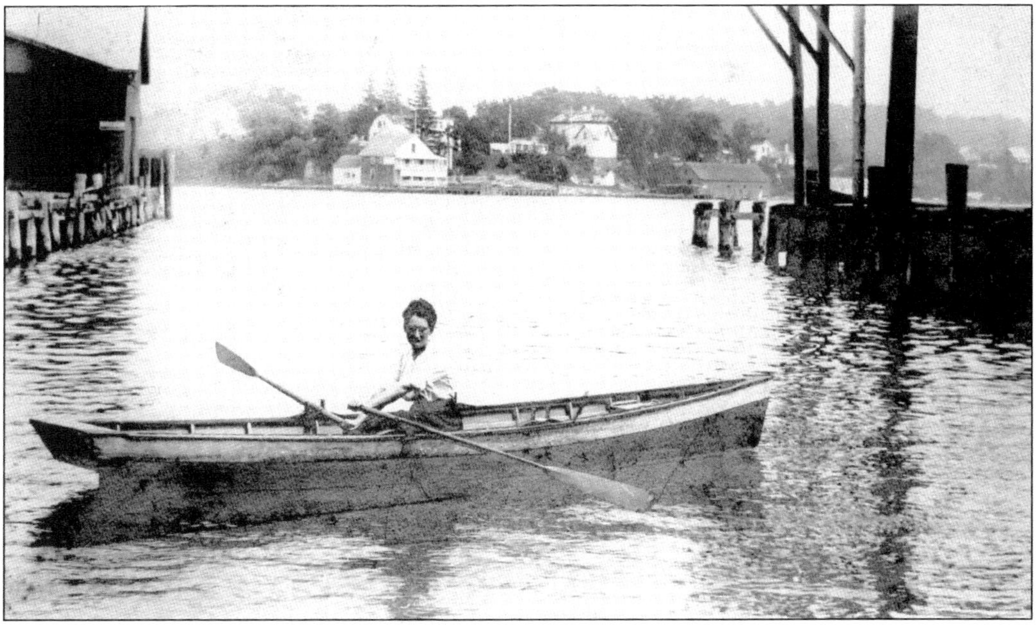

Over the years, two wharves developed in Gales Ferry. The ferry landing itself was Upper Wharf, located at the end of what is now Hurlbutt Road. This view of Gertrude Bolles leaving the ferry slip on the Montville side of the river shows the buildings of Upper Wharf in the background.

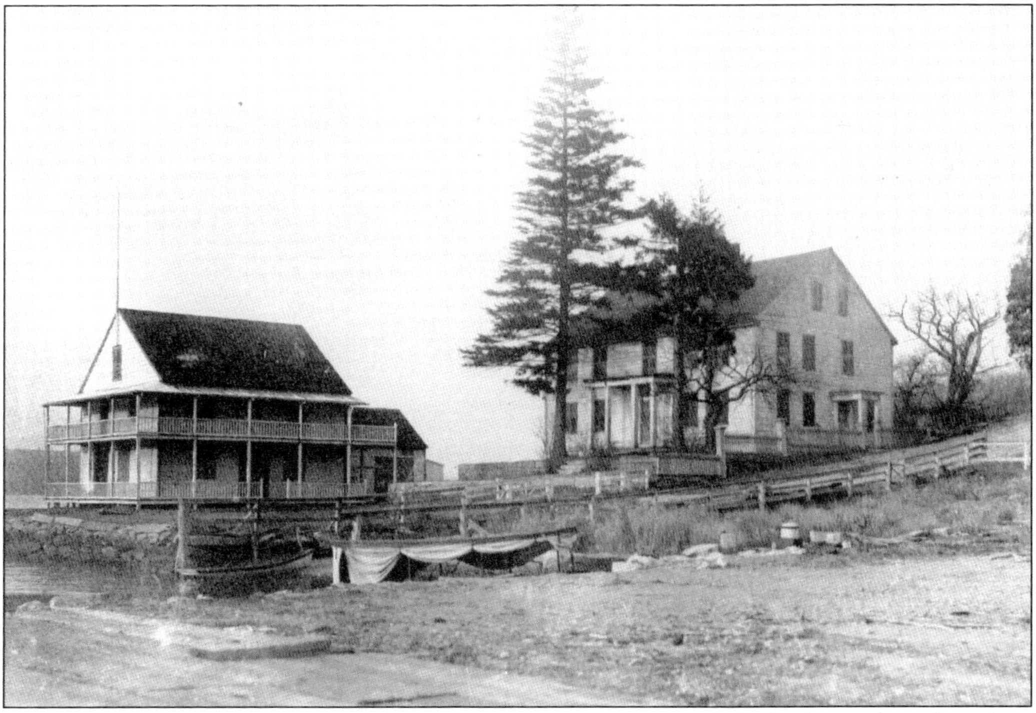

At Upper Wharf were the Bragaw house (right) and store. Likely built much earlier than when Isaac Bragaw resided there (1865–1887), they may be the "store" and "dwelling house" mentioned in an 1808 deed. Both buildings were razed c. 1908.

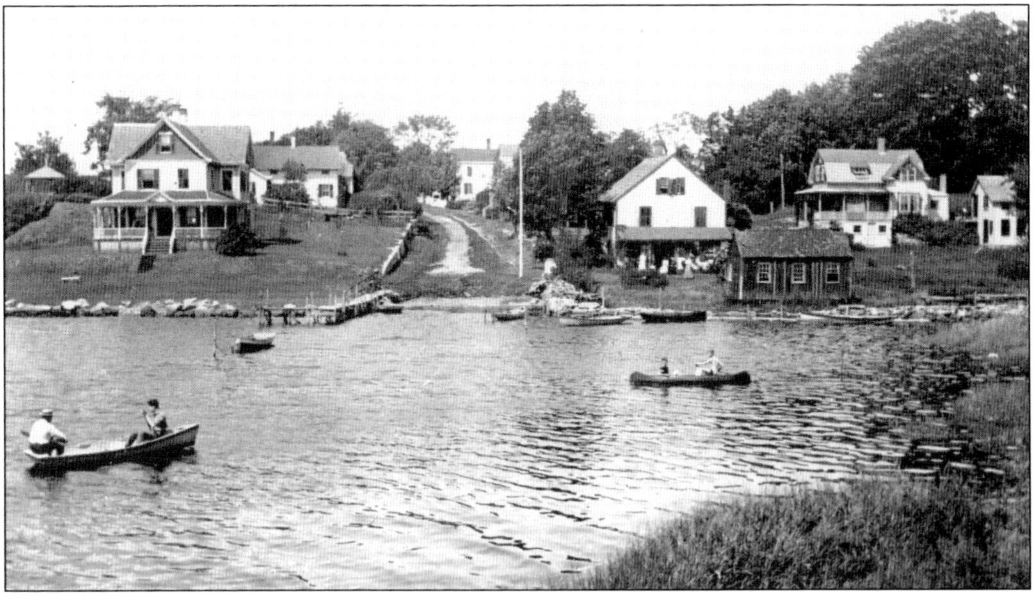

Lower Wharf was at the south end of what is now Riverside Place. The house to the right was built by Guy C. Stoddard *c.* 1820. The house to the left was constructed in 1903.

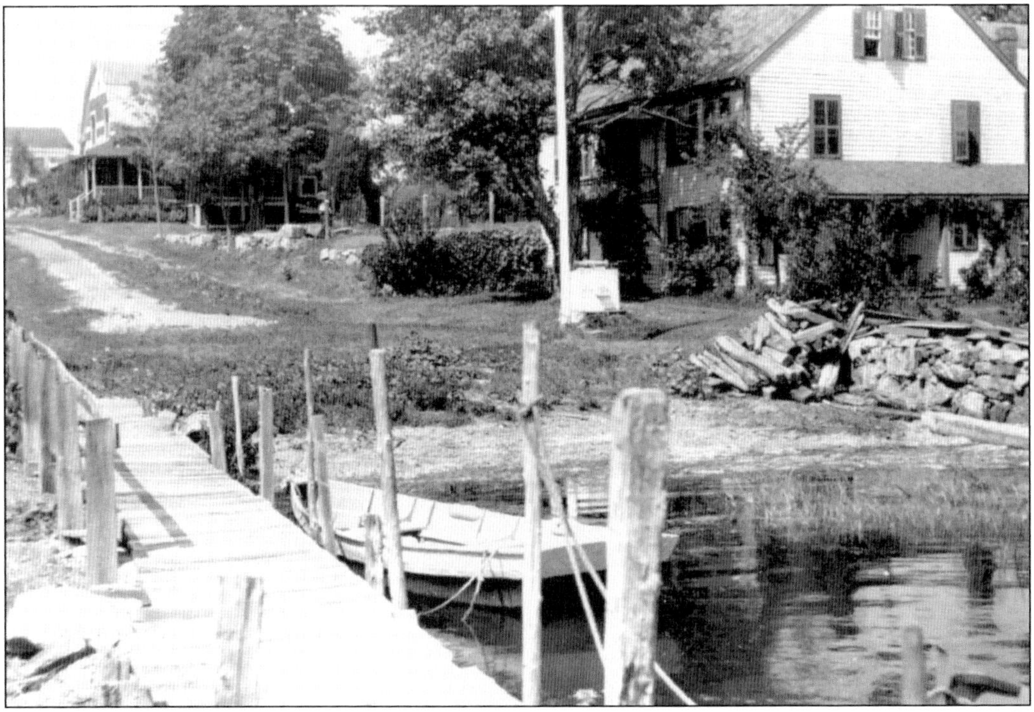

The Guy Stoddard house at Lower Wharf (right) was later owned by Capt. Charles Crandall, pilot of the steamer *Atlantic* when it was wrecked at Fishers Island. From 1871 to the late 1940s, the house was owned by the Perkins family.

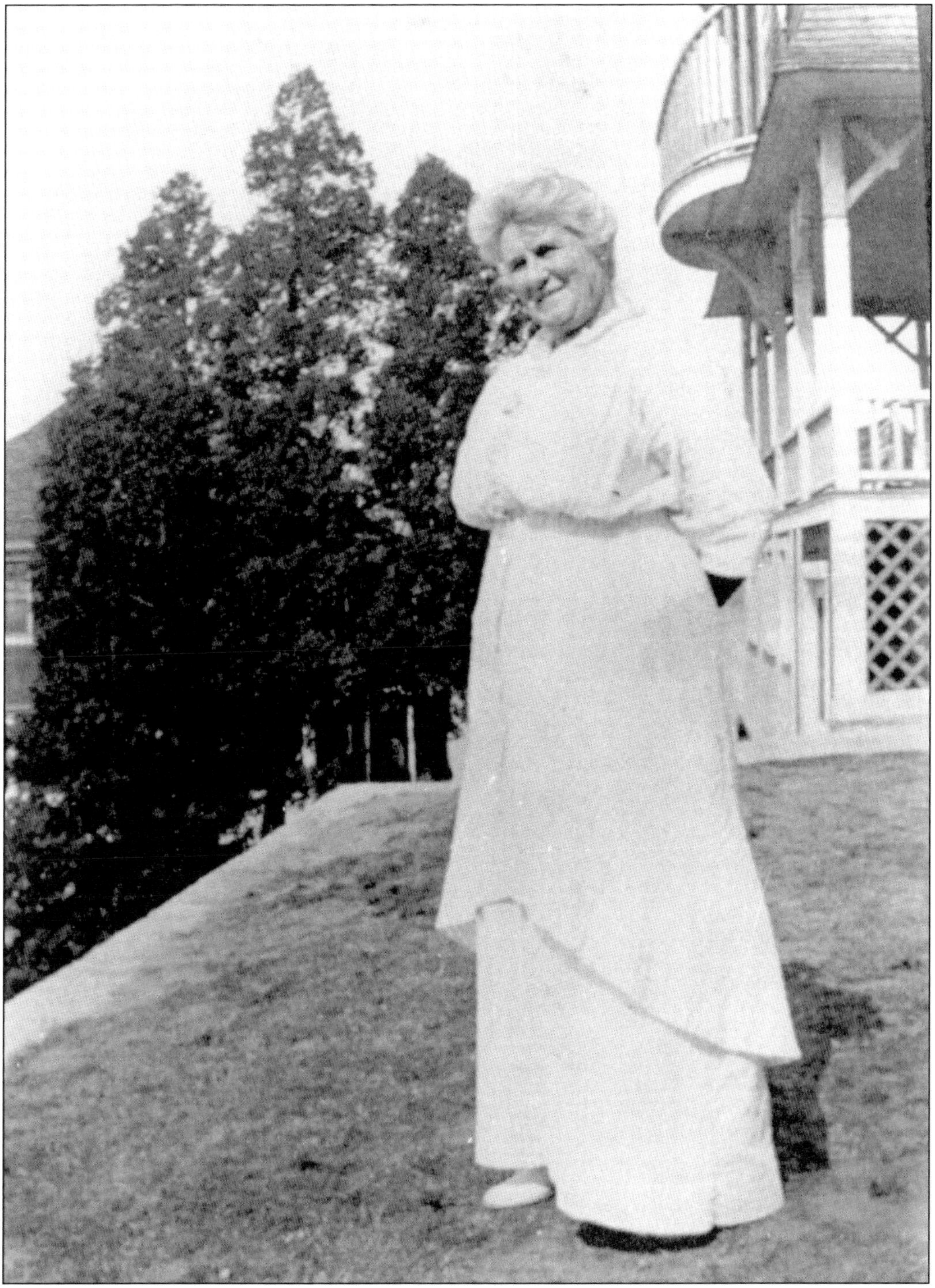

Gertrude Bolles married Edward Latimer of Gales Ferry and moved to a house overlooking the eastern ferry slip. She continued her informal ferry service as long as she was able, into the 1940s. She died in 1965 at age 87. This later photograph of her was taken at the Yale rowing quarters adjacent to the slip, originally a house built by Thomas Geer *c.* 1796.

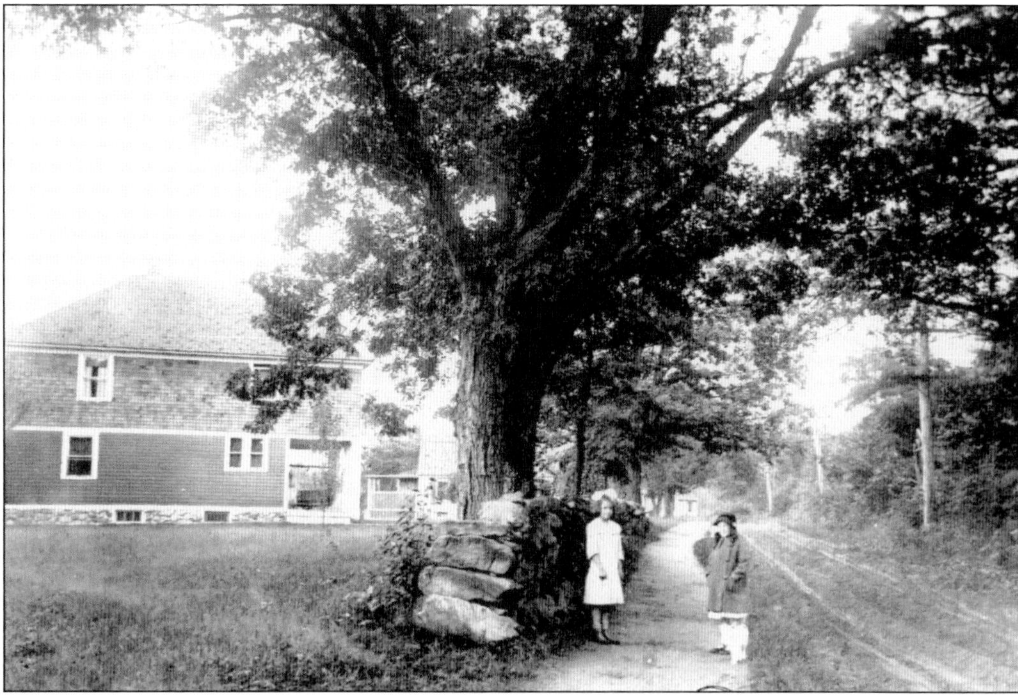

By 1914, the "road . . . through ye farm of Mr. Ralph Stoddard" had become a scenic, tree-lined lane with a broad walking path and a boundary of stone walls. These girls enjoy a walk on August 3, 1914. The house to the left is currently designated 36 Hurlbutt Road.

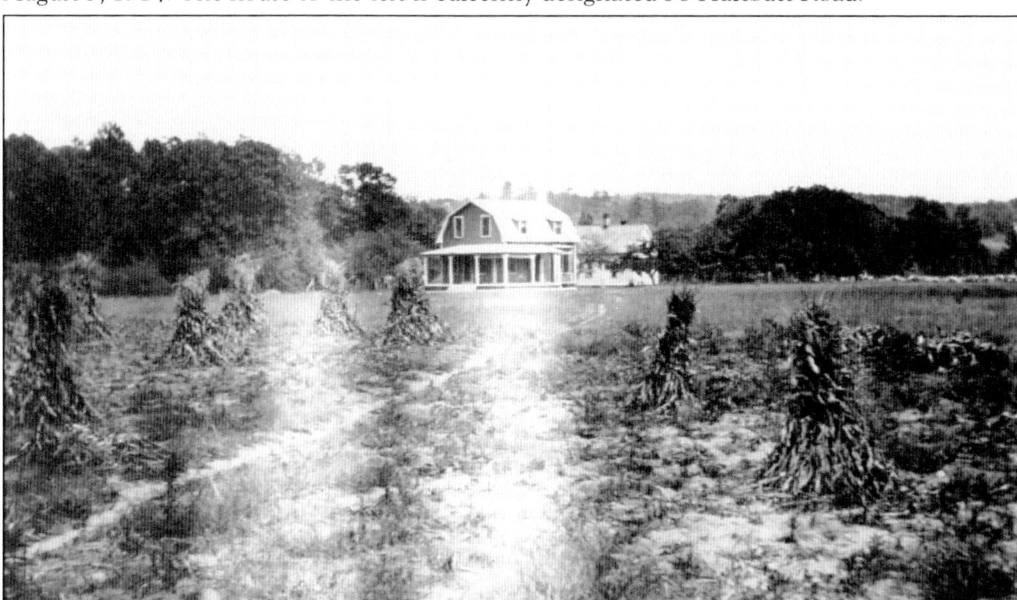

The Povey cottage, on Library Lane, was built in 1910 as a summer cottage for the widowed mother and maiden aunts of Richard G. Povey, son of a Methodist minister. Richard's brother Danzy later became postmaster of Gales Ferry, and his aunt Gracy was the first librarian for the village's new library, which opened in 1921. The cottage is still a seasonal dwelling, owned by relatives of the Povey family.

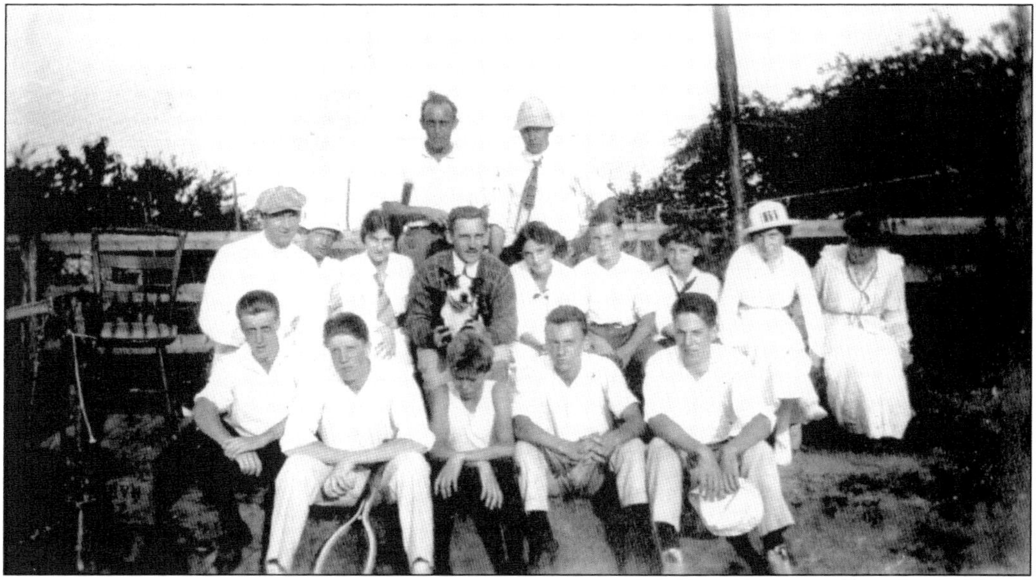

Villagers formed a tennis club and constructed courts, the upkeep of which was the responsibility of club members. The sport became very popular in the village and was a source of keen competition.

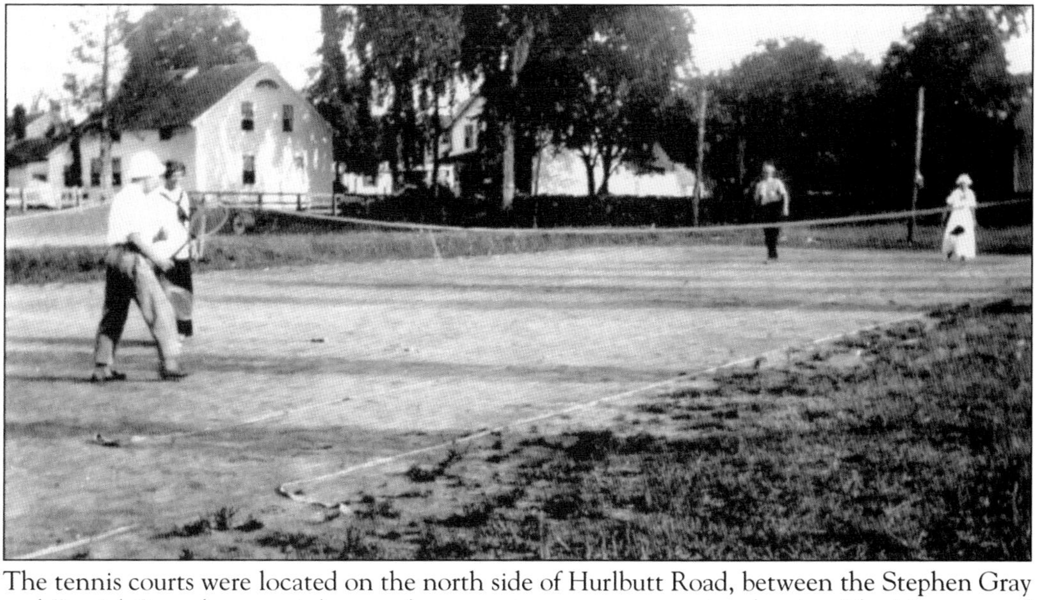

The tennis courts were located on the north side of Hurlbutt Road, between the Stephen Gray and Daniel Copp houses. A house of recent vintage now occupies the site. The Norman and Povey Store can be seen in the background of this 1919 photograph.

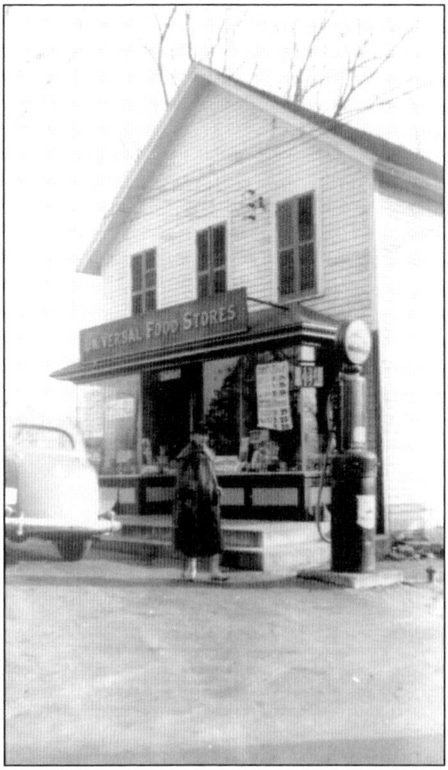

The first post office in Gales Ferry was likely located at Lower Wharf, at the foot of Riverside Place. Norman Brown, known to be the first postmaster, owned a store there with Christopher Allyn in the early 19th century. Later, the post office was at the top of the ferry slip; by 1916, it was in the Norman and Povey Store, just west of the railroad tracks on Hurlbutt Road. Danzy Povey served as postmaster until his final illness in 1941. The building is now a private home.

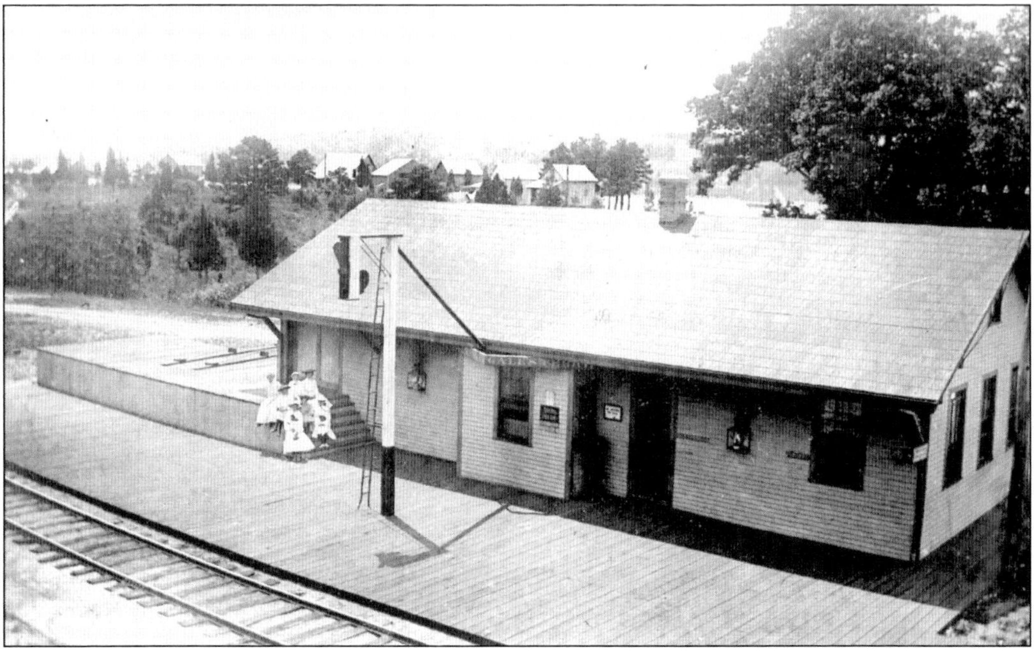

The railroad came to Gales Ferry in 1899, when the New York, New Haven and Hartford assumed and extended the bankrupt Norwich and Worcester line, which had reached Allyn's Point in 1844, to Groton. The station was located just south of the Hurlbutt Road overpass, from which this view was taken.

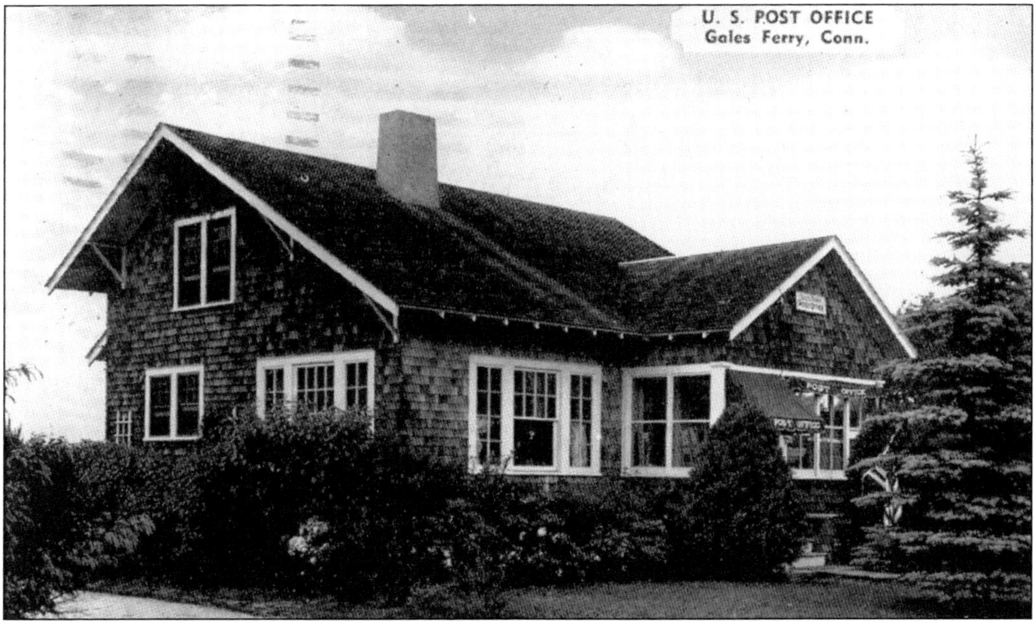

When Danzy Povey gave up the job of Gales Ferry postmaster, his duties were assumed by Stanley Faford, who lived on Allyn Lane. Faford's home was established as the new post office, and a small ell was constructed on the front for that purpose. It continued as such until 1944, during which time this postcard view was published. The building survives in this configuration as a private home.

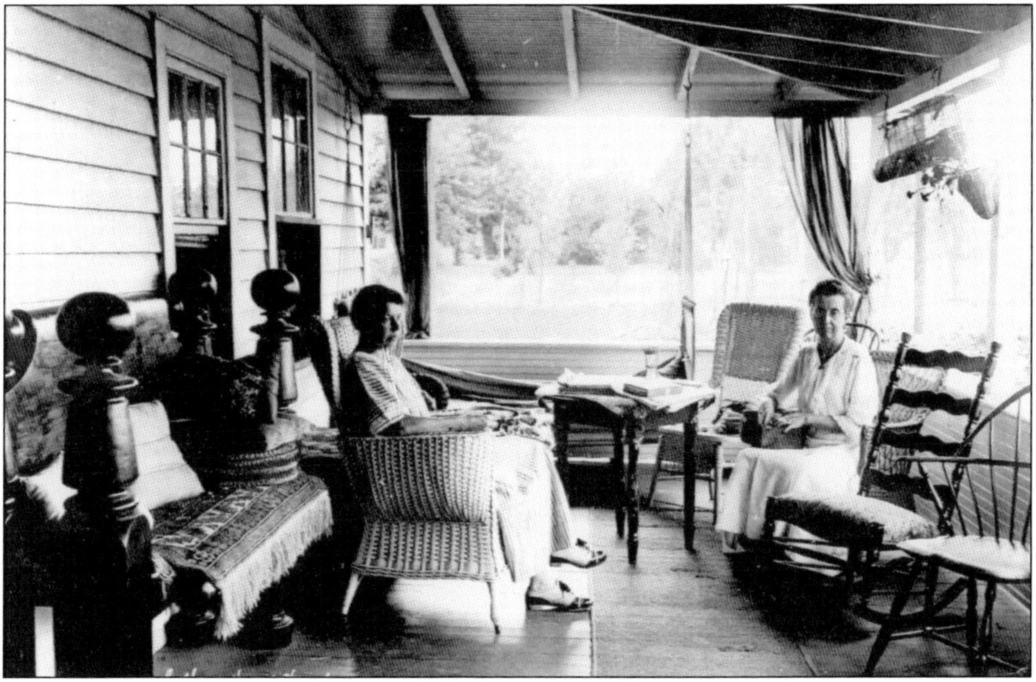

The veranda was an important feature of the Victorian-era house, a pleasant place to sit in summer. In this August 1912 photograph, Mabel Buckingham chats with a friend on the veranda at the Stephen Gray house on Hurlbutt Road.

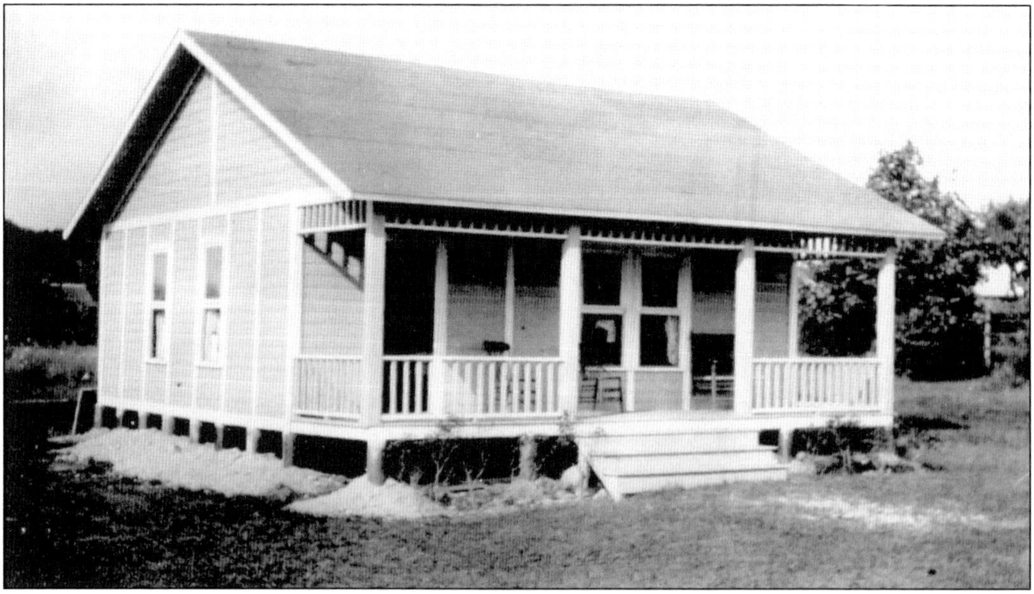

The Gales Ferry Country Club originated from the very successful production of a play organized by village residents Charles Satterlee and Walter and Mabel Buckingham. Joining with other young families, they formalized their association by founding the country club. In 1916, Noyes B. Allyn donated land at the corner of Hurlbutt Road and Allyn Lane for a clubhouse and ordered this building from Sears Roebuck.

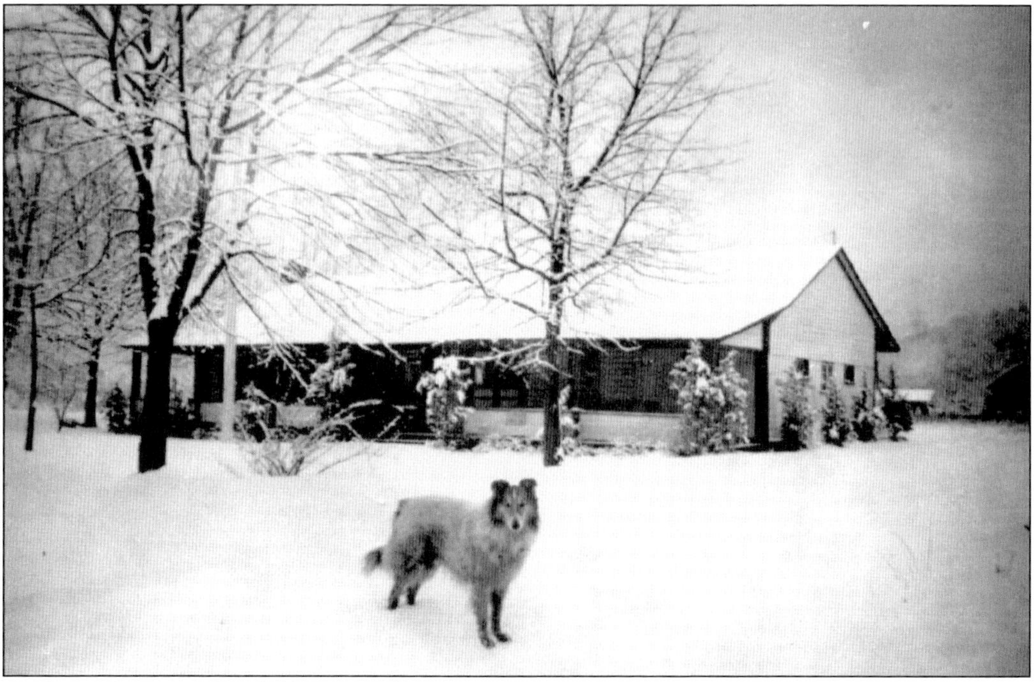

By the early 1920s, the clubhouse had been enlarged to include a fireplace, a kitchen, and a stage. In 1920, this group of civic-minded people formed the Village Improvement Association, which undertook the laying of new sidewalks, installing streetlights, and providing fire protection.

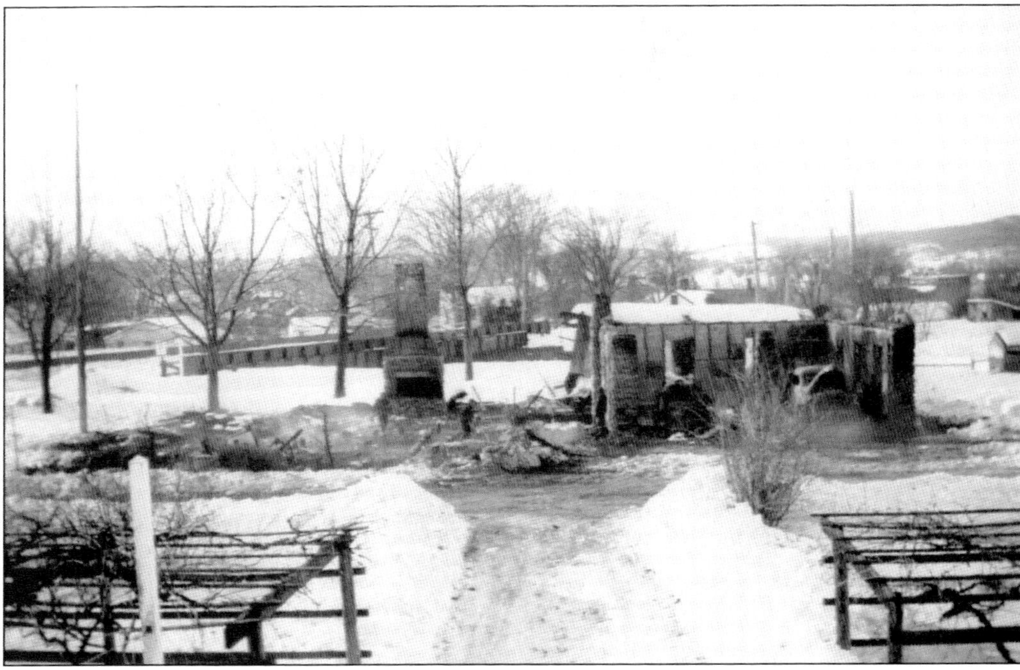

The first piece of fire apparatus, a hand-propelled chemical cart, was housed in a shed built onto the country club. After the formation of a separate volunteer fire company in March 1942, a new International fire engine was purchased by the town, and the building was further enlarged to house it. In January 1948, the clubhouse, fire station, and fire engine were destroyed by a blaze of indeterminate origin.

After the disastrous fire, the firehouse was rebuilt of reinforced concrete and fieldstone. Before the advent of fire sirens and radios, the village was alerted to emergencies by gongs made of old locomotive wheels, one of which can be seen to the left. The building was converted to a private residence in 1986 after a new fire station was built on Route 12.

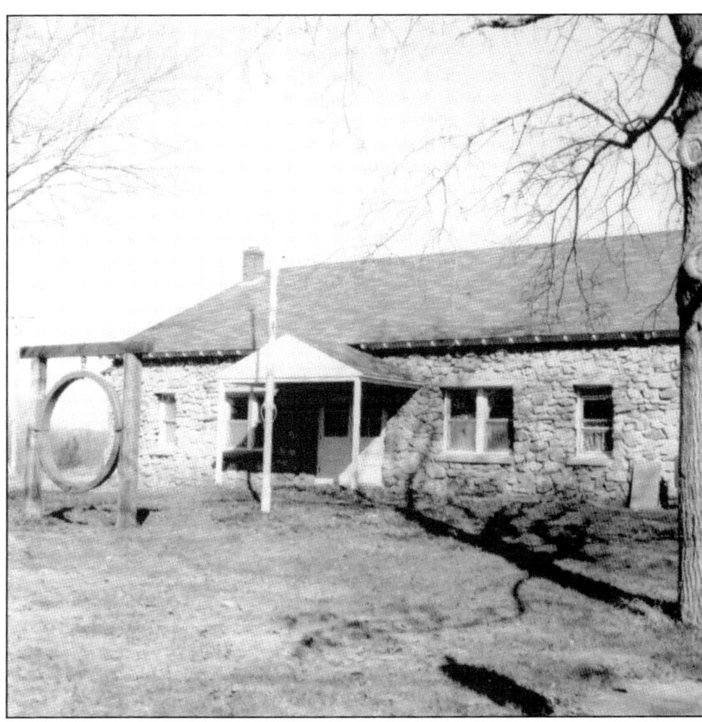

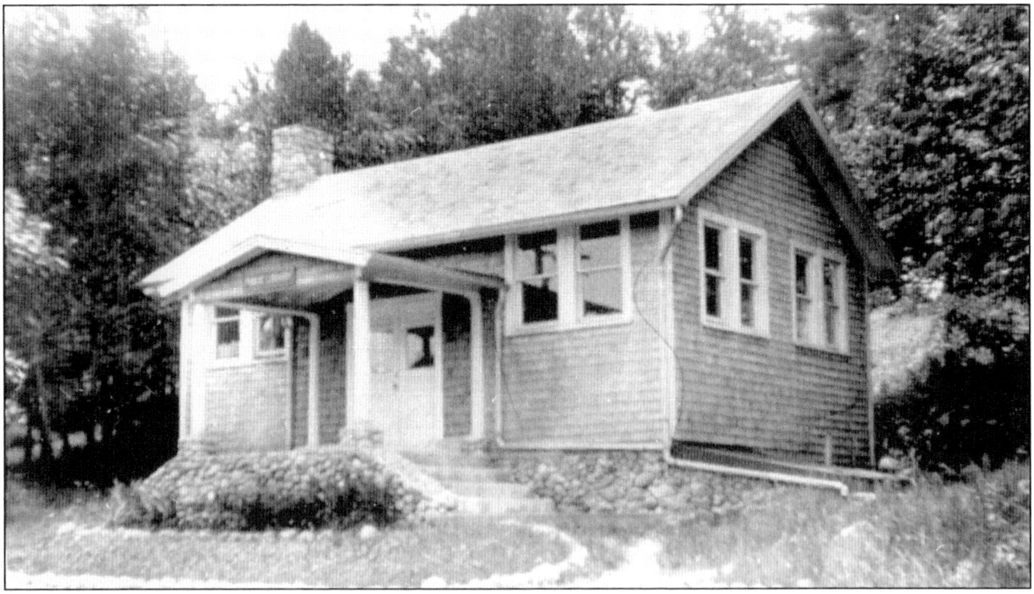

A circulating library was established in the Gales Ferry Country Club clubhouse in 1917, instigated by Hettie Way, a summer resident. It was so successful that a formal organization was begun on July 1, 1920, with the formation of the Gales Ferry Free Public Library. Charles Brown donated a parcel of land on Hurlbutt Road, and by April 1921, a foundation had nearly been completed. The building opened on June 28.

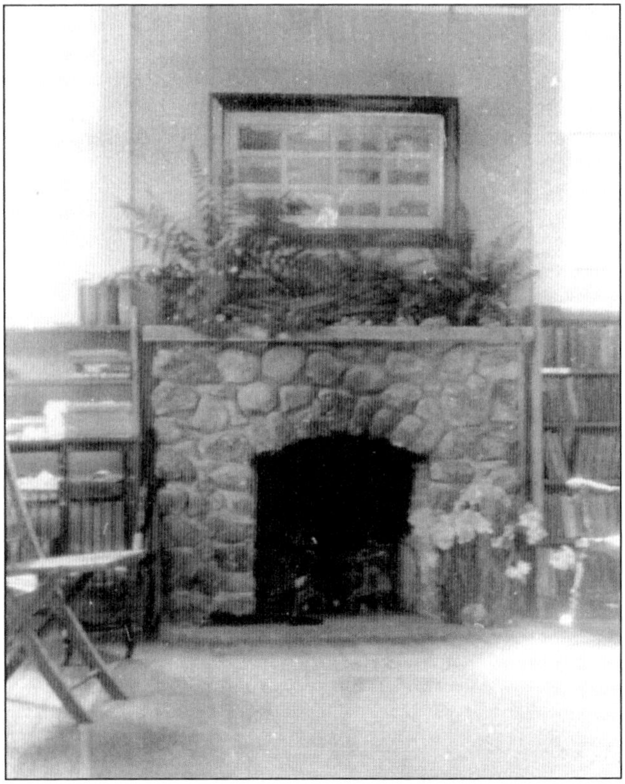

The interior of the original Gales Ferry Library was well furnished with shelves and seating arrangements, made more cozy by a fieldstone fireplace. The building is now a private home.

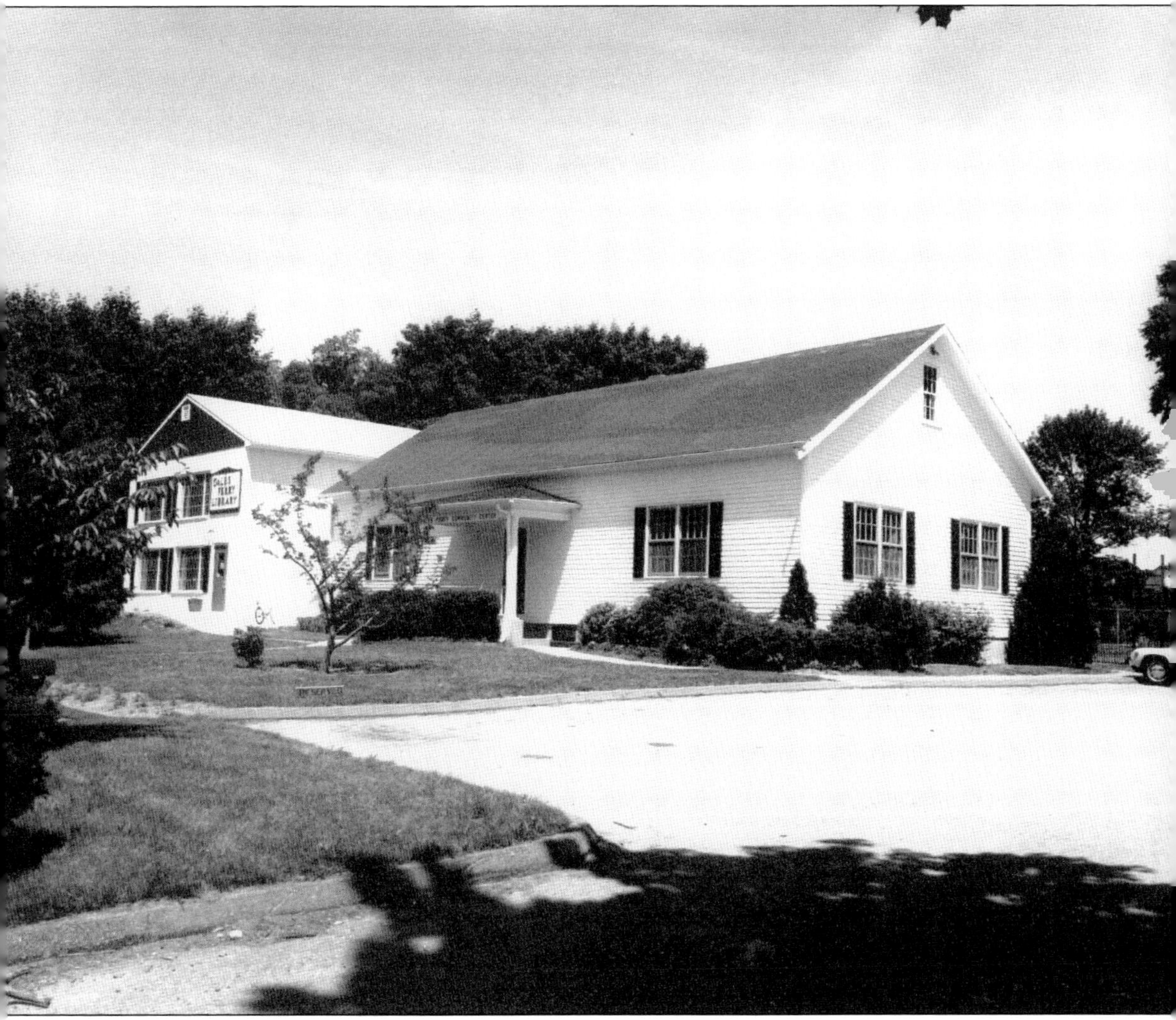

By the early 1970s, the reading and reference needs of the town had outpaced the ability of the Gales Ferry Free Public Library, and a campaign for a new consolidated town library was initiated. It was not successful, however, due in large measure to townspeople's preference for convenient village libraries. In 1973, the Gales Ferry Fire District (successor to the Village Improvement Association) and the Gales Ferry Free Public Library collaborated to provide a site and raise money for a new Gales Ferry Library. The building (left) was attached to the district's community center, a former school. The new library opened in 1974 and was leased to the town.

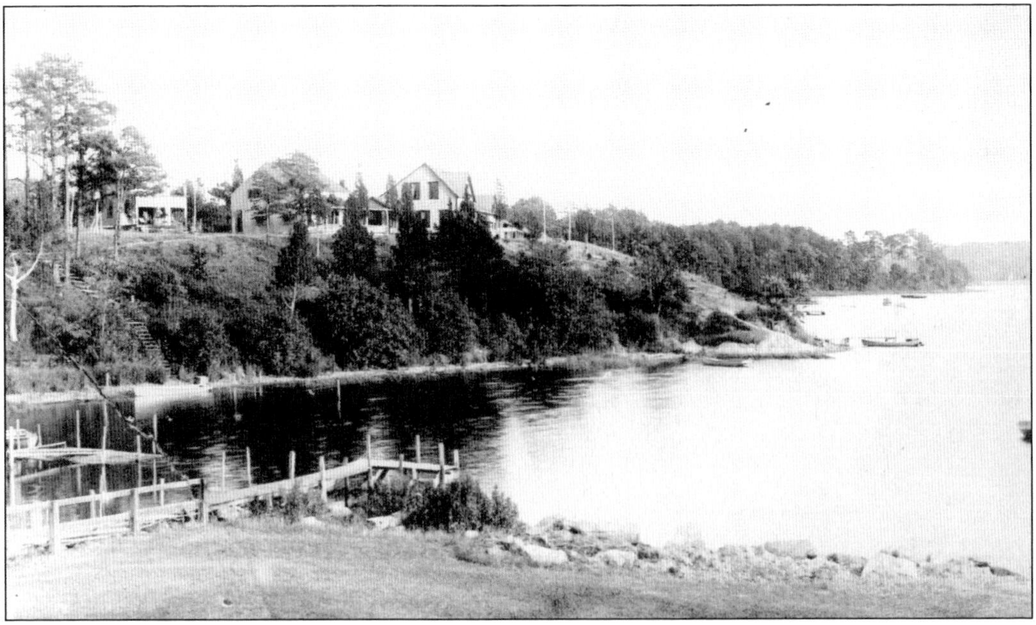

The Bluff began as a summer community on land overlooking the river just south of the Ferry. The land was acquired from Noyes B. Allyn by the New York, New Haven and Hartford Railroad at the time of the rail line extension through the Ferry and was leased to workers for the construction of cottages.

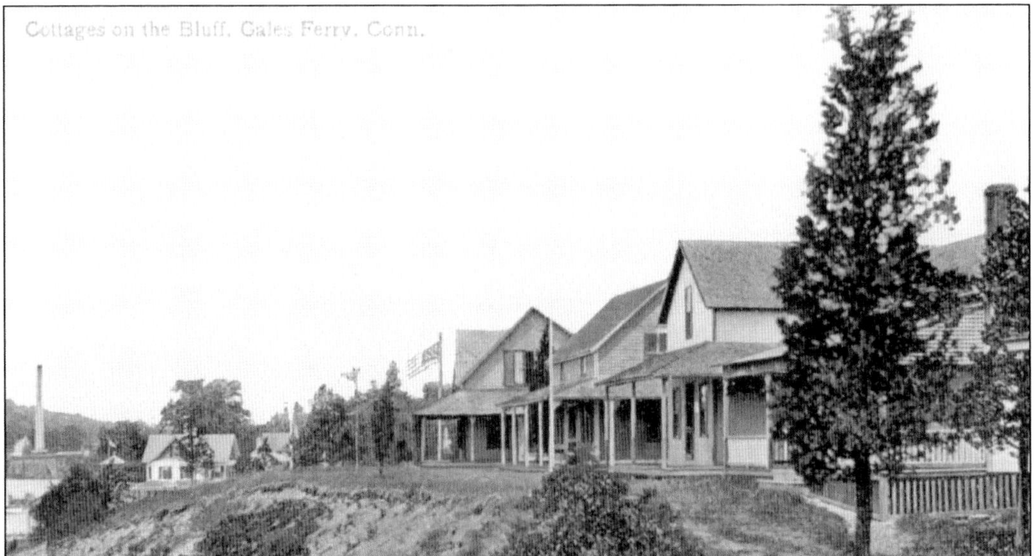

The first cottage was built in 1901. By 1911, 22 of the 24 Bluff lots had buildings, which were owned by the tenant householders. When the railroad decided to sell the land in 1926, the Gales Ferry Realty Association was formed to administer and maintain the community and act as landlord for the cottage owners. Private ownership of the land did not come until 1955.

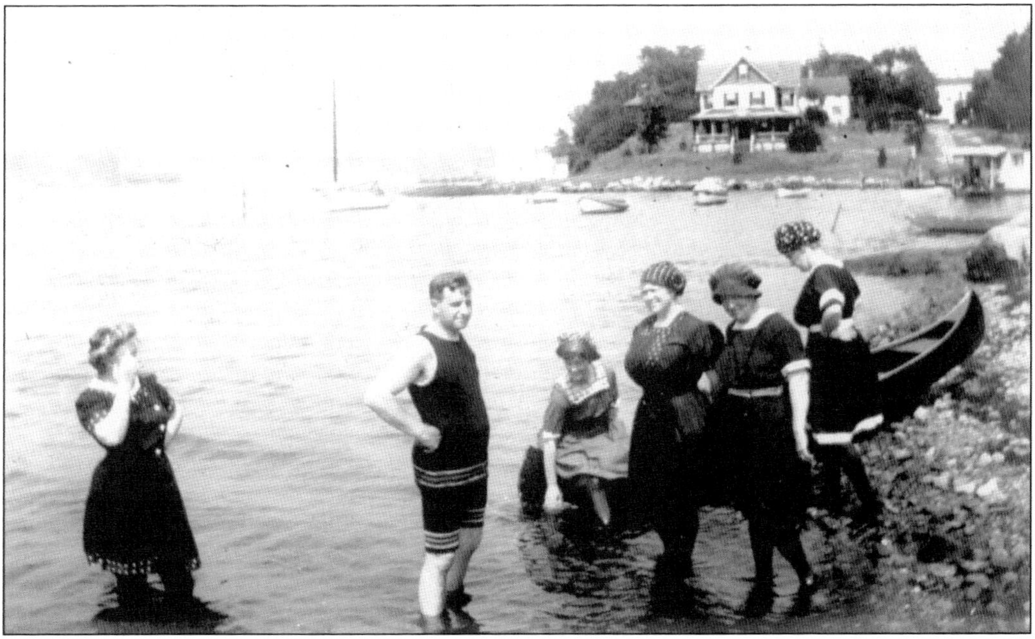

Bathing was a popular pastime for seasonal residents, and boating and diving docks were built at the foot of the Bluff. This *c.* 1915 photograph was captioned "Ladies in Bathing (also Mr. Woodruff)" in the photograph album of a Bluff family. Lower Wharf can be seen in the background.

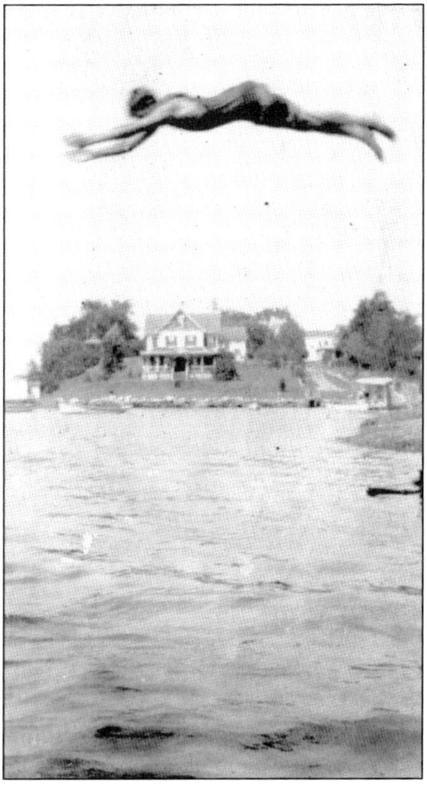

Oliver Wulf (1897–1987), whose family owned one of the Bluff's cottages, was an athlete and scholar. He later became a scientist with the U.S. Weather Bureau, forerunner of the National Weather Service. Here, he executes a swan dive from the dock at the foot of the Bluff.

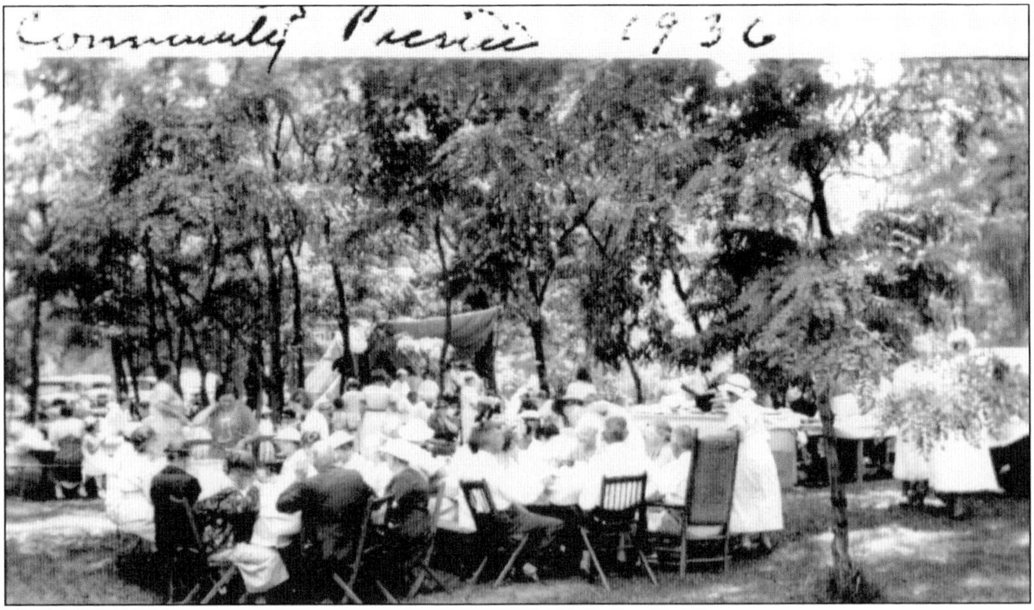

The Methodist church held picnics in Gales Ferry starting in the 1890s, eventually settling into a permanent spot on the lawn beside Noyes B. Allyn's house. These broadened into community affairs, with the whole village attending and other organizations setting up booths and activities. The picnics were a village tradition until World War II.

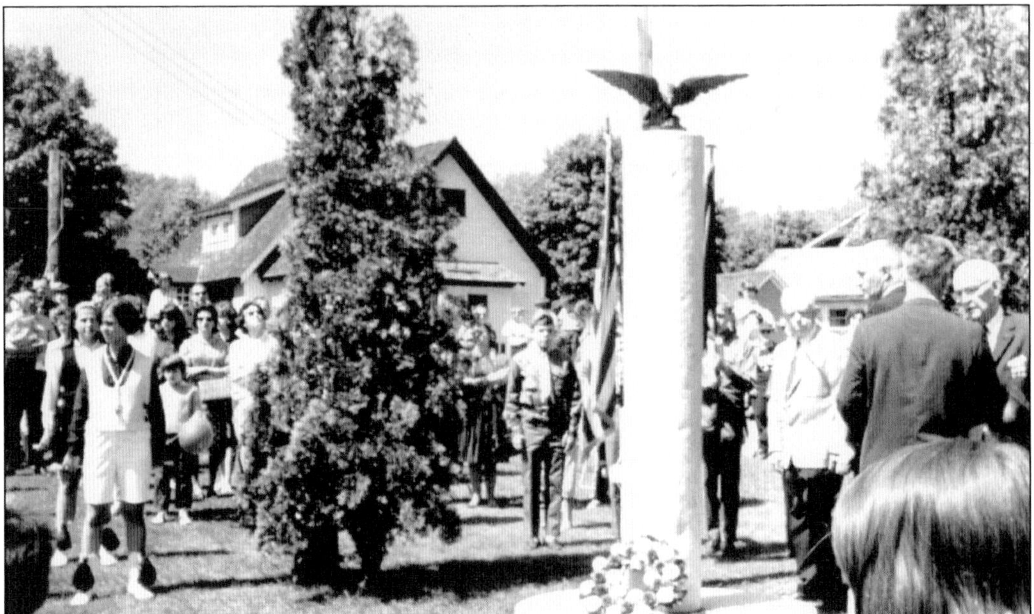

The Gales Ferry Memorial Parklet began as a small piece of land deeded to the Village Improvement Association by Henry Hurlbutt in 1920 to memorialize those lost in World War I. In 1942, an honor roll was placed on the parklet. The wooden roll had deteriorated by 1956, and a stone memorial was constructed of a granite column (a 1942 gift by Courtland Colver Sr.) and placed on a millstone from the Stoddard Mill on Route 12. This photograph was taken during a Memorial Day observance in 1966.

Four

Decatur's Mountain

Though hardly a native son, Stephen Decatur is remembered in Gales Ferry by a street, a hill, and a monument bearing his name. Captain Decatur, distinguished for his audacious capture of the British frigate *Macedonian* in October 1812, took command of a squadron at New York. Attempting to escape a British blockade, he sailed his small fleet up Long Island Sound. Encountering British warships near Block Island, Decatur, now a commodore, sought refuge in New London Harbor in June 1813.

New London and Groton, scenes of fierce battles during the American Revolution, had become placid, their forts fallen into disrepair. This new war was not popular in New England, and Decatur's efforts to organize the citizenry were largely fruitless. He weighed anchor and moved his fleet up the Thames, finding a permanent refuge at Allyn's Point, just north of Gales Ferry. Sand bars forced him to lighten the ships, but the shallow water also provided an impediment to pursuit by the enemy.

There, he was sheltered by Allyn's Mountain, the top of which offered a splendid view all the way to New London. He proceeded to erect breastworks at the crest, armed with cannon transported from the ships. Tradition holds that he stretched a heavy chain across the river as a further shield, and rings implanted in riverside rocks support this story. The Decatur fleet attempted to leave the river in the spring of 1814 but was unsuccessful. Leaving his fleet behind, he traveled by land to New York, taking command of the USS *President*. Outgunned by the British in the West Indies, he was taken prisoner. Elsewhere, however, negotiations were under way to end the war, resulting in the signing of the Treaty of Ghent on December 24, 1814. News of the peace, though, did not arrive in America until February 1815. New London celebrated with a George Washington Birthday Ball, and Decatur, by coincidence recently paroled by the British, came ashore to participate. The embargoed ships finally set sail.

The artifacts of history have mostly weathered away, but the hill overlooking Gales Ferry is still known as Mount Decatur.

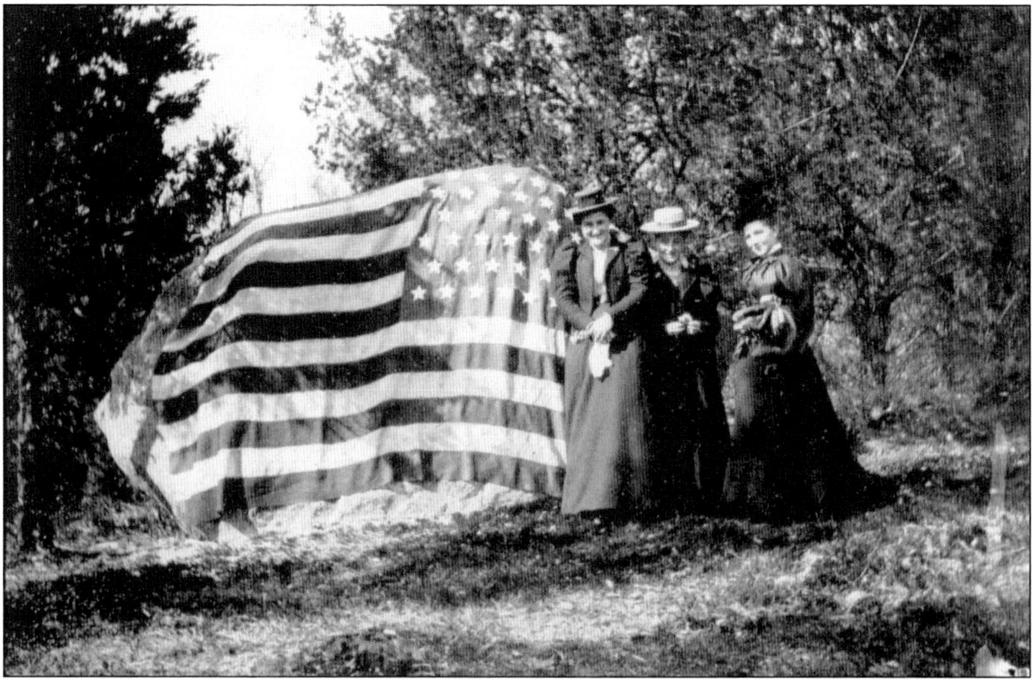

In 1898, the Belton Allyn Society, Children of the American Revolution, dedicated a stone atop Mount Decatur to commemorate the commodore's time in Gales Ferry.

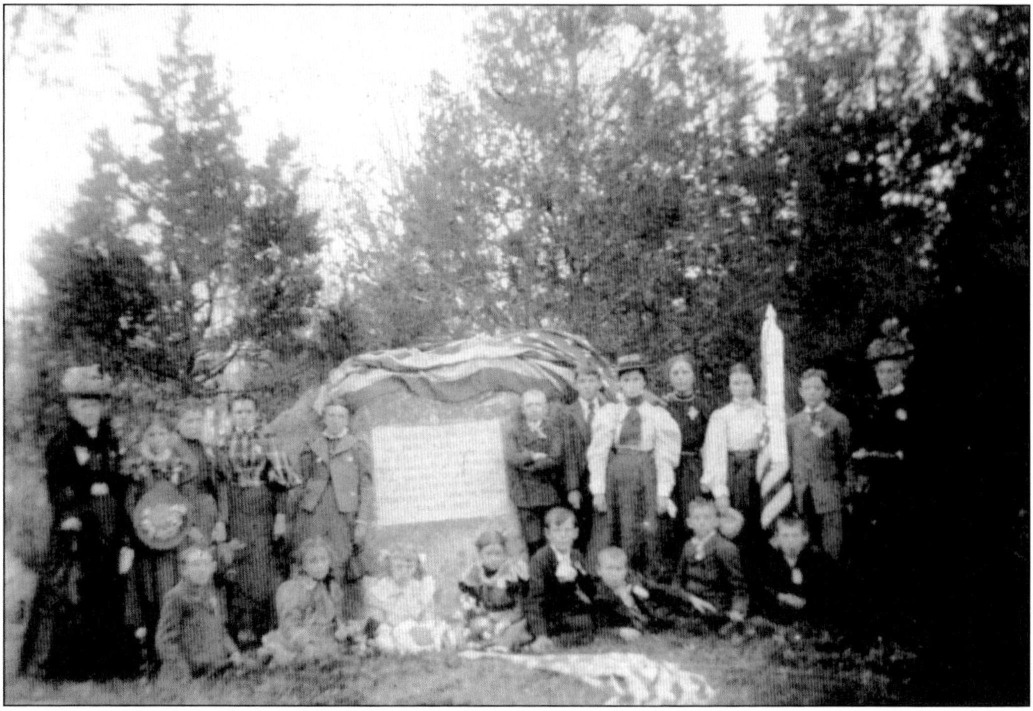

Dated February 28, 1898, the Decatur stone was unveiled later that year. The National Society of Children of the American Revolution, formed in 1895, is today the oldest patriotic association for the nation's youth.

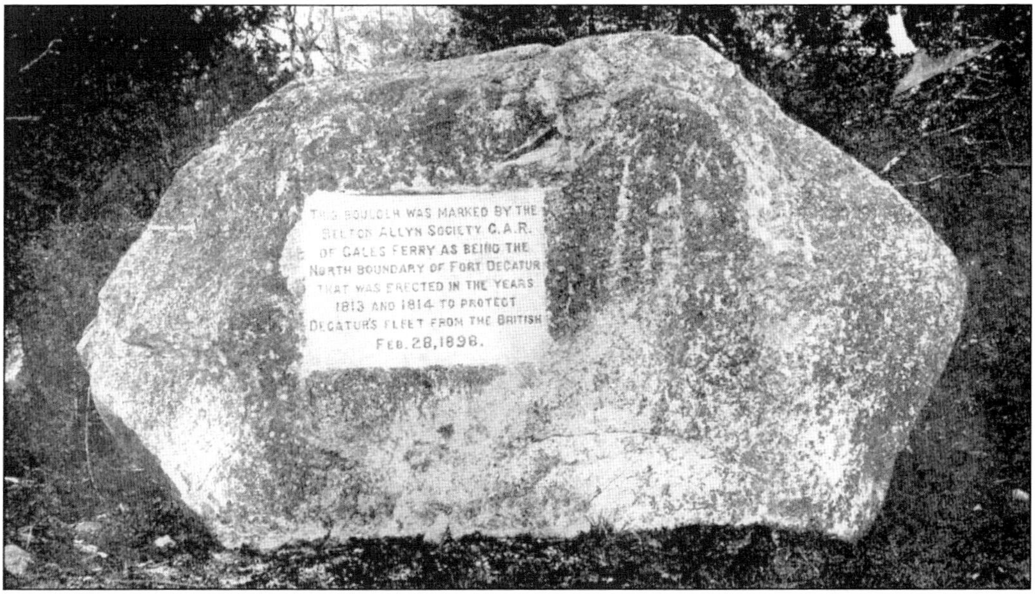

The commemorative stone is inscribed as marking "the north boundary of Fort Decatur that was erected in the years 1813 and 1814 to protect Decatur's fleet from the British." The Belton Allyn Society is no longer active, and the nearest local group is the General Ebenezer Huntington Society in Norwich. Below is a closeup of the inscription.

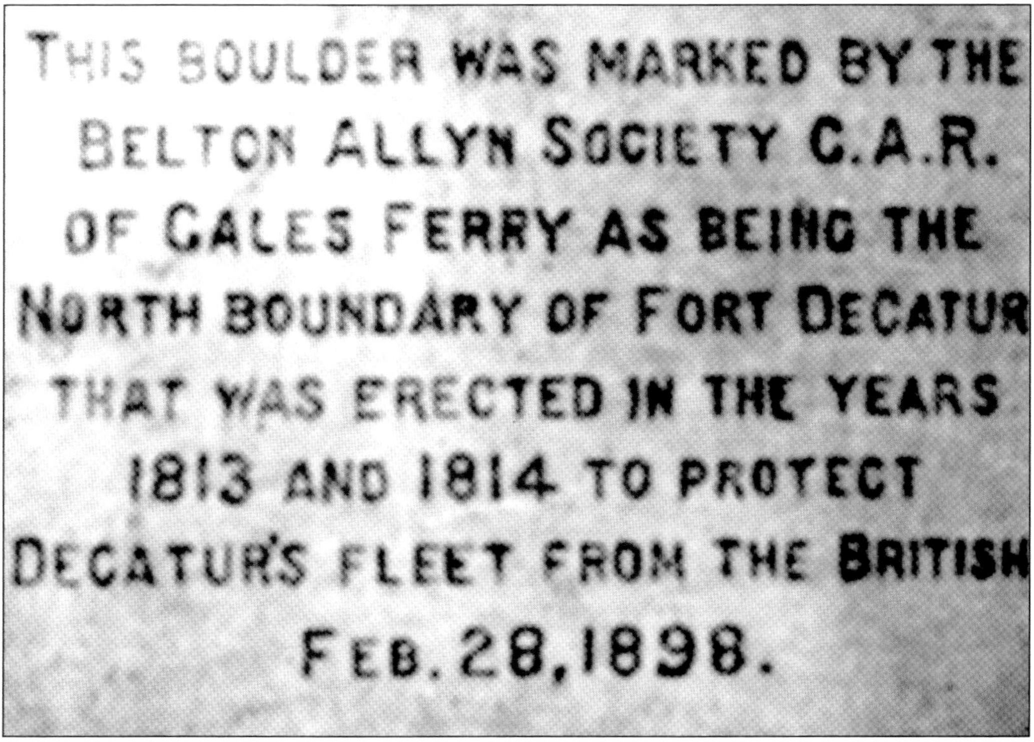

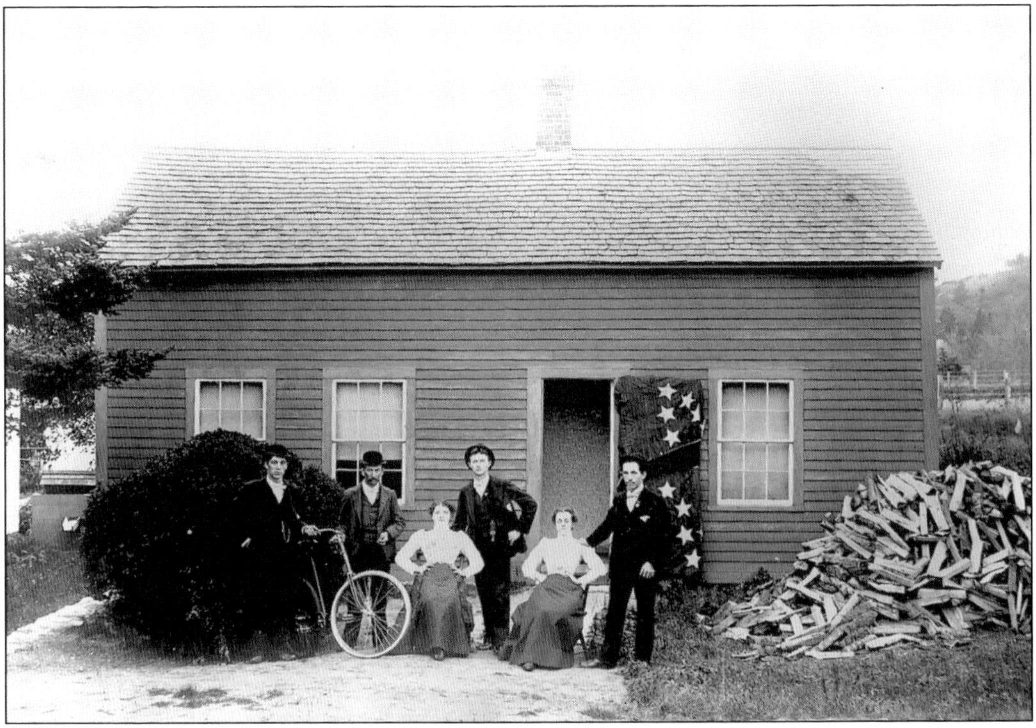

Legend states that Stephen Decatur taught his midshipmen navigation at the so-called Ichabod Cottage in Gales Ferry. Built by John Allyn Jr. in 1795, the cottage takes its name from Ichabod Babcock, who lived there from 1815 to 1848.

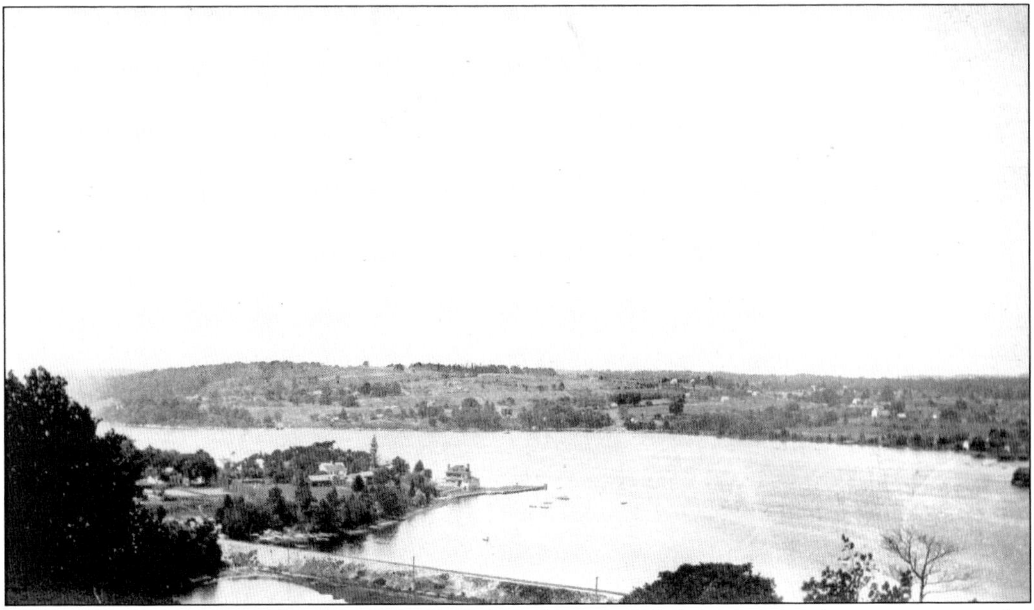

This view southward from Mount Decatur is indicative of the mountain's attraction to the commodore. From the top, one has a commanding view of any vessels coming up the river.

The tradition of a chain across the river is substantiated by artifacts embedded in stones along the shore. Ledyard town historian Janice Bell stands by a ring on the Montville side of the Thames River in 1968.

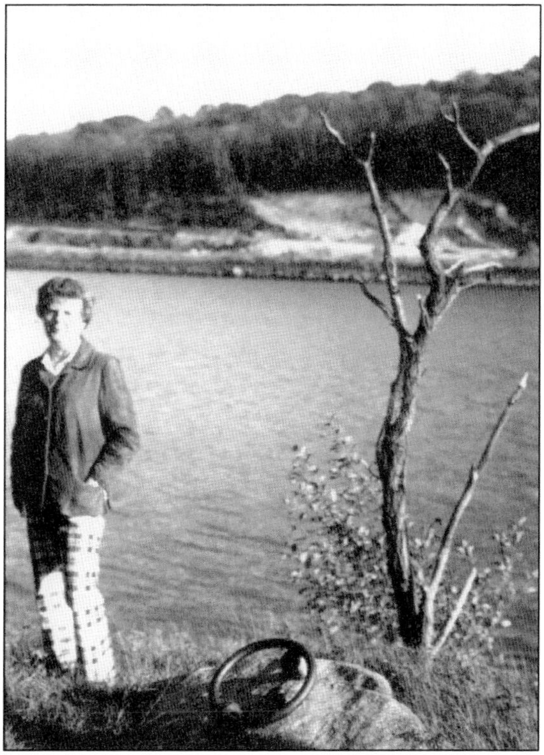

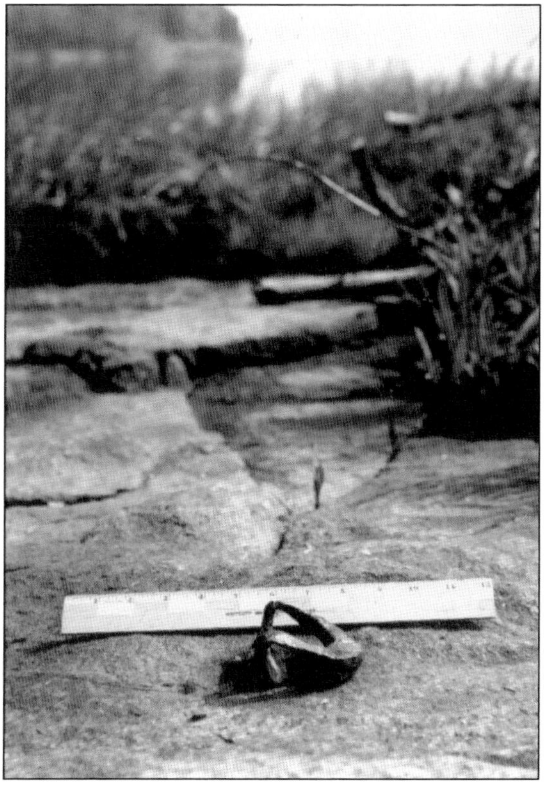

A line of hasps is embedded in the rocks on the Gales Ferry side of the Thames River. Prominent at the time this 1961 photograph was taken, the hasps are now but iron stains on the rocks.

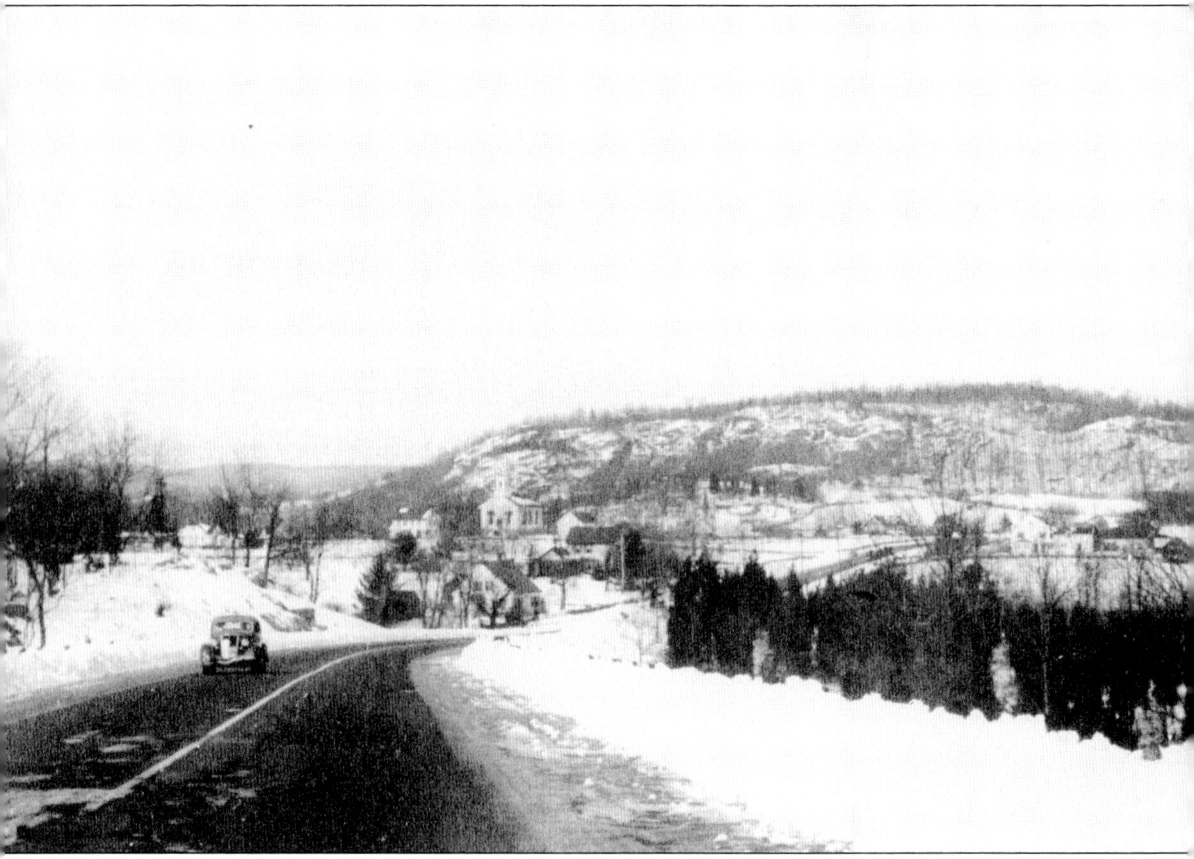

Gales Ferry lies in the shadow of Mount Decatur. This wartime photograph, taken soon after the December 1943 opening of Connecticut Route 12, shows a much less intensely developed community and a mountain free of the high-tension power lines that now cross its summit.

In earlier times, Mount Decatur was a popular place for outings from the village. This young man atop the mountain in 1920 is Allen DuMont, a summer resident of the Bluff. Allen Balcom DuMont (1901–1965) was a television pioneer and founder of the DuMont Television Network, the nation's first, in 1946.

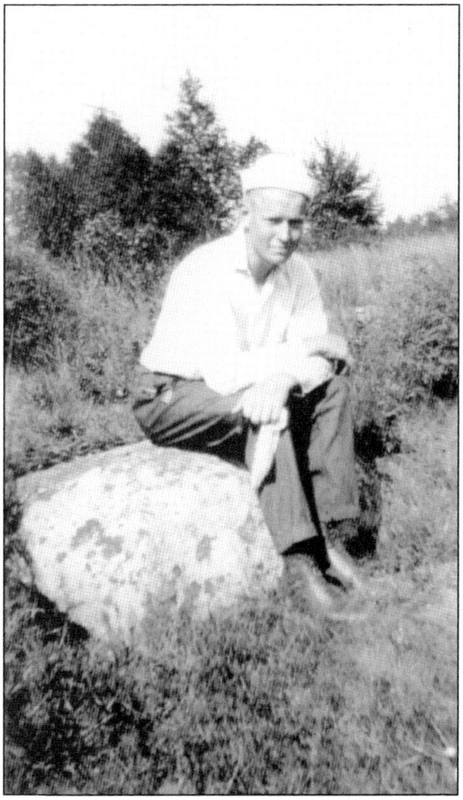

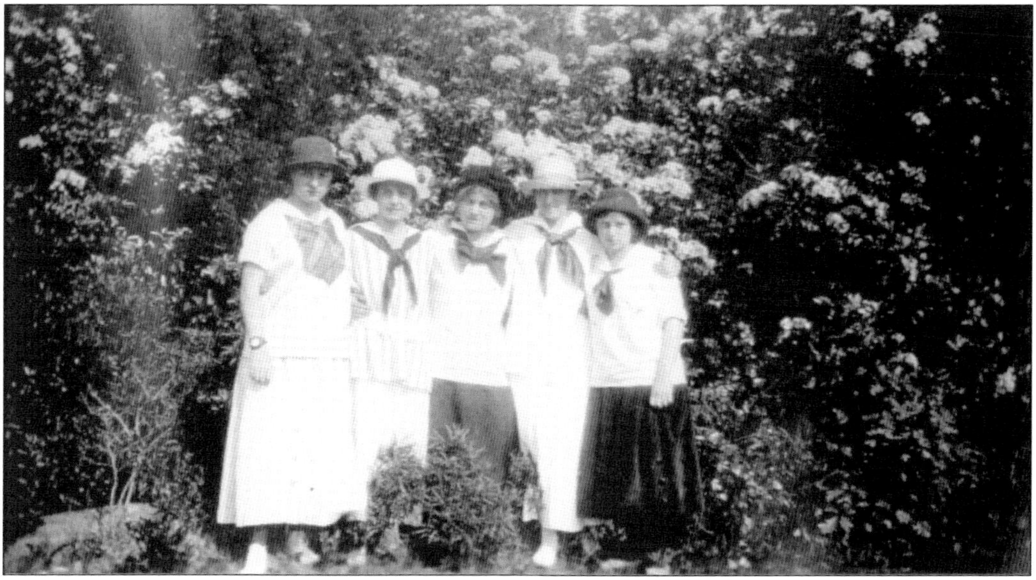

Spring laurel blossoms give a festive background to a Wulf family outing on Mount Decatur in 1915. Family members shown here are, from left to right, Dot, Faith, Daisy, Ede, and Helene.

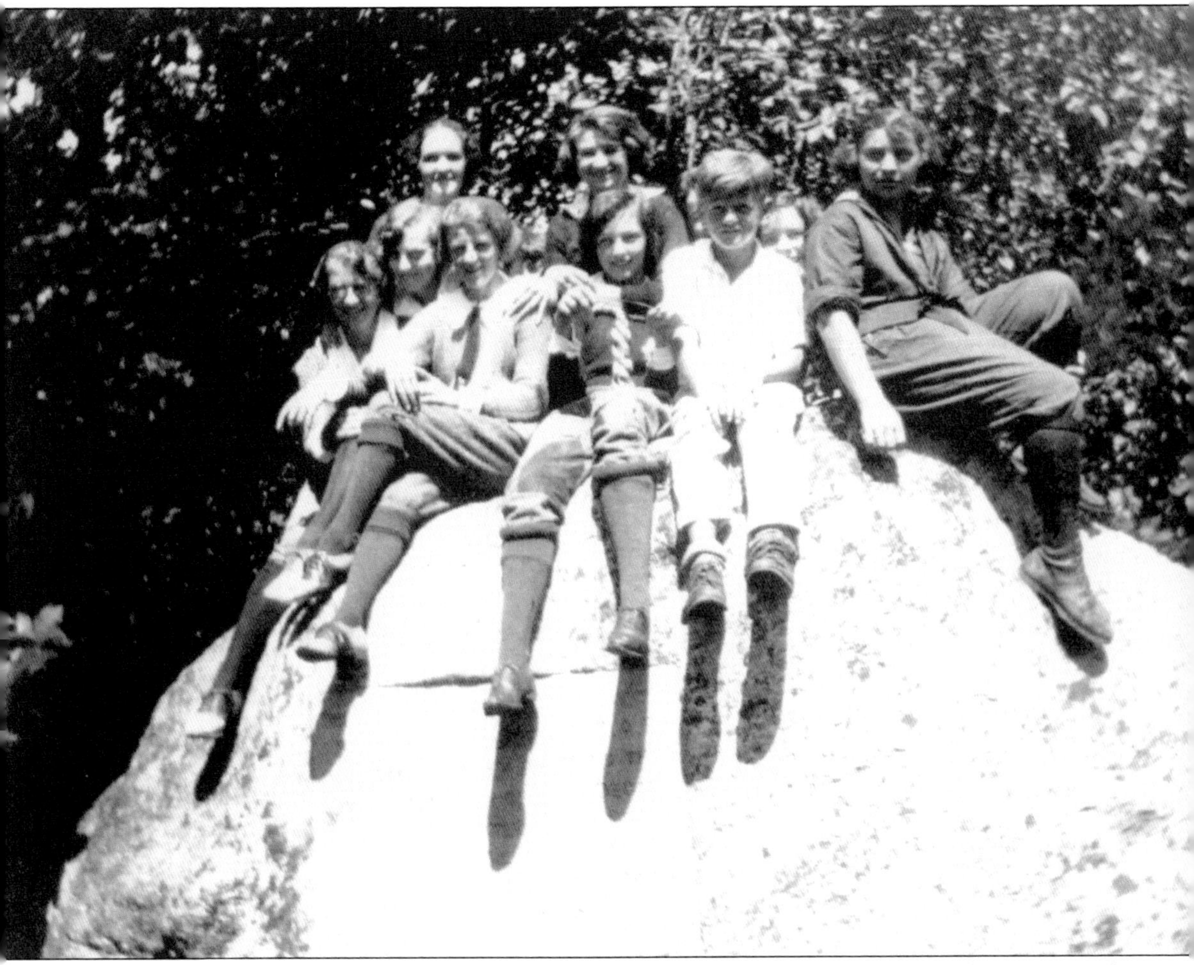

Family outings to Mount Decatur were common in the early part of the 20th century. This group from the Bluff sits on the commemorative stone for a photograph c. 1918.

Five

Boat Race Day

The Harvard-Yale Regatta, America's oldest intercollegiate athletic event, has been rowed on the Thames River, between New London and Gales Ferry, since 1878. The two universities first met on the water in 1852, at Lake Winnepesaukee in New Hampshire. The early years of the contest were held at erratic intervals at various New England venues, but in 1864, a race on Lake Quinsigamond at Worcester began an annual tradition that has rarely been interrupted.

An unusual, four-mile course on the Connecticut River was adopted in 1876, and two years later, the first event was held on the Thames. The Yale crew arrived 12 days prior to the race, boarding at the house of Latham Brown in the Ferry. Harvard set up camp at the farmhouse of Charles Stoddard at Long Cove, about a mile to the south.

For a time, the Thames was the place to be for college rowing. Cornell, Columbia, and the University of Pennsylvania all raced here, though only Harvard and Yale have remained. Crews boarded in local homes, families moving their children into temporary quarters in outbuildings during the race season. The inaugural 1878 Harvard-Yale race drew 25,000 spectators; by 1925, the crowds numbered 100,000, a 500-yacht spectator fleet lay at anchor, and two observation trains followed the race, one on each side of the river.

By this time, the two universities had taken permanent quarters, Yale purchasing the houses of Latham and Christopher Brown and Harvard constructing Red Top Cottage on the bank of the river, north of Cow Point. Boathouses at both camps were rebuilt and enlarged, and in 1930, Harvard acquired the Charles Brown farm at Brown's Crossing, constructing a large dining hall and several dormitories there.

Although Boat Race Day on the Thames no longer draws the crowds of earlier years, it remains the high point of the rowing season at both Harvard and Yale and is still considered a holiday by many in Gales Ferry.

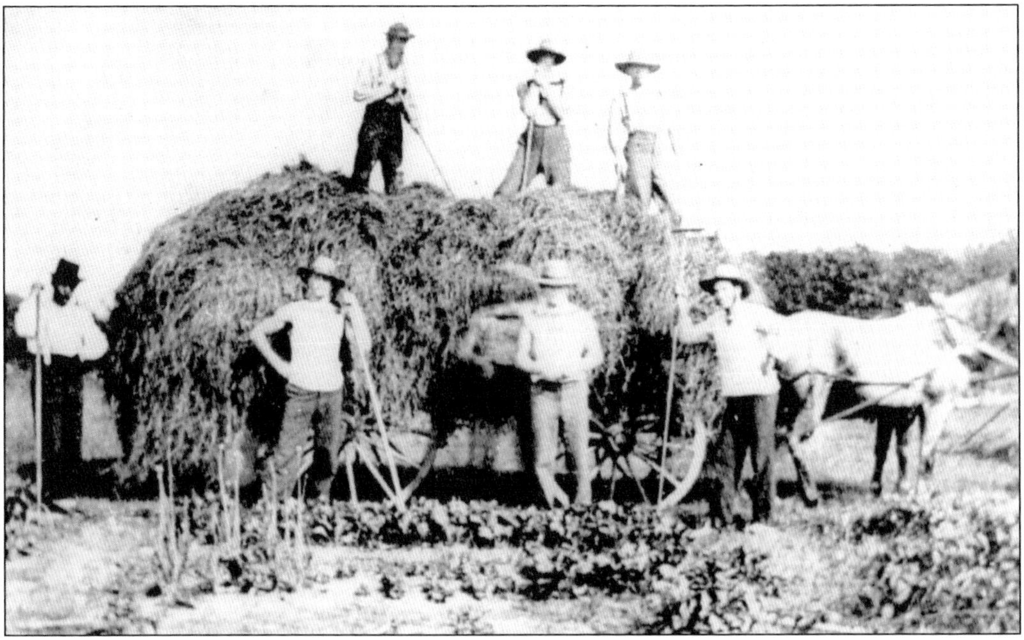

The first Harvard crews to train on the Thames boarded at the farmhouse of Charles Stoddard at Long Cove. It is not certain whether they were expected to work on the farm in exchange for their board or were merely exercising a photographic opportunity.

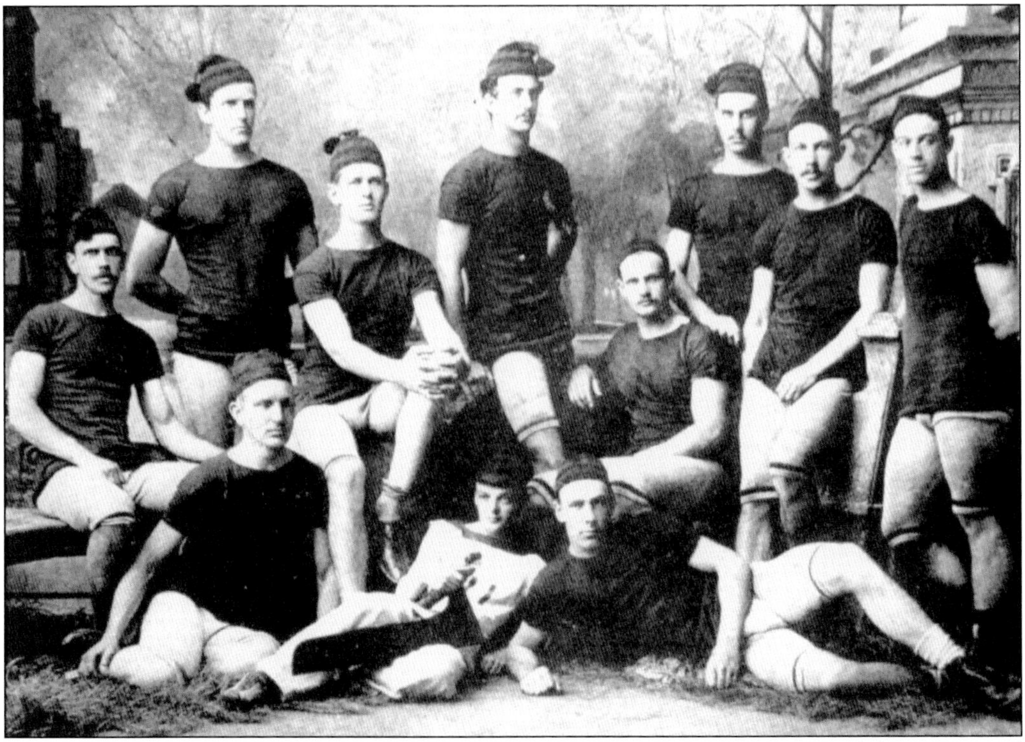

The Harvard crew of 1883 poses for a group photograph against a studio backdrop. Harvard crews have won nearly two-thirds of the regattas since 1852.

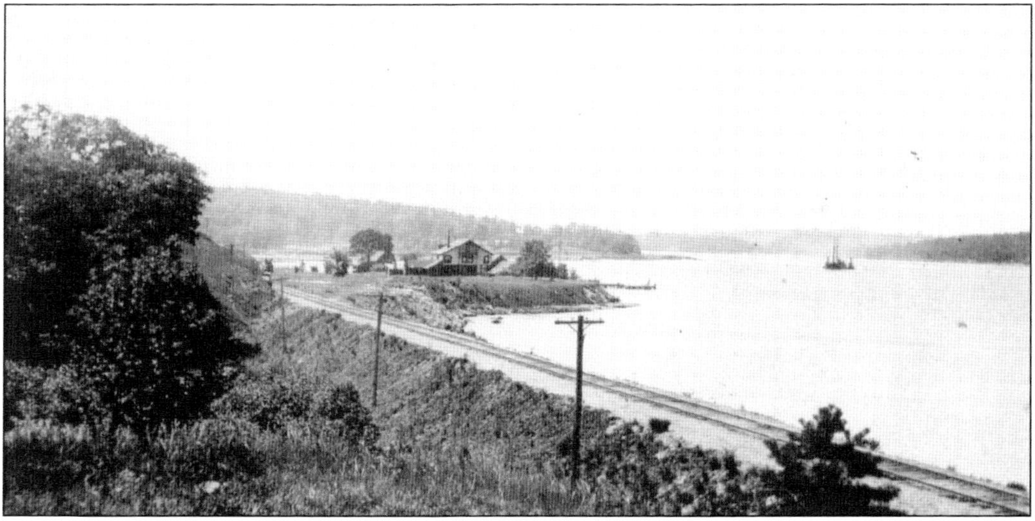

Harvard acquired property north of the icehouse in 1881 and built Red Top Cottage on the rise overlooking the boathouse. This served as the crew's headquarters until the acquisition of adjacent property in 1930.

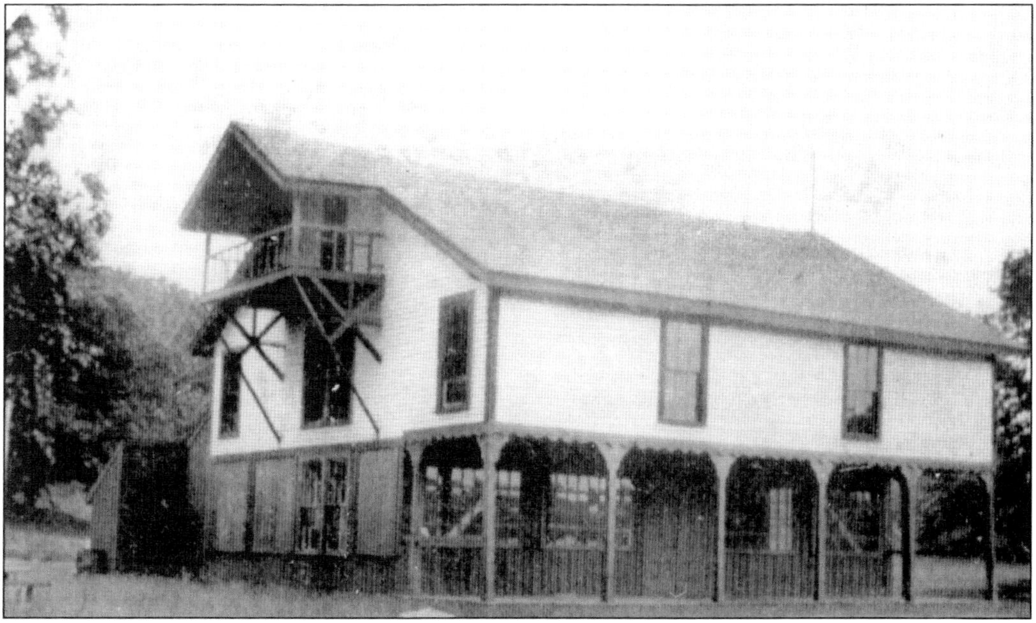

As evidenced here, Red Top Cottage had sleeping quarters on the upper floors and dining below.

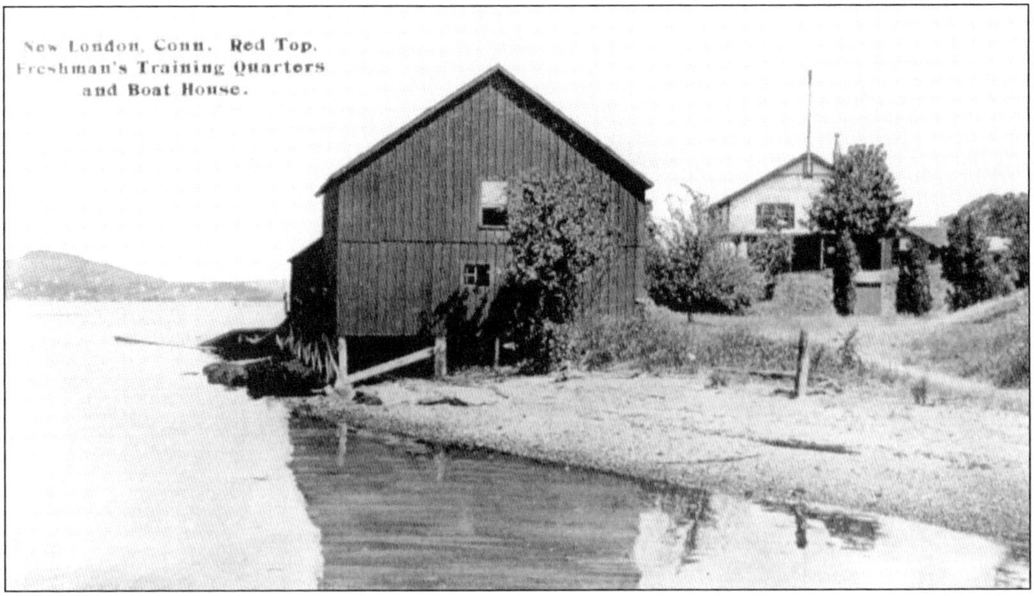

Harvard's first boathouse was located at Cow Point, but by the time Red Top was built in 1881, a new structure had been built at the site of the present boathouse. Crews arrived for training about two weeks before the regatta.

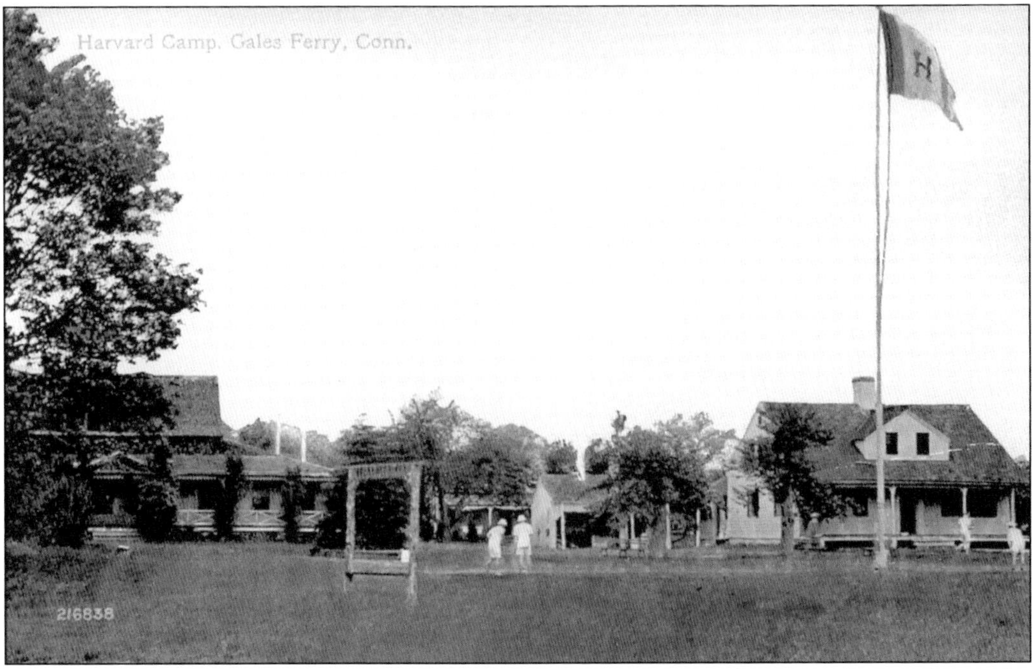

In 1930, Harvard purchased the farm of Charles Brown on Military Highway, above the site of Red Top. Brown's house (left) burned, after which large dormitories and a dining hall were constructed.

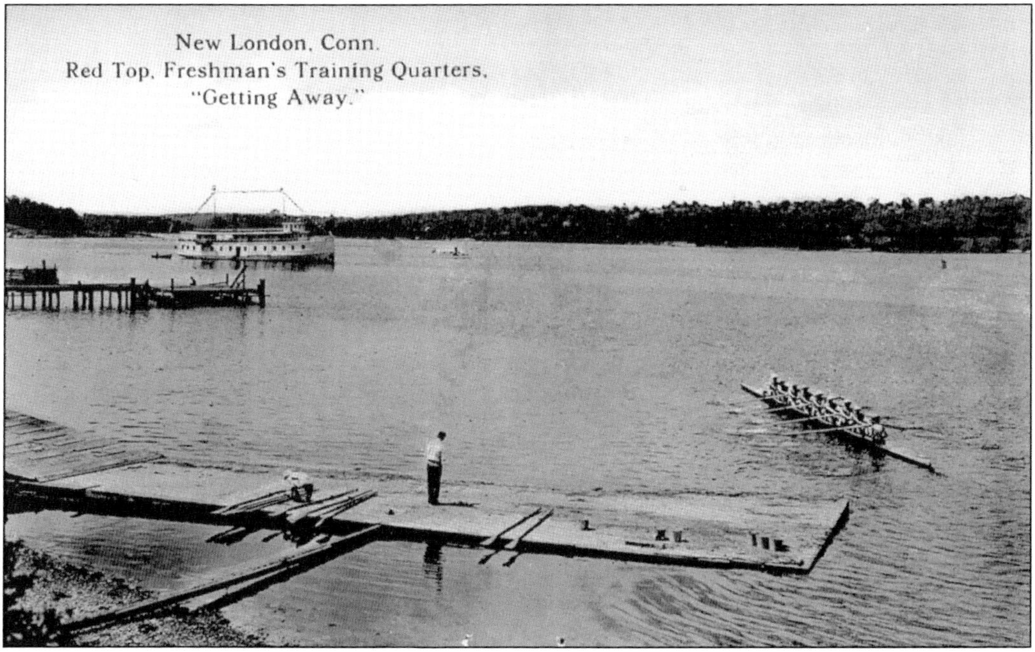

This early postcard, entitled "Getting Away," shows a freshman crew leaving the launch ramp for a row on the Thames.

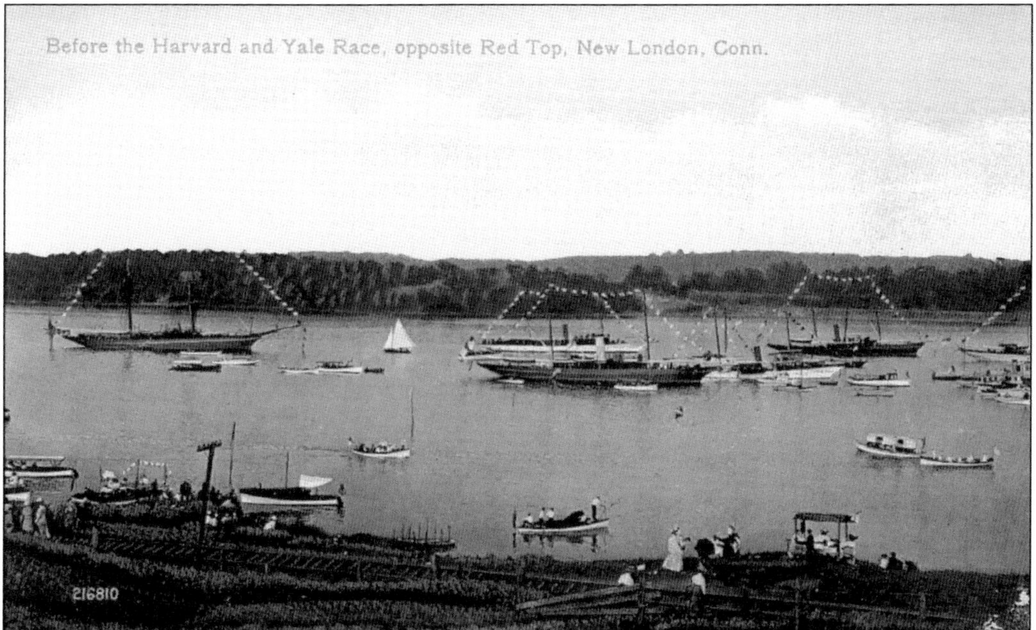

By the 1920s, the Harvard-Yale Regatta drew a sizeable spectator fleet bedecked with flags and pennants. In 1925, some 500 yachts lay at anchor.

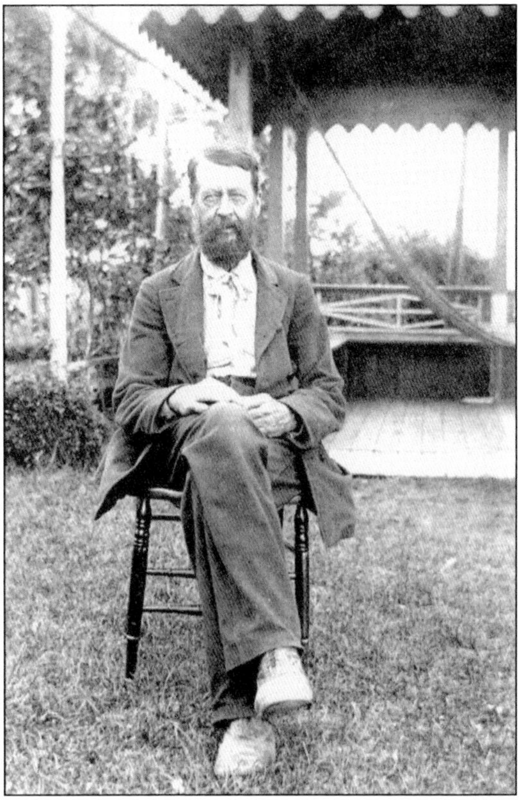

Latham Brown, a Civil War veteran, was caretaker of the navy yard in Groton. The Yale crew began boarding at his house in the Ferry in 1878. The house was later acquired by the university as permanent training quarters.

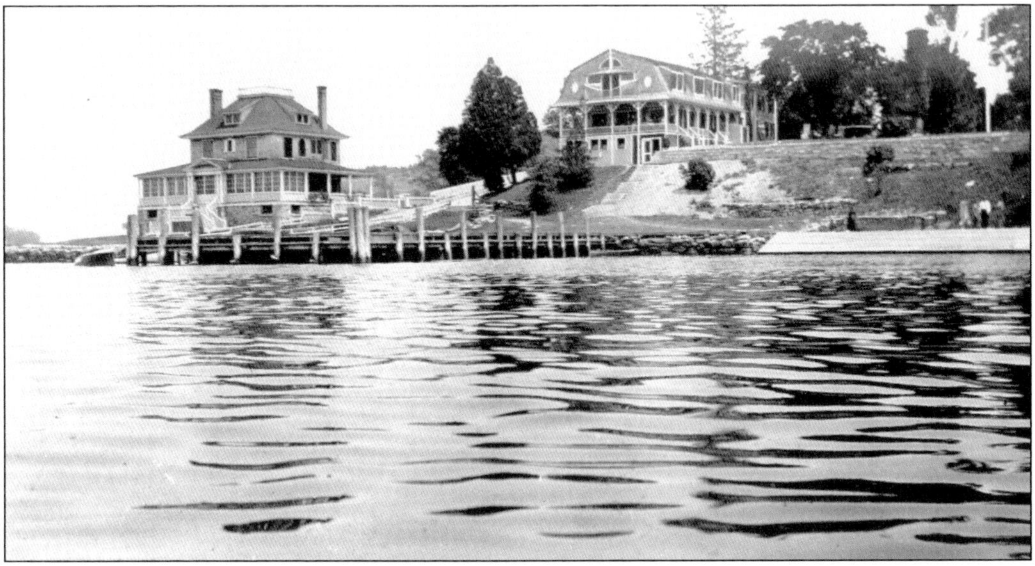

The Yale quarters at Gales Ferry consisted of the Whitney cottage (left) and the Thomas Geer house (center) in addition to Latham Brown's house (out of frame to the right). Built *c.* 1908 as the Voorhees cottage, the Whitney cottage was renamed after it was purchased by Payne Whitney in 1911. The university purchased the Geer house from Christopher "Kit" Brown in 1907.

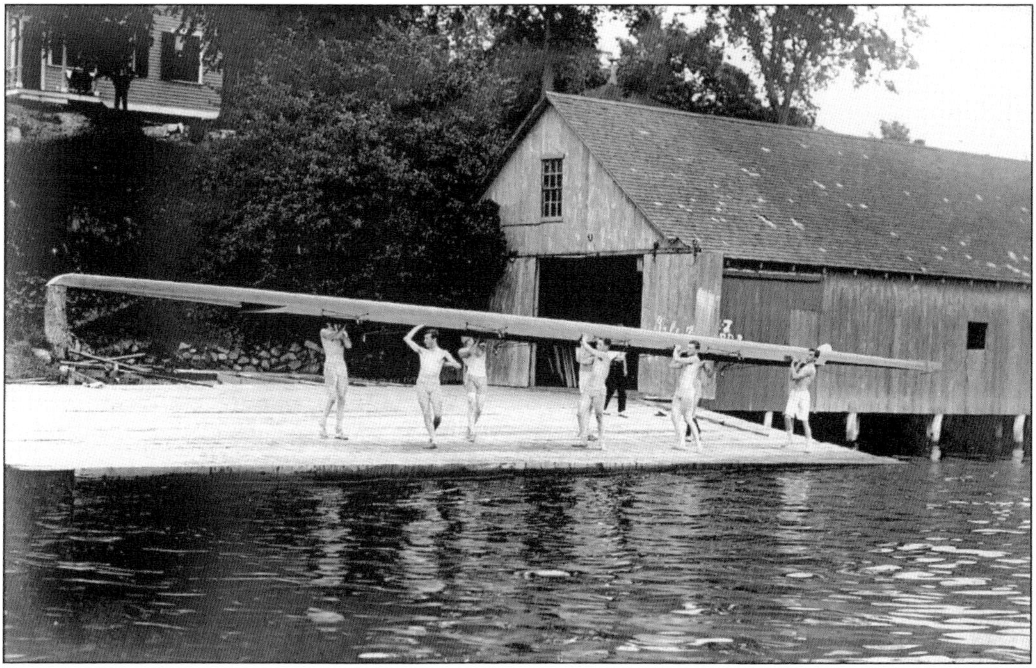

Yale's old boathouse was located slightly to the south of the present structure. Here, a crew lifts its shell into the water *c.* 1915.

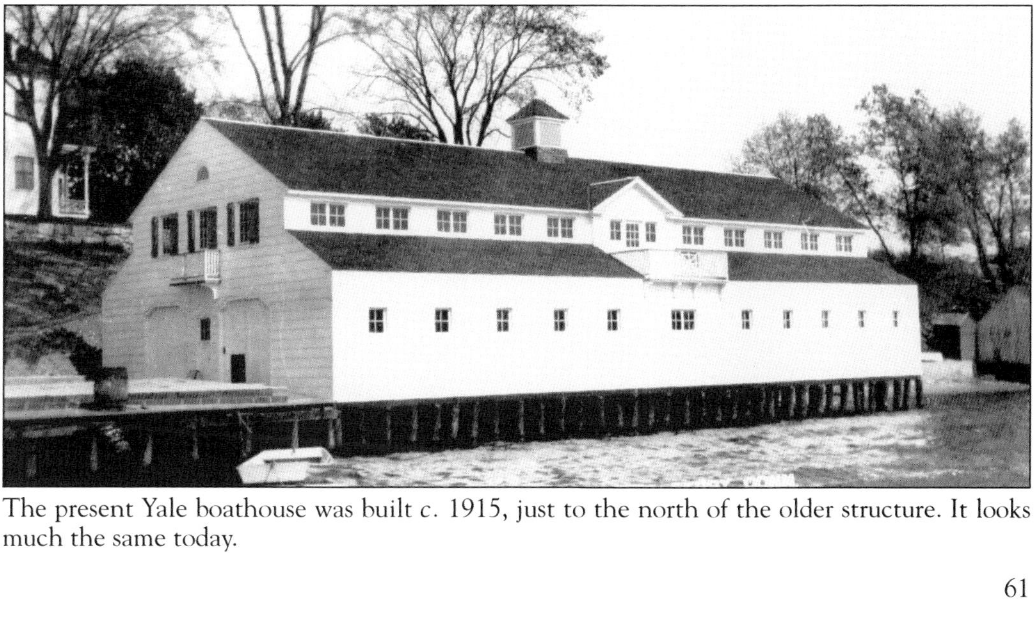

The present Yale boathouse was built *c.* 1915, just to the north of the older structure. It looks much the same today.

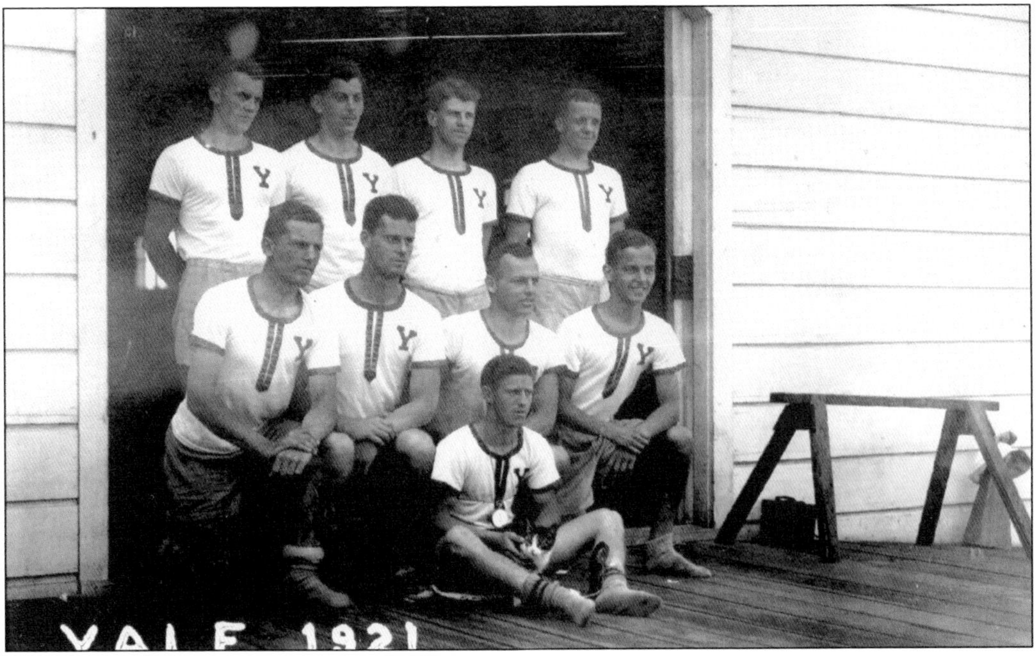

The 1921 Yale crew poses in the doorway of the boathouse prior to rowing to victory. That year, Yale began a six-year winning streak.

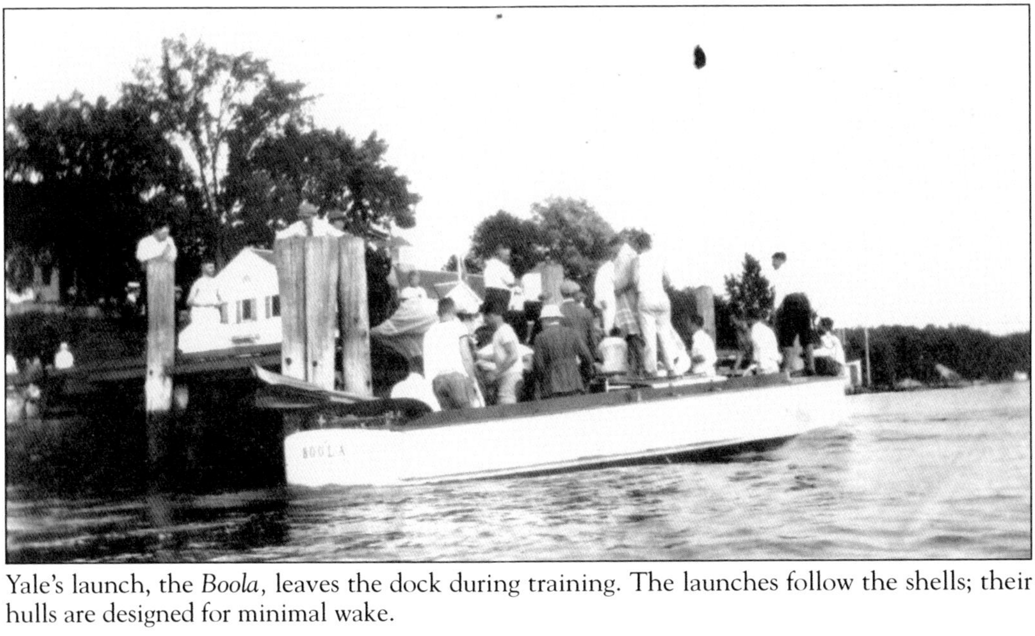
Yale's launch, the *Boola*, leaves the dock during training. The launches follow the shells; their hulls are designed for minimal wake.

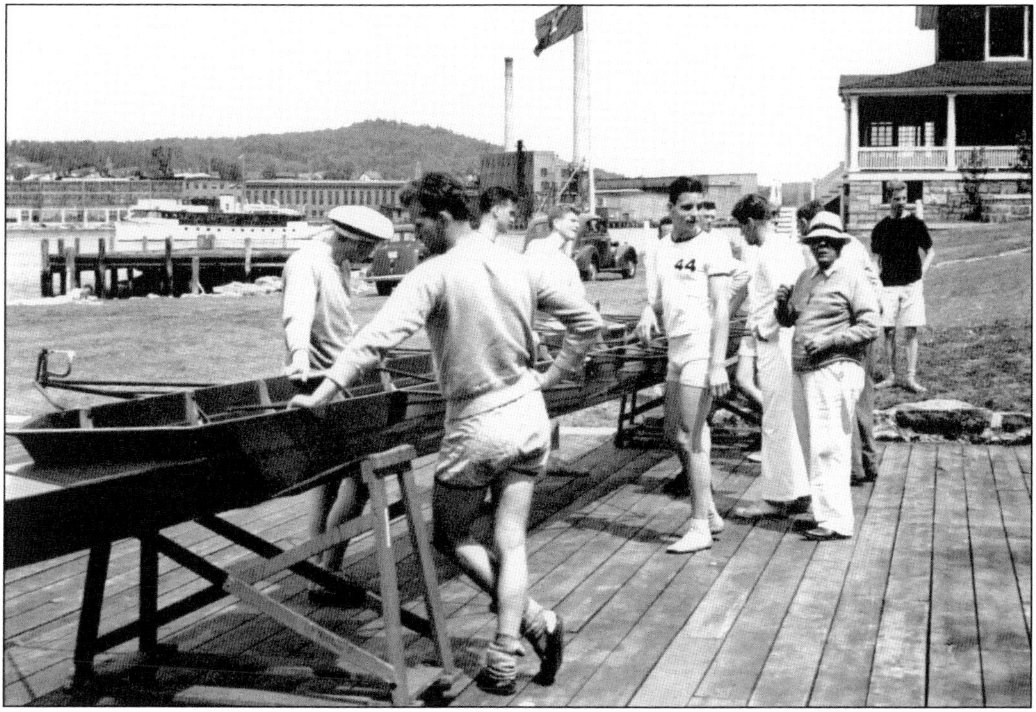

A Yale racing shell is outfitted in 1943. The Whitney cottage, used as the coaches' quarters, can be seen to the right.

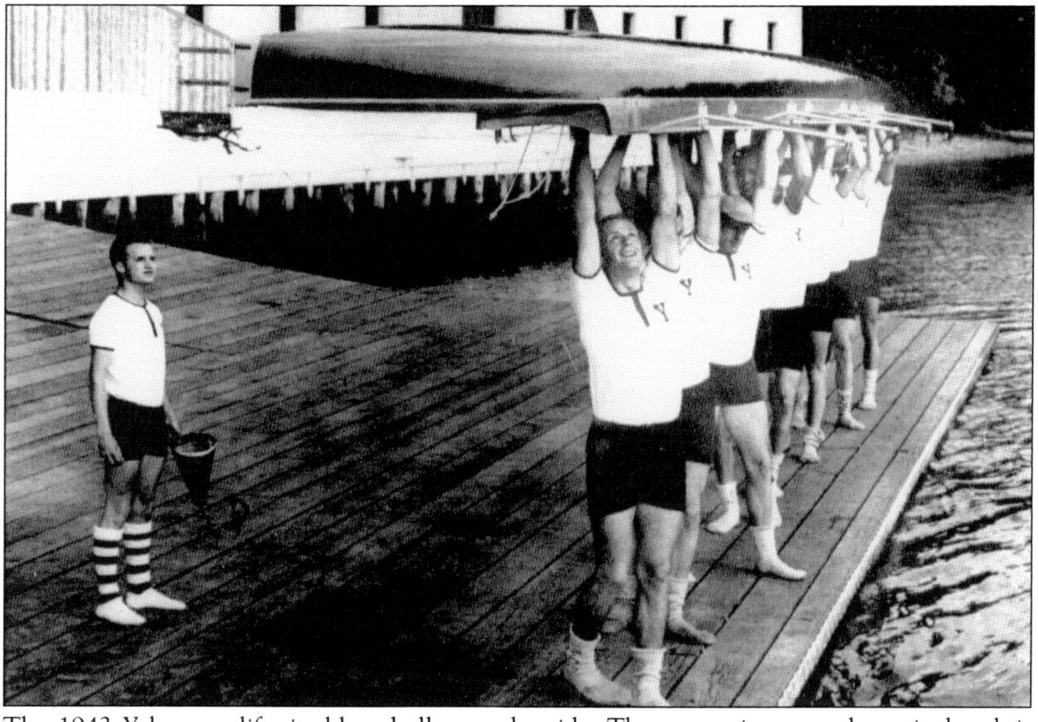

The 1943 Yale crew lifts its blue shell over the side. The coxswain, megaphone in hand, is to the left.

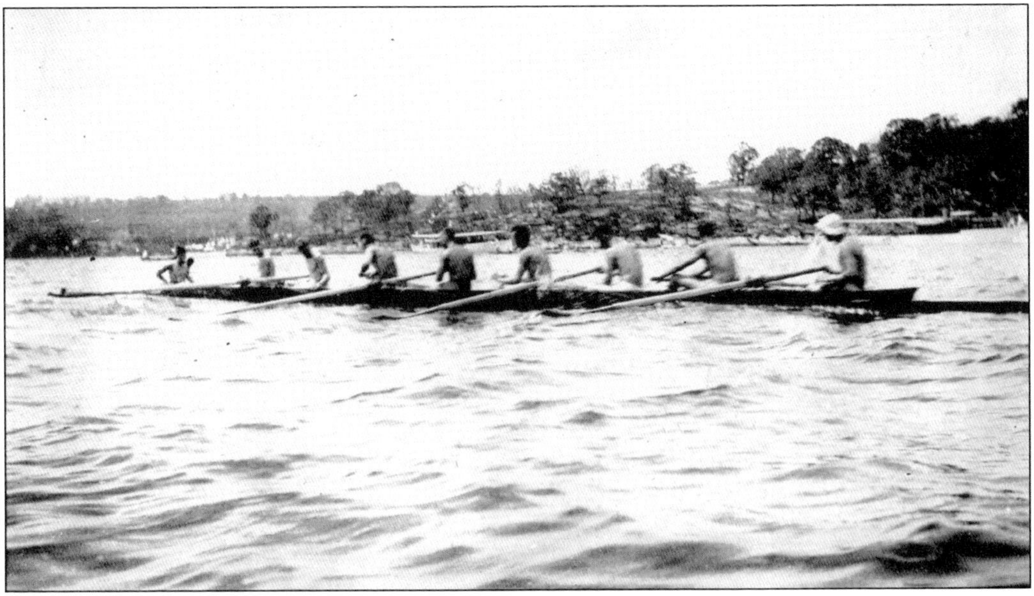

A freshman crew prepares to start the 1916 race opposite the navy yard in Groton. Junior varsity and varsity teams row longer races.

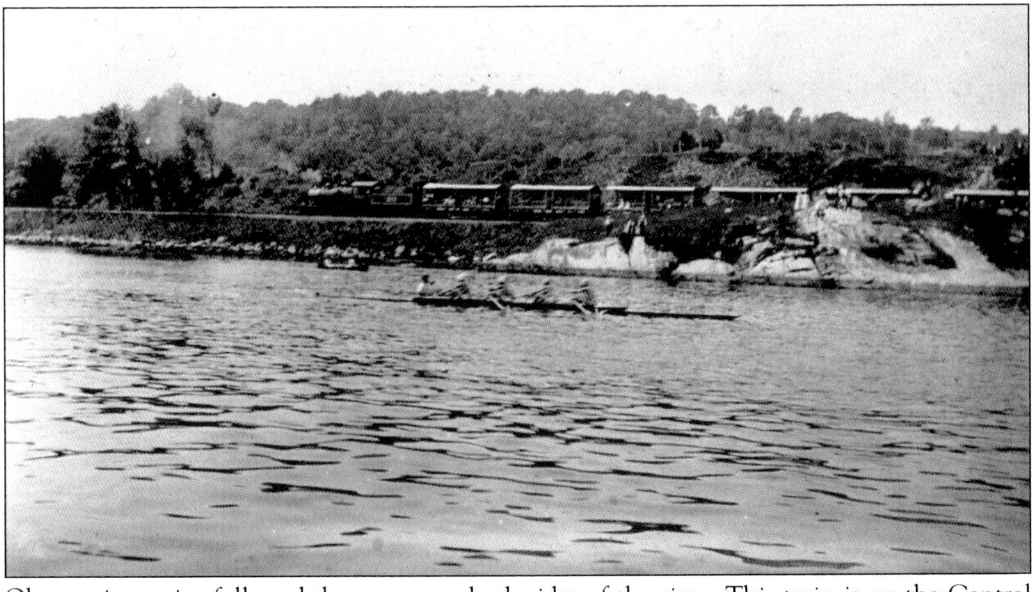

Observation trains followed the course on both sides of the river. This train is on the Central Vermont tracks on the west side. A similar excursion was run by the New York, New Haven and Hartford Railroad on the east side.

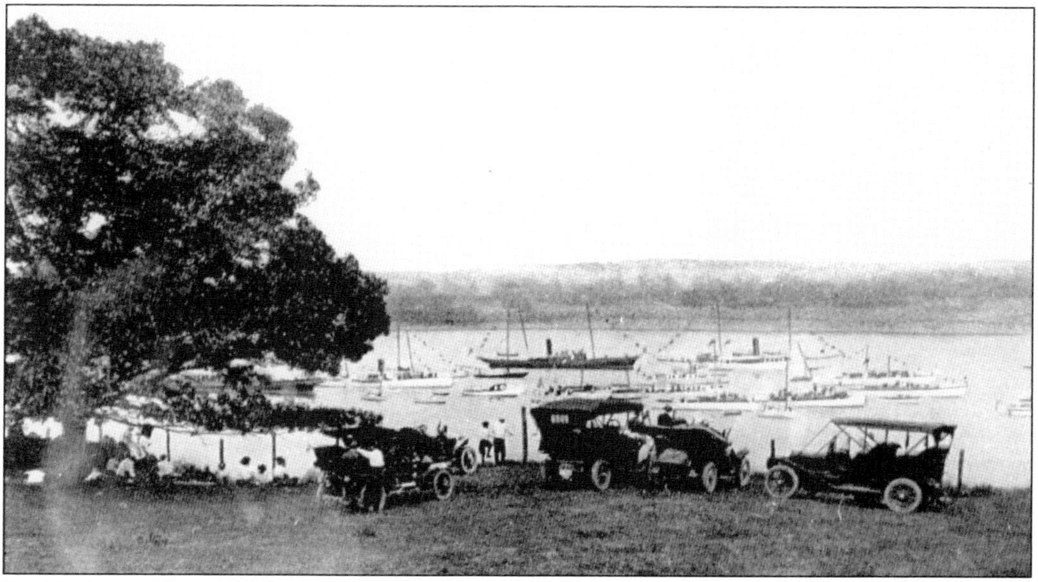

By 1915, crowds regularly drove to the races. These early cars are parked at Red Top Cottage, with the spectator fleet anchored offshore.

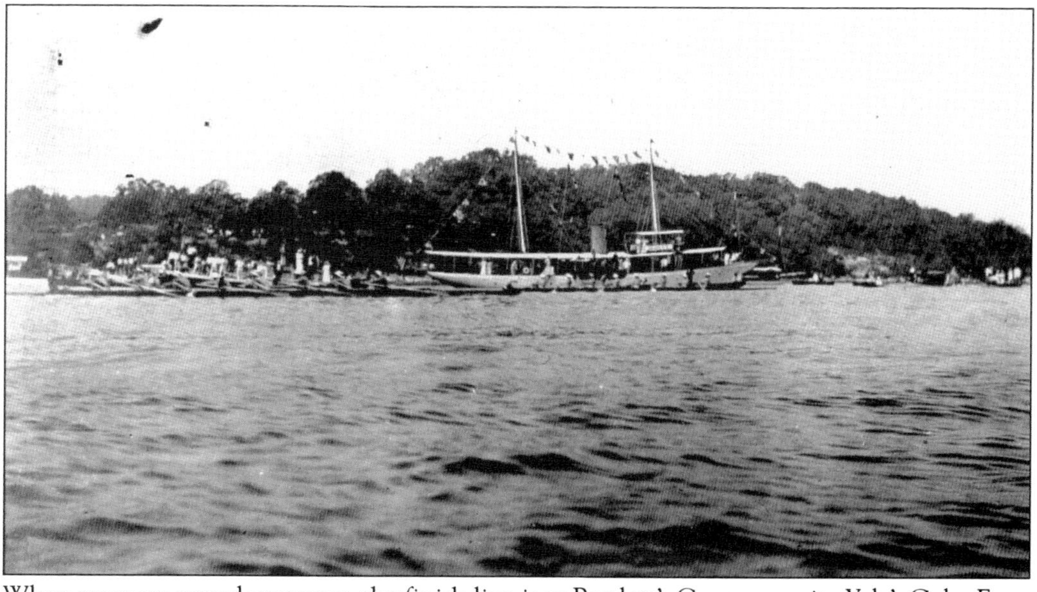

When races are rowed upstream, the finish line is at Bartlett's Cove, opposite Yale's Gales Ferry camp. The large yacht is the committee boat from which the races are administered.

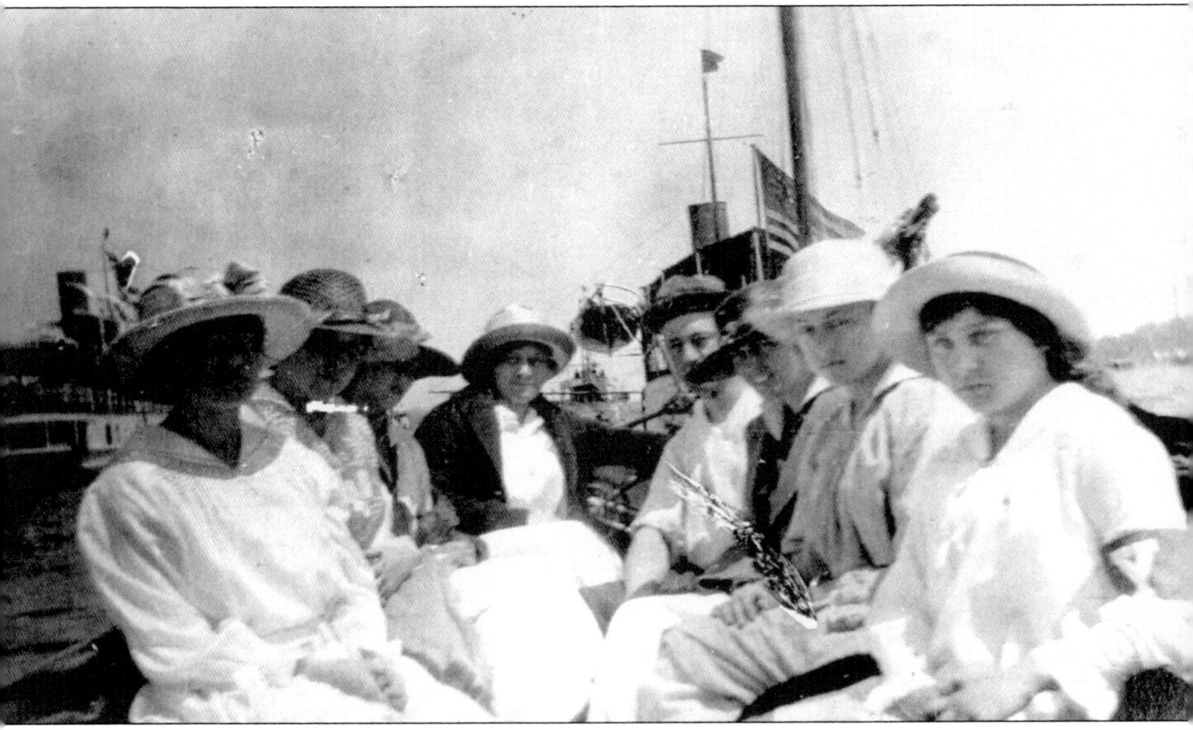

Residents of Gales Ferry take to the water to get a better view of the races. A group from the Bluff watches the 1917 regatta from the launch *Togo*.

Six

In the Shade of the Great Oak

Ledyard takes as its symbol the Great Oak, once the second-largest tree in Connecticut. Believed to be more than 400 years old, the oak, at its prime, had a circumference of 21 feet and a spread of 105 feet, shading nearly a quarter-acre.

Tradition tells that native tribes held their councils under the oak, which stands on the edge of the mystical land called Gungywamp.

The property on which the oak stands was purchased by Peter Lester of New London *c.* 1738. Upon Peter's death in 1789, Nathan, his third and youngest son, received half the land, and his wife and three unmarried daughters received the farmhouse and the land on which it stood. Under the terms of Peter Lester's will, Nathan was to keep one cow and one hog annually for his sisters and to allow them to "procure sufficient firewood for their necessary consumption [and] privilege in the cellar for their cider."

Nathan built a new house on his land in 1793, and there he and his bride, Susanna Gallup, raised their only child, Hannah. Nathan Lester was a successful farmer and a man of some means, evidenced by the size and style of his house. Hannah and her husband, Capt. Adam Larrabee, a distinguished veteran of the War of 1812, had nine children, one of whom became governor of Iowa. Hannah died in 1837, after which Adam remarried. He sold the farm in 1880 and moved to Windham.

After a series of undistinguished owners, the property was purchased by Dr. Charles Graves, a botanist at Connecticut College, in 1908. The Graveses' daughter Elizabeth Hill inherited the farm, and she and her husband, Norbert, raised three sons there. The Hills gave the 11-acre tract on which the Great Oak stands to the town of Ledyard in 1965. In 1967, the town purchased the farmhouse and 100 surrounding acres, now open to the public as the Nathan Lester House and Farm Museum.

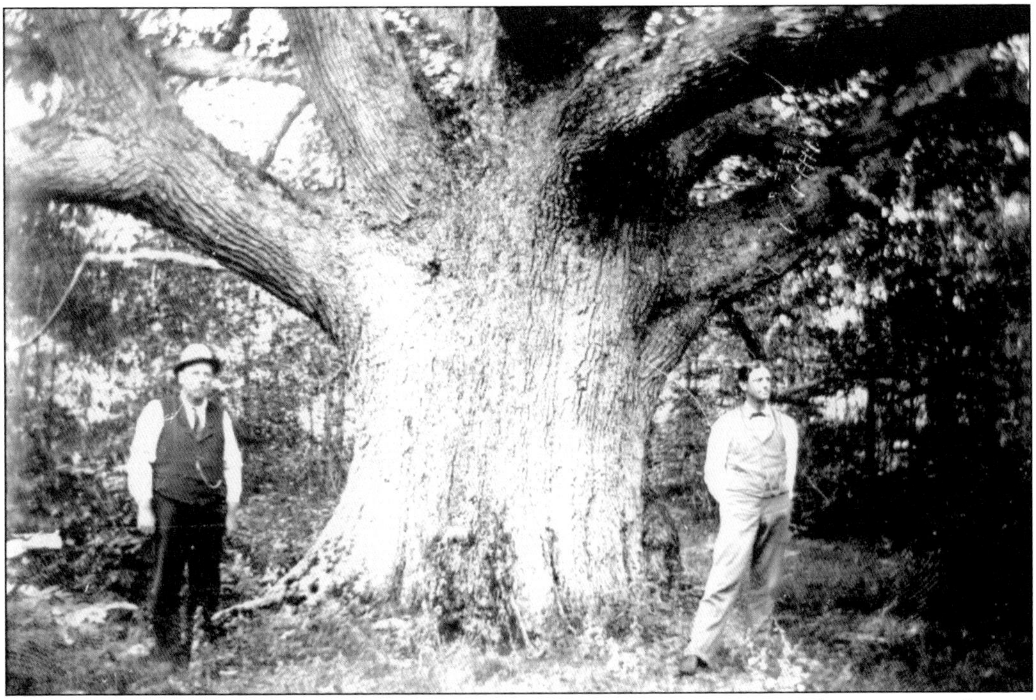

In its prime, the Ledyard Oak was the second-largest tree in Connecticut. These two gentlemen posing in 1898 give proportion to the trunk, whose circumference measured 22 feet.

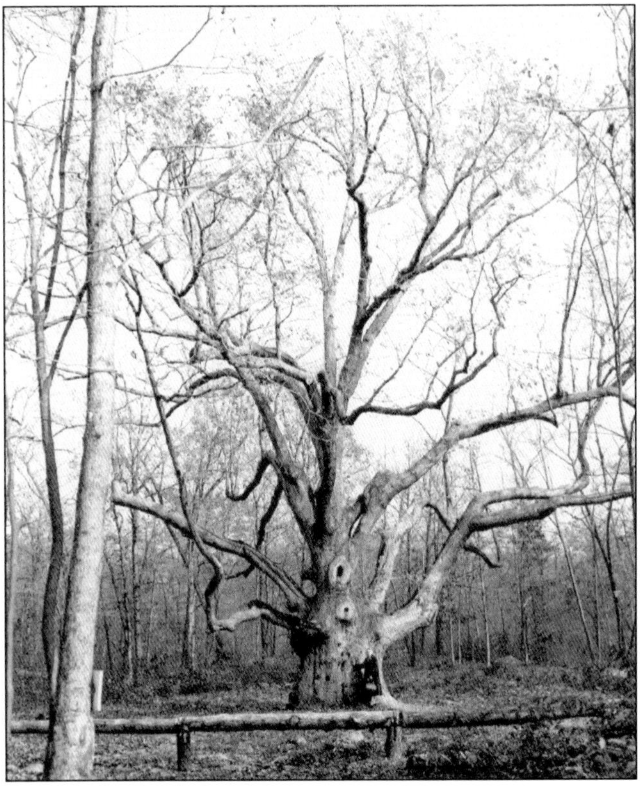

By the 1950s, pruning had left the oak with ugly scars, but the breadth of its branches was still readily apparent.

"Hands around the Oak" was a popular family pastime. Pictured here in 1923, Dr. Charles Graves (left), owner of the tree, adjacent homestead, and surrounding acreage, joins hands with Mr. and Mrs. Charles A. Weatherby to show the magnitude of the tree.

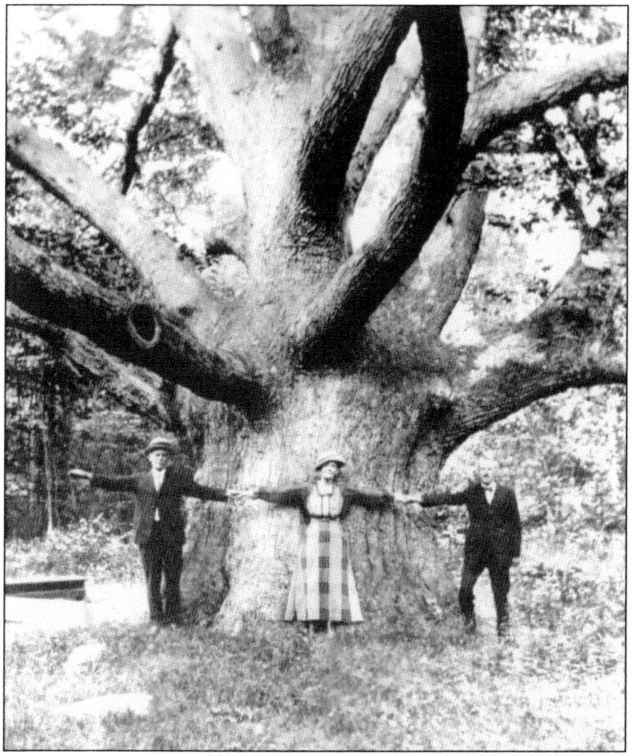

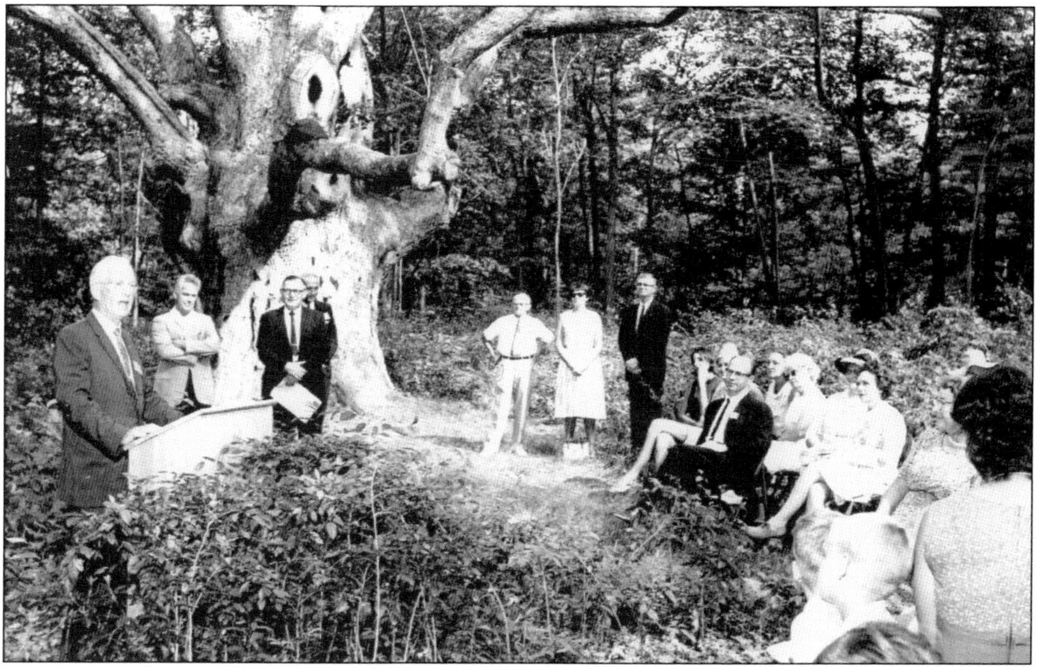

In 1965, the Graveses' daughter Elizabeth Hill and her husband, Norbert, gave the tree and 11 surrounding acres to the town of Ledyard. Here, Norbert speaks at the presentation ceremony. At the base of the tree is Commissioner Joseph N. Gill of the Connecticut Department of Natural Resources.

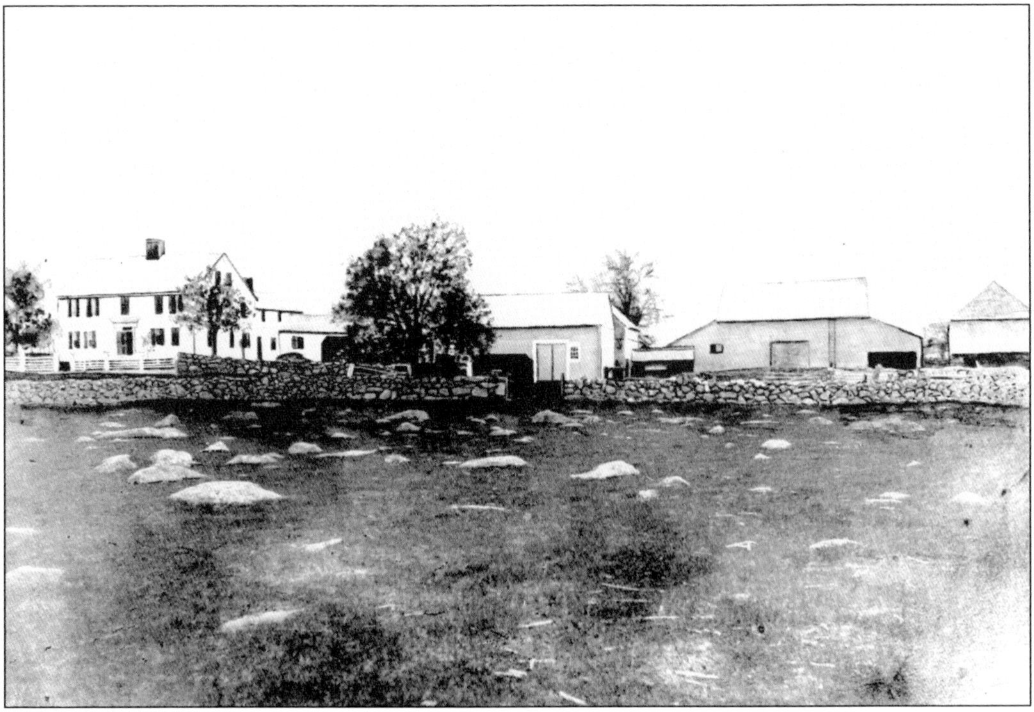

The Ledyard Oak stood by the homestead built by Nathan Lester in 1793. This view from the south pasture early in the 20th century shows the extensive series of barns that once stood to the east of the house.

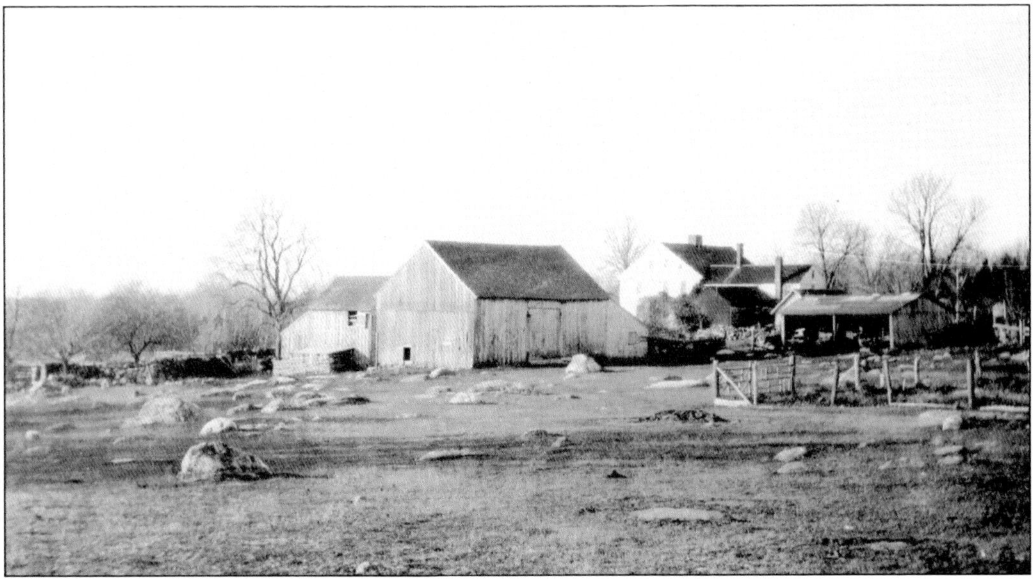

By the time this photograph was taken c. 1940, some of the barns in the previous view were gone. Today, only two connected barns remain.

Elizabeth Graves (later Hill) and her mother sit with a family friend on a rock. The Graves family purchased the Great Oak property in 1908.

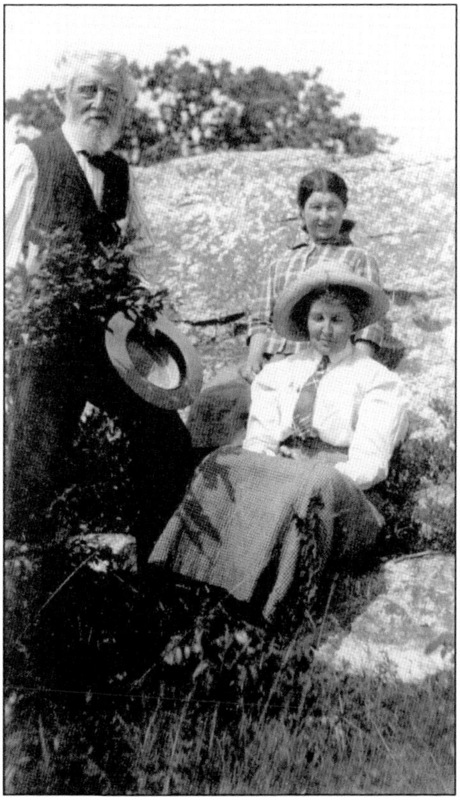

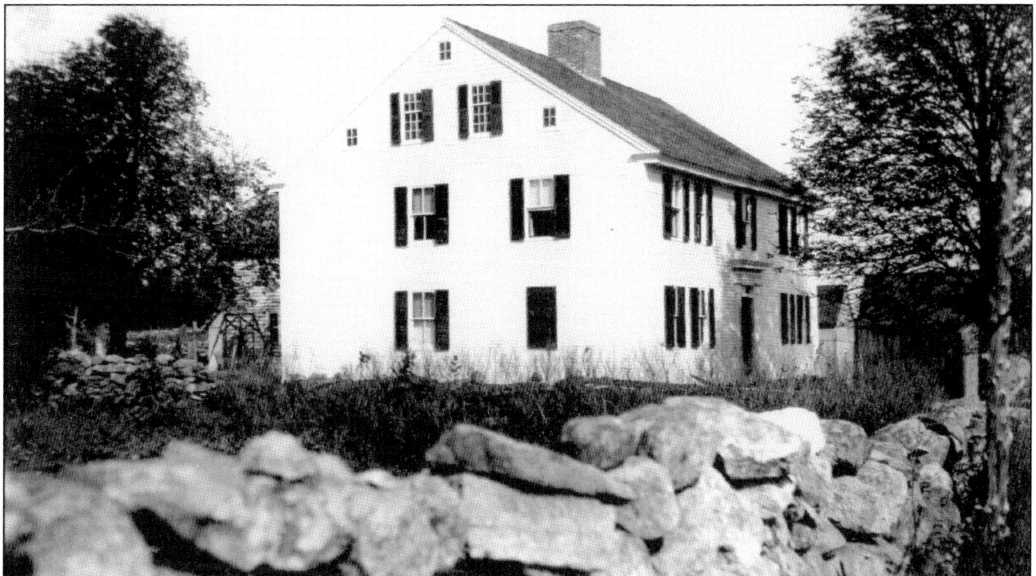

Although largely unchanged through the centuries, the Nathan Lester House was subjected to some minor modifications. This view from the 1930s shows that some windows had been "modernized."

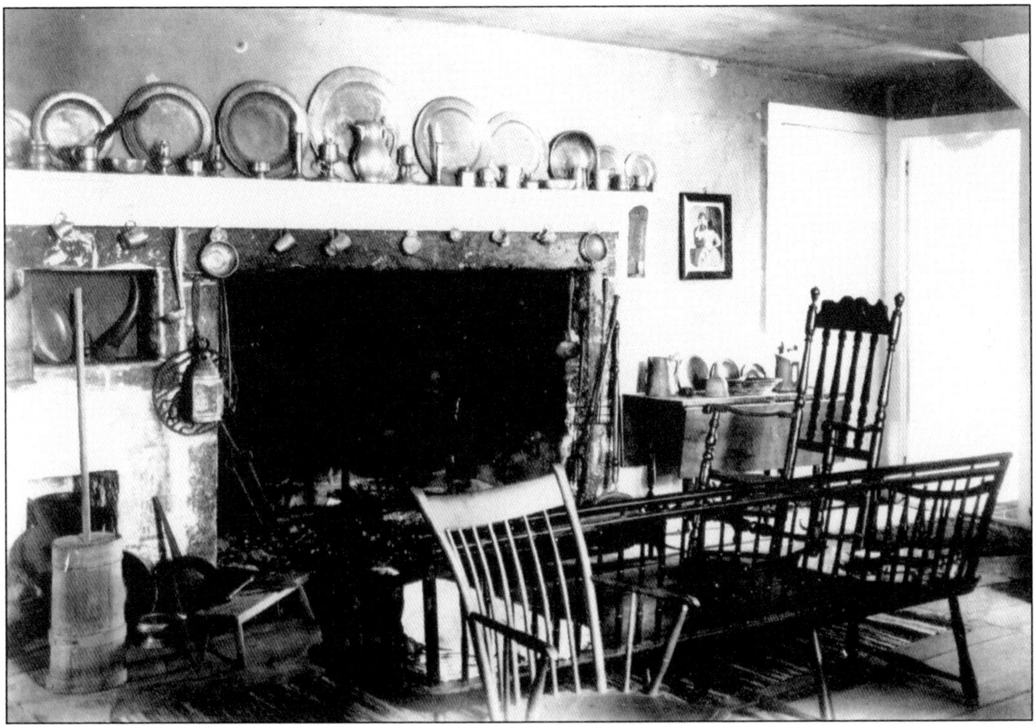

But for ornamentation, this 1910 photograph of the Nathan Lester House kitchen might have been taken recently. It points out the originality of much of the structure.

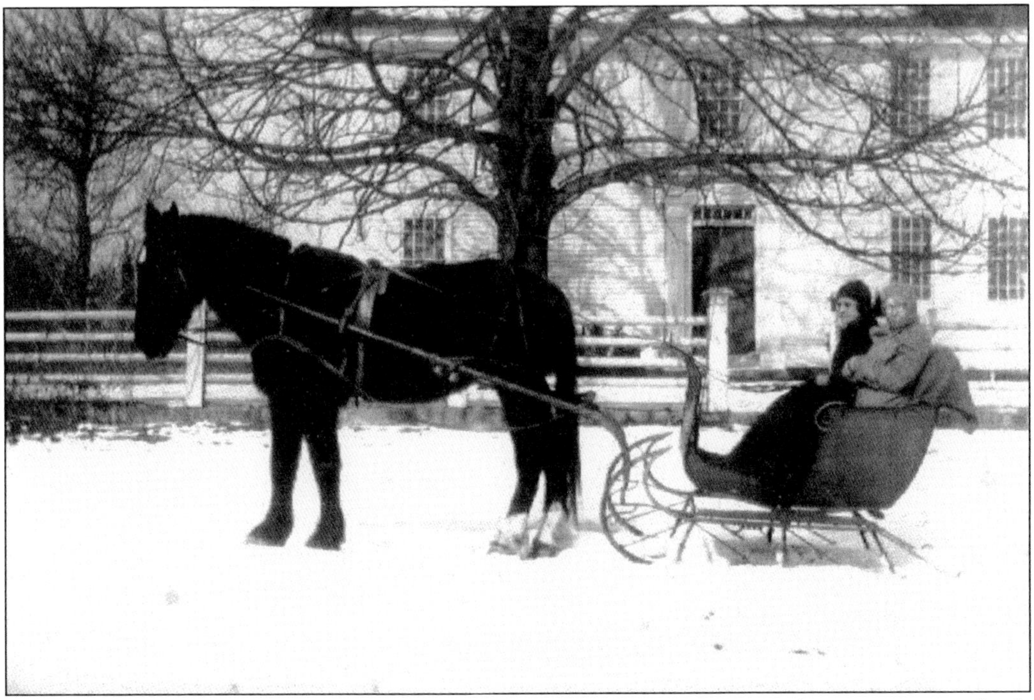

Norbert and Elizabeth Hill pause in front of the Nathan Lester House during a winter sleigh ride. The Graveses and the Hills gradually restored the house.

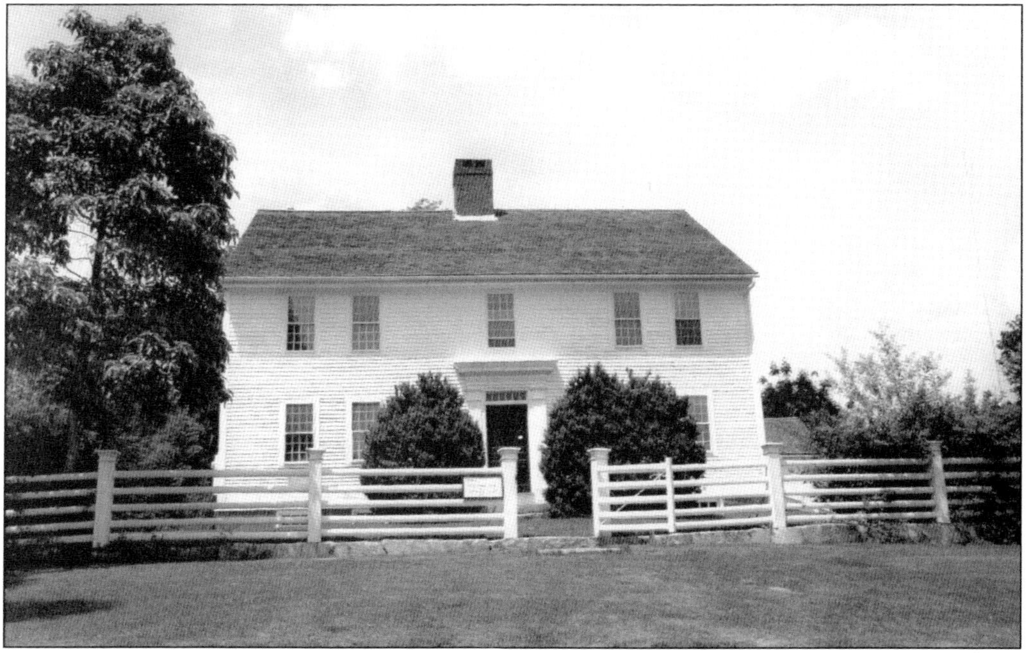

Following the town acquisition in 1967, restoration work was continued to return the house to its 18th-century appearance. This photograph was taken in 1976. The house is now overseen by the Ledyard Historic District Commission and is open to the public during summer months.

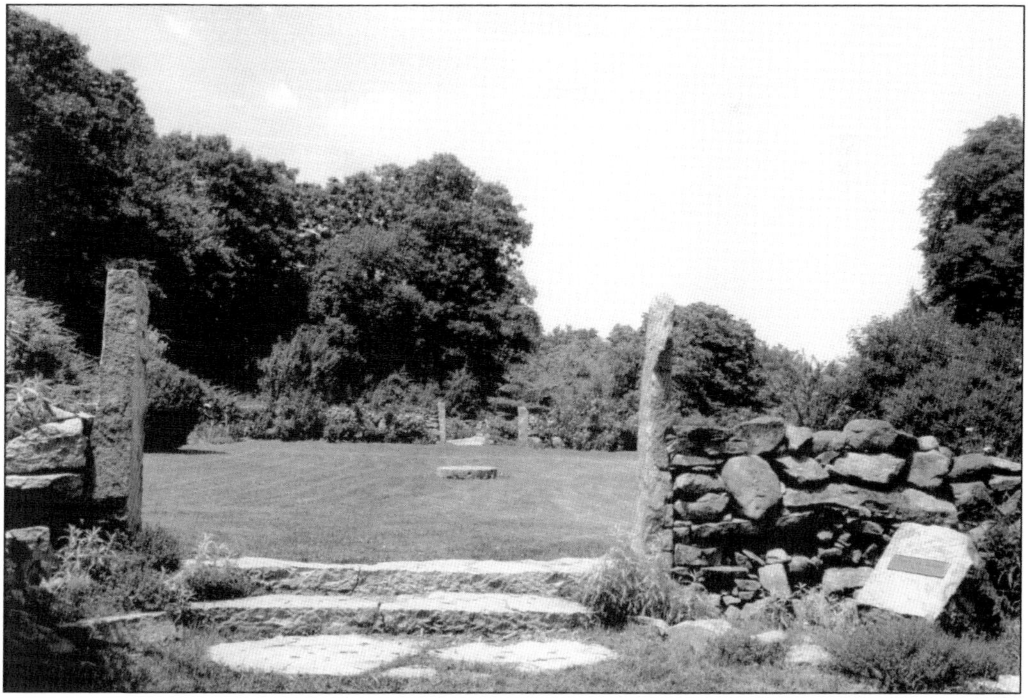

The Great Oak Memorial Garden was developed in 1970 by five local garden clubs and the Ledyard Historical Society. Designed by landscape architect Rudy Favretti, it is a faithful rendition of an 18th-century Colonial garden.

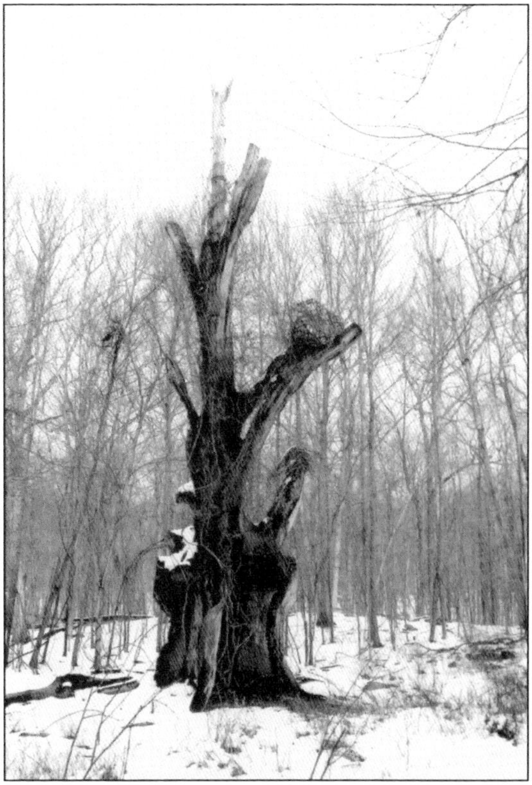

After several successive years of defoliation by gypsy moths, the Ledyard Oak was officially declared dead in June 1969. Although its spreading branches are long gone, the massive trunk gives an indication of the scale of the tree.

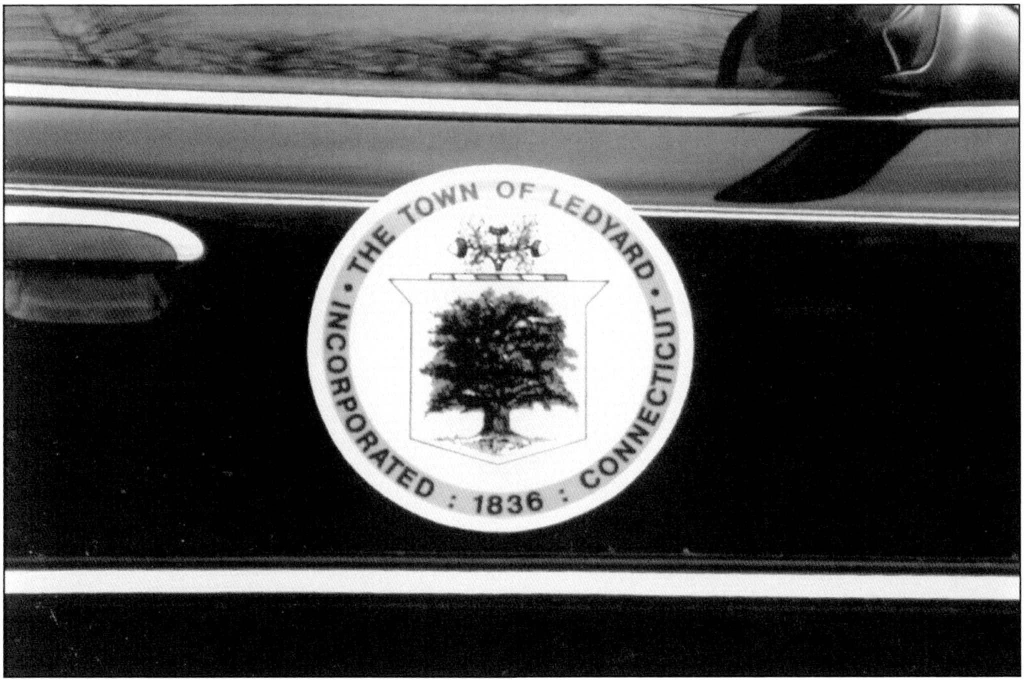

The tree is dead, but the Great Oak lives on as the symbol of the town of Ledyard. The town seal, with tree and acorns, heads official stationery and is proudly displayed on town vehicles.

Seven

We Gather Together

In Colonial Connecticut, the church was not separated from the state. The 1650 Connecticut Code of Laws carried biblical references, and the governor was required to be "of an accepted congregation." Taxes were levied for the upkeep of meetinghouses and the salaries of ministers, as well as for public education. Towns were formed within the boundaries of the ecclesiastical societies, and governmental activities revolved around the Congregational church.

In 1724, 36 residents of the northern portion of Groton petitioned the Connecticut General Assembly for establishment of their own ecclesiastical society. Citing the "extreme difficulties we are under in attending ye place [of worship] by reason of our great distance and the imposebility of our familys constant atandance for want of a sufficient number of horses," the petitioners had their treaty honored, and the Second Ecclesiastical Society of Groton was founded in January 1825. Two years later, the society began the construction of a meetinghouse at the geographical center of its territory.

An Episcopal church was built near the Crossroads in 1837. This occurred after the Reverend Ebenezer Punderson, first minister of the new Congregational church at Ledyard Center, felt a call to be "a conformist to the Church of England" and crossed the sea to be ordained. The area around the new church came to be known as Church Hill. The building was taken down *c.* 1775, and its materials were used in construction of a new church at Shingle Point in Poquetanuck. The present Episcopal Parish of St. James at Poquetanuck traces its history directly from this "conformist" church in North Groton.

The first religious observance in Gales Ferry came in July 1793, when George Roberts, a Methodist circuit rider, preached at an outdoor service. In 1803, Gales Ferry was accepted into the New London circuit, and a class meeting was formed with Ralph Hurlbutt as leader. In 1806, Hurlbutt was "licensed to exhort" and, by 1910, had obtained a preacher's license. Hurlbutt gave land next to the schoolhouse for a church to be erected.

A Baptist church was built in 1843 on what is now Iron Street. Its congregation splintered from the church at Old Mystic for the same reason that the Congregational church had been established at Ledyard Center—an opportunity to worship closer to home.

John Waterhouse, a Rogerene Quaker from New London, established a community of talented and industrious people in the southeastern part of town, north of Burnett's Corners.

But for the dissolution of the Baptist church *c.* 1940, the religious life of Ledyard remained relatively unchanged from the 19th century until the mid-1950s, when growth of the town brought people from other places and other backgrounds. Over the next 40 years, new Roman Catholic, Episcopal, Lutheran, American Baptist, and Southern Baptist churches, among others, were established to serve their spiritual needs.

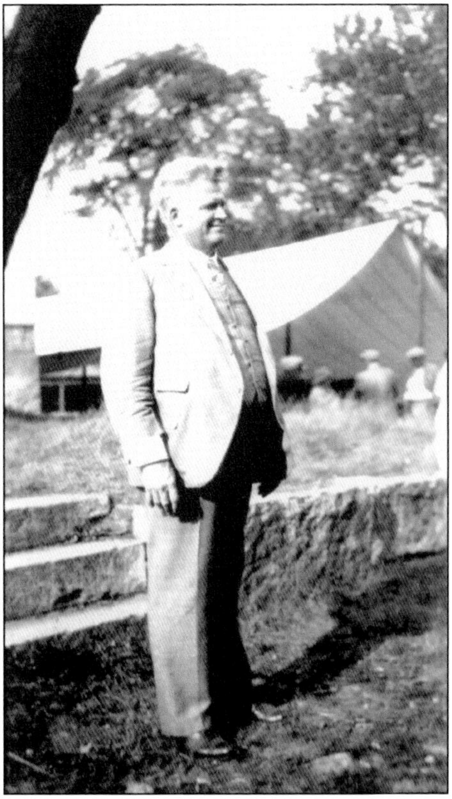

Rev. Giles Goodenough was pastor of Ledyard Congregational Church from 1914 to 1926. In this photograph, he stands in front of the church during a Bill Dinner.

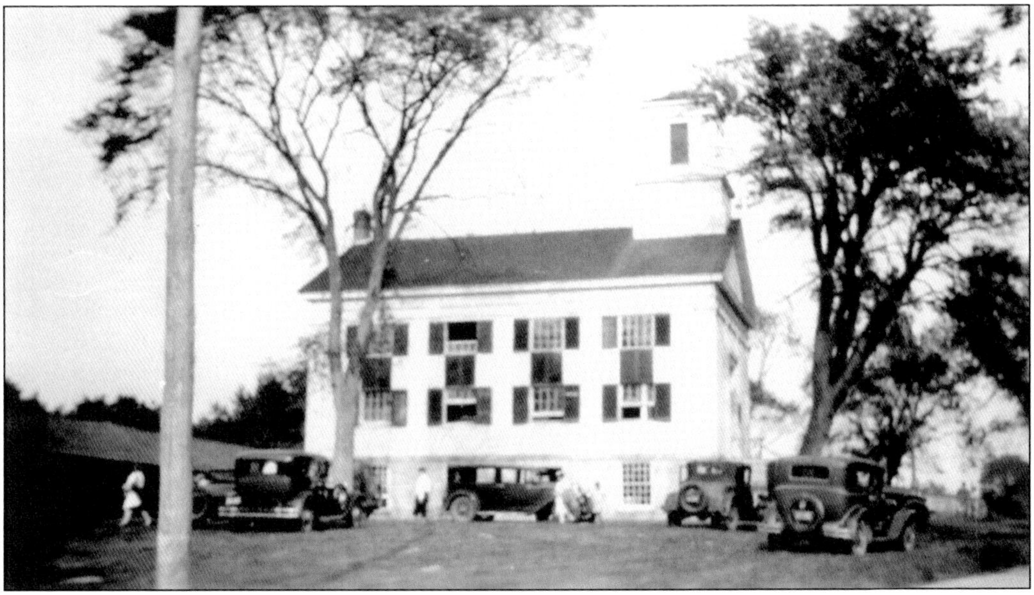

The present Ledyard Congregational Church is the second on the site, completed in 1843. By 1930, when this photograph was taken, it had become commonplace to arrive at church by automobile.

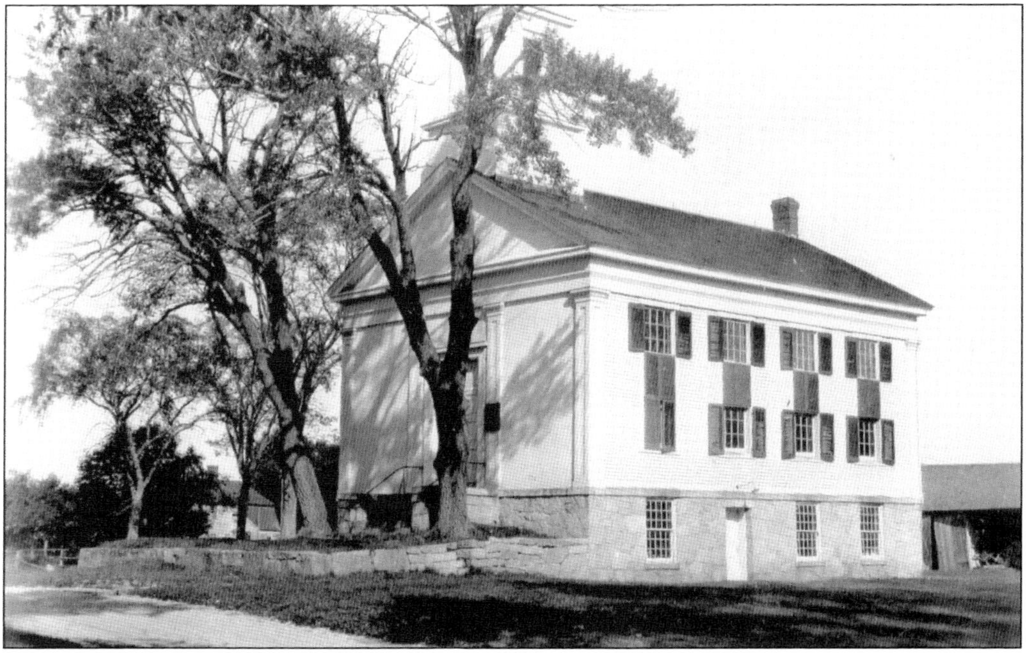

Until the 1938 hurricane, tall trees flanked the front of the church. In recent years, the building has been enlarged successively with ground-floor wings, appearing to the right in the photograph.

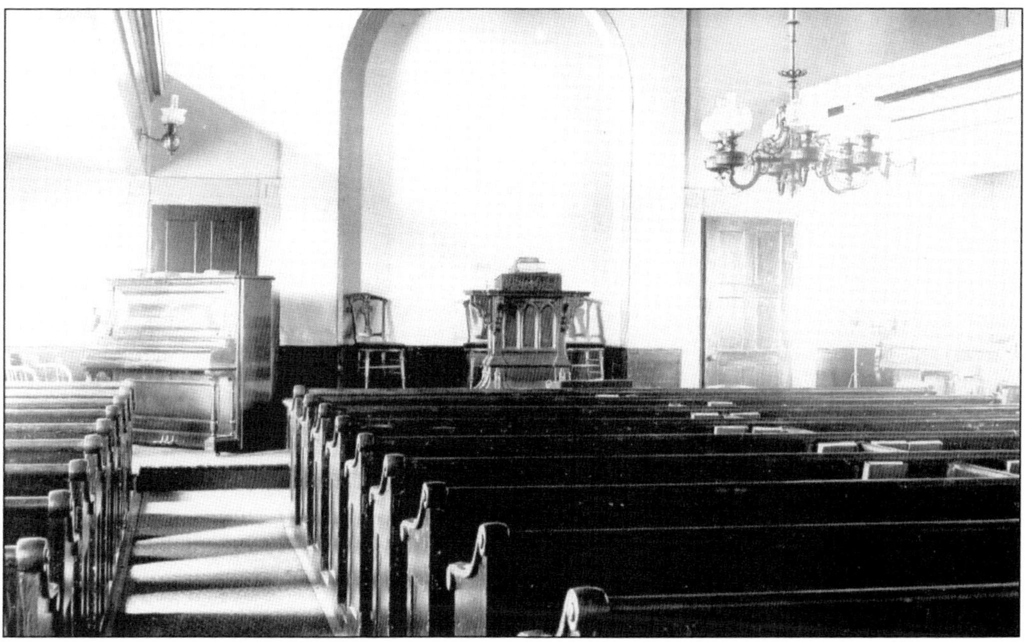

Since the 1920s, when this photograph was taken, redecoration has made the sanctuary of the Congregational church much brighter, though the general configuration remains the same.

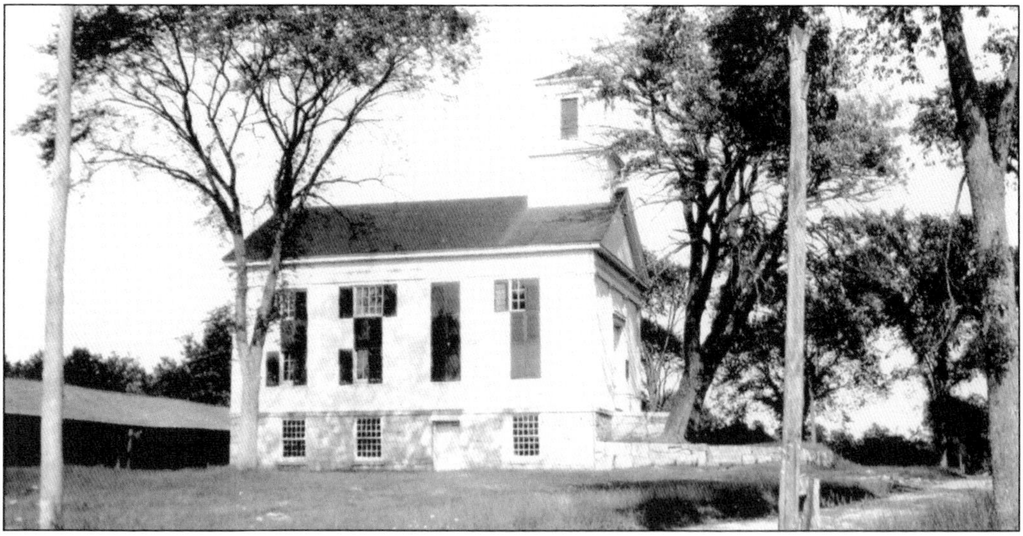

Located to the back of the Congregational church were carriage sheds, important protection in a time when worshipers arrived by horse-drawn buggy. Today, buildings used by the Ledyard Fair occupy that space.

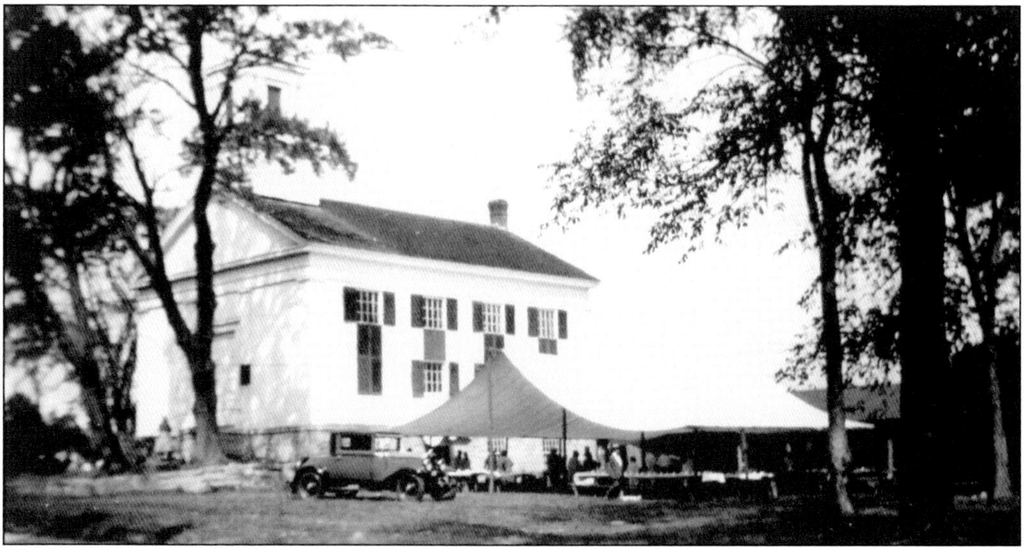

The church was home to the Bill Dinners, held outdoors in order to serve the large crowds of townspeople. After World War II, the dinners became smaller affairs for the Bill trustees only, and the Ledyard Fair took their place on the social calendar. This photograph dates from c. 1930.

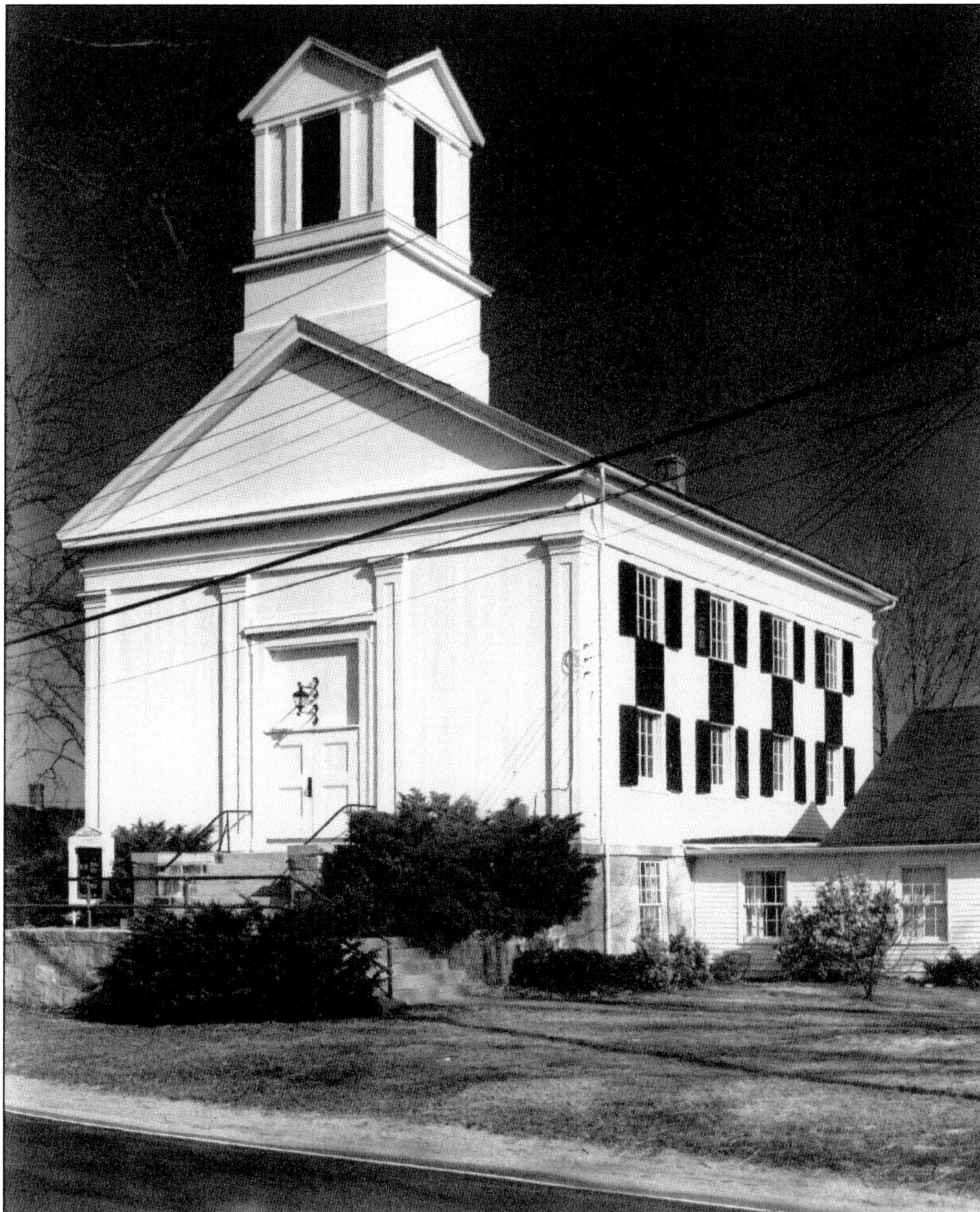

The trees in front of the Congregational church were long gone by the time this photograph was taken at the bicentennial celebrations in 1976. The growing space needs of the church were being met by additions on the east side.

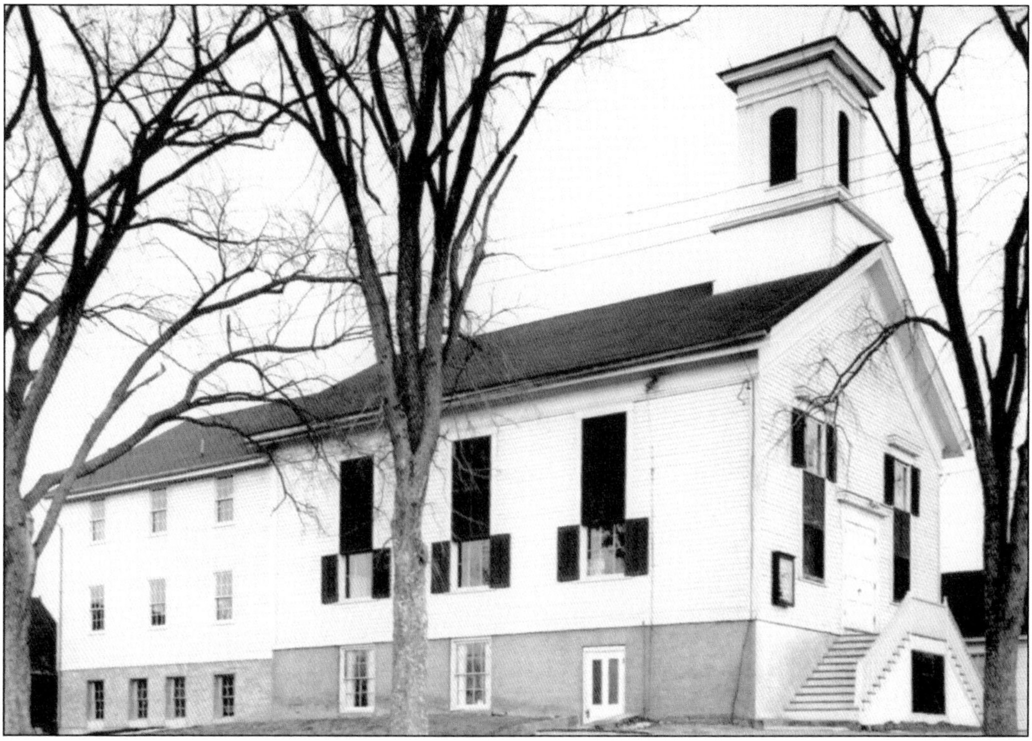

The Gales Ferry Methodist Church traces its beginnings to 1803, though this, its second building, was constructed in 1857. This view from the west side shows the three-story addition to the back, completed in 1954.

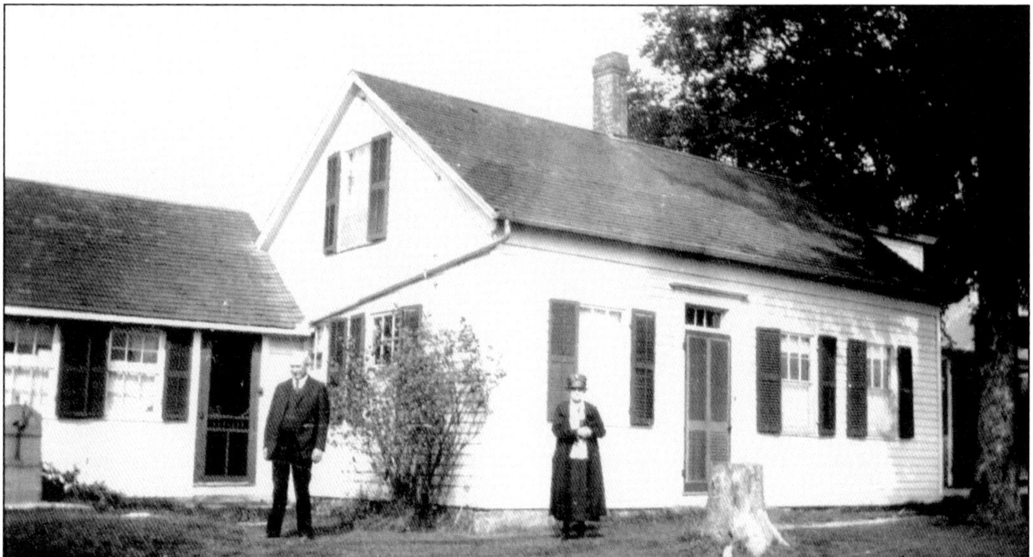

The first parsonage for the Methodist church was built prior to 1850 and occupied the land immediately to the west of the church building. This photograph was taken on September 21, 1927, shortly before it was replaced by a new parsonage. In front of the parsonage are Rev. Jerome Greer, pastor from 1927 to 1930, and Phoebe Benham of New London.

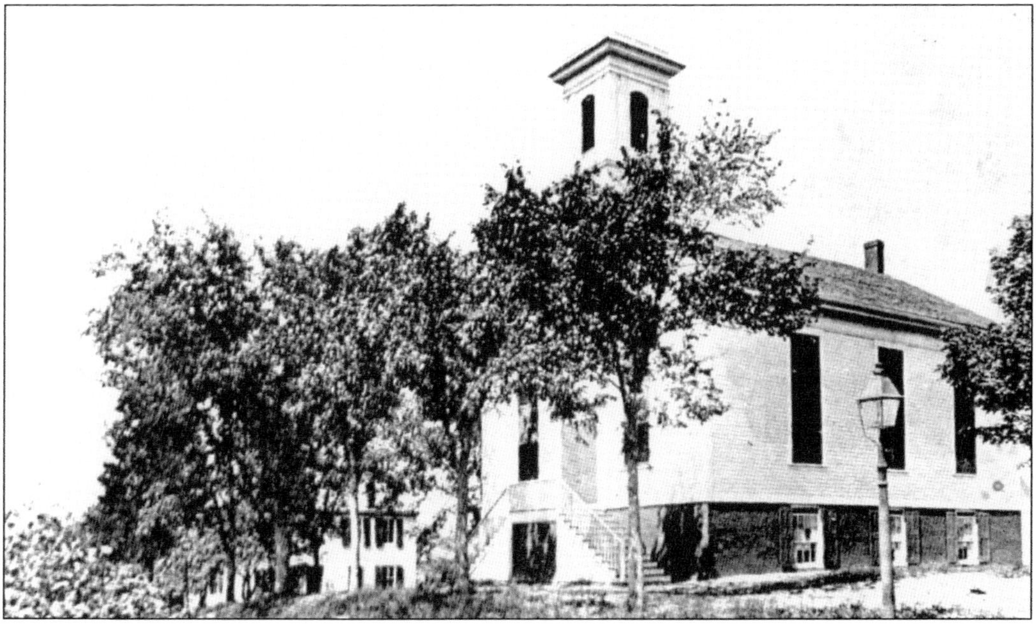

At the time of the church's 100th anniversary in 1903, trees still lined Hurlbutt Road. The old parsonage can be seen to the left of the church. Since the congregation moved to a new building on Chapman Lane in 1972, the church building has become a funeral home.

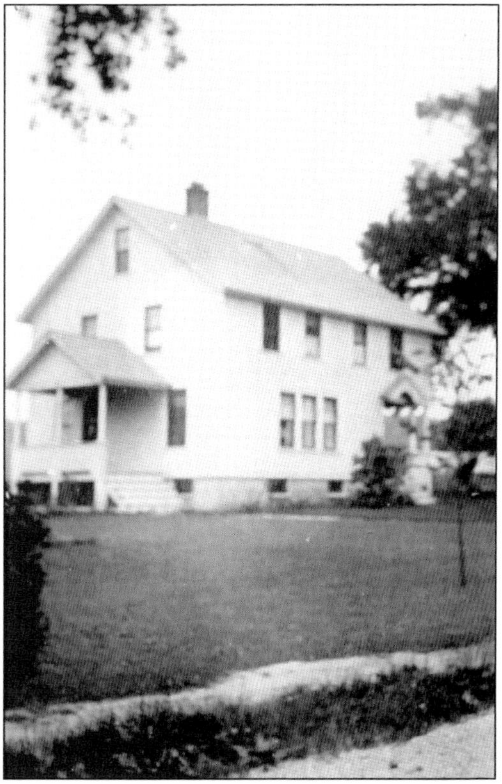

The new parsonage was built in 1928 on the site of the earlier building. Home of the pastor until the church moved to Chapman Lane, it has since served retail and professional uses.

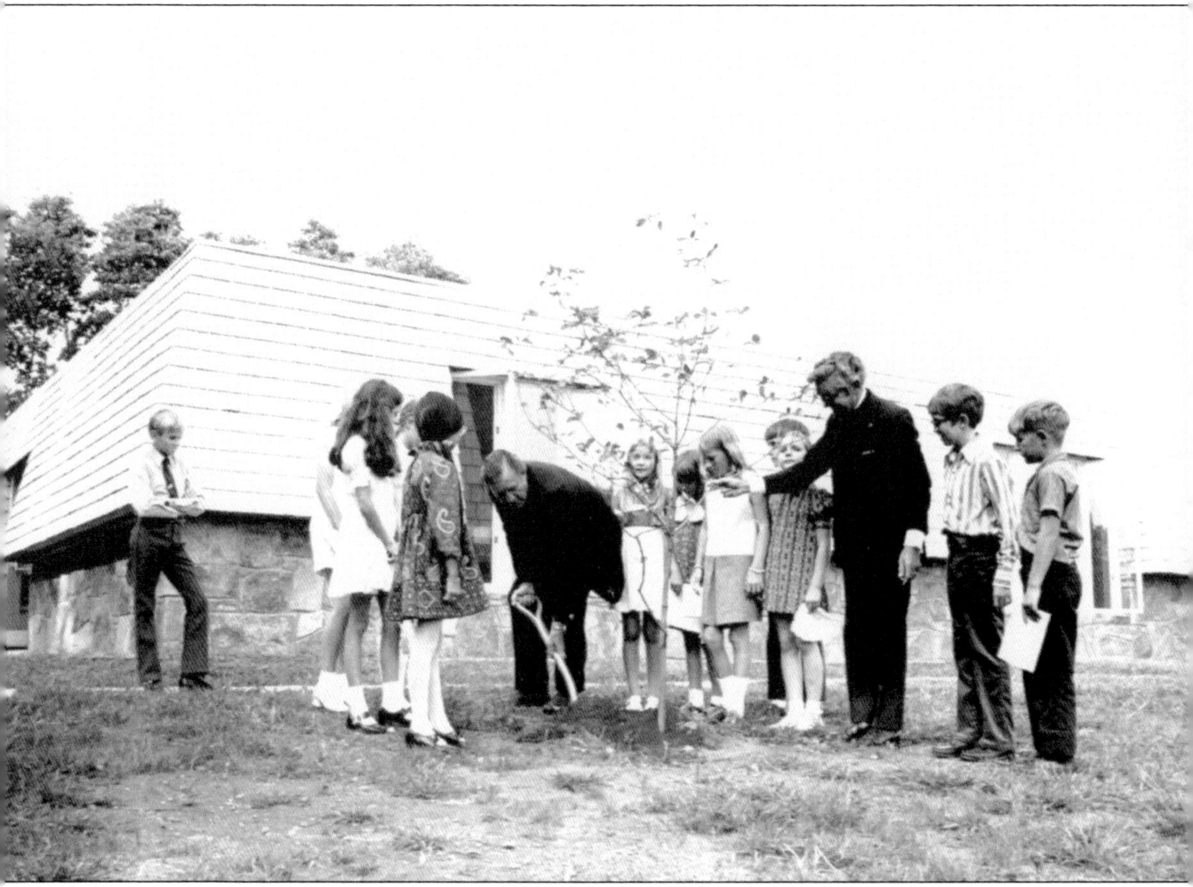

The first building for the new Methodist church was a modern and utilitarian structure on Chapman Lane. A contemporary sanctuary has since been added, along with a large, multistory multipurpose wing. Here, Rev. Gale Williamson (third from right), affectionately known as "Rev" during his 20-year pastorate, plants a tree with children of the parish. (Courtesy United Methodist Church of Gales Ferry.)

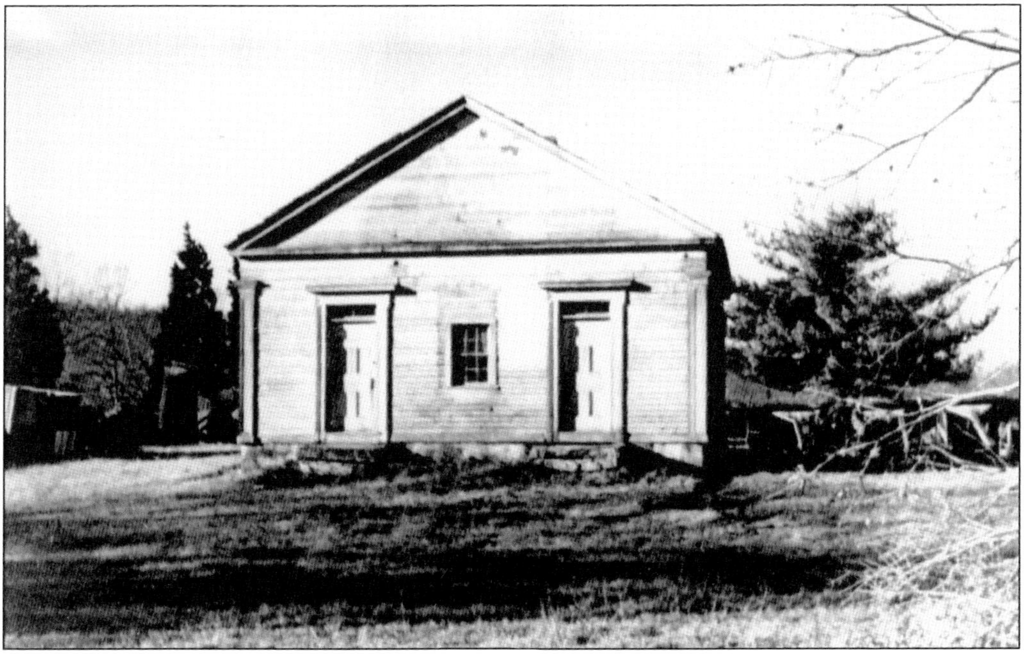

Ledyard's first Baptist church was built in 1843 on Iron Street, near the Main Cemetery and sawmill. The congregation disbanded *c.* 1940; the building later became a private home and remains so today. This photograph was taken as part of a Work Projects Administration project in 1938.

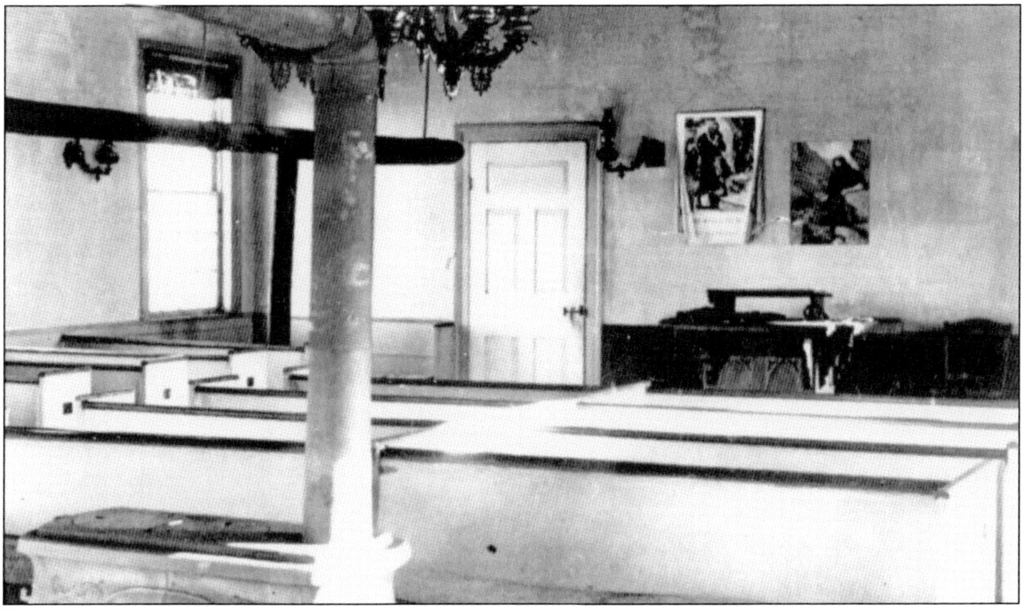

The interior of the first Baptist church is pictured here in 1938. It had not yet been converted to residential use.

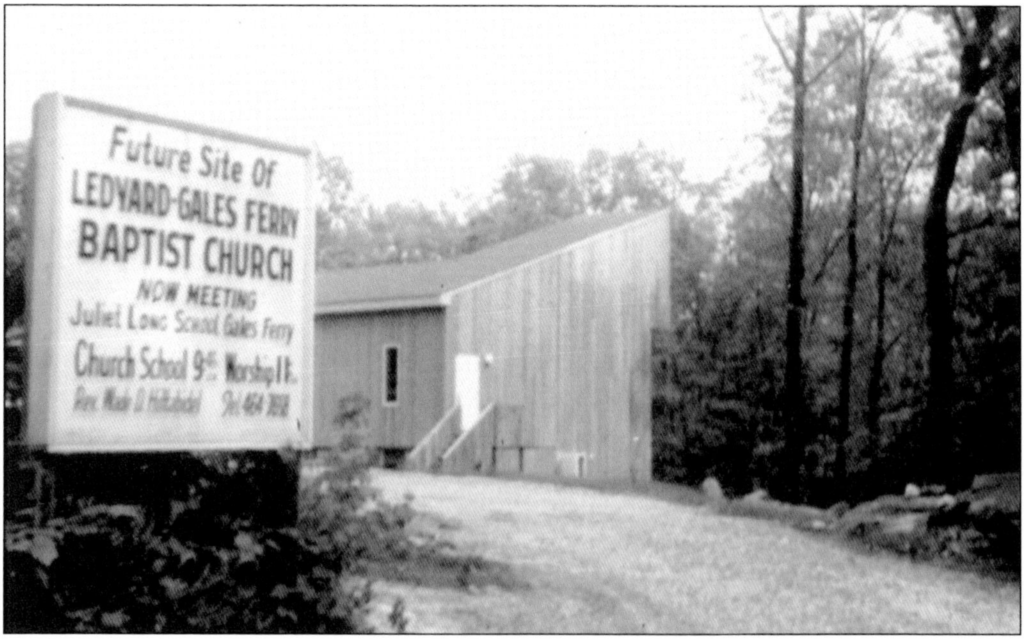

In the 1960s, many new churches were founded in Ledyard. Like the Ledyard–Gales Ferry Baptist Church on Christy Hill Road, most of them met in schools or the Gales Ferry Community Center before constructing their own buildings. The Baptist church is shown under construction in 1969.

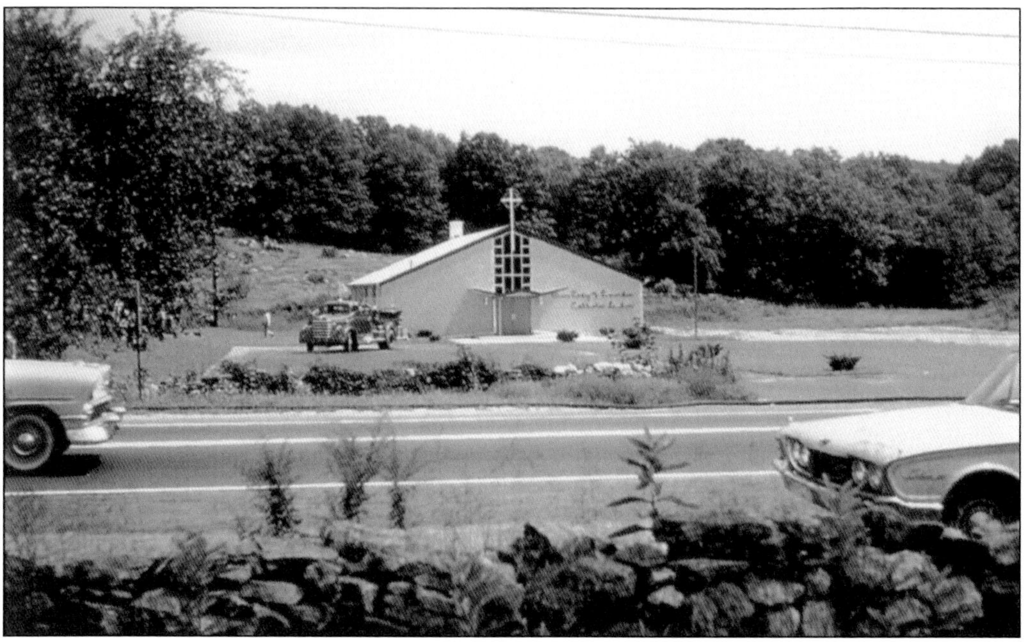

Our Lady of Lourdes Roman Catholic Church was formed in 1957 as a mission of Sacred Heart Church in Groton. A chapel was erected on a section of the Hurlbutt farm, and mass was first celebrated there in 1960. Successive additions have enlarged the parish complex, culminating in the construction of a 700-seat church in 1980. This photograph was taken in 1961. (Courtesy Our Lady of Lourdes Parish.)

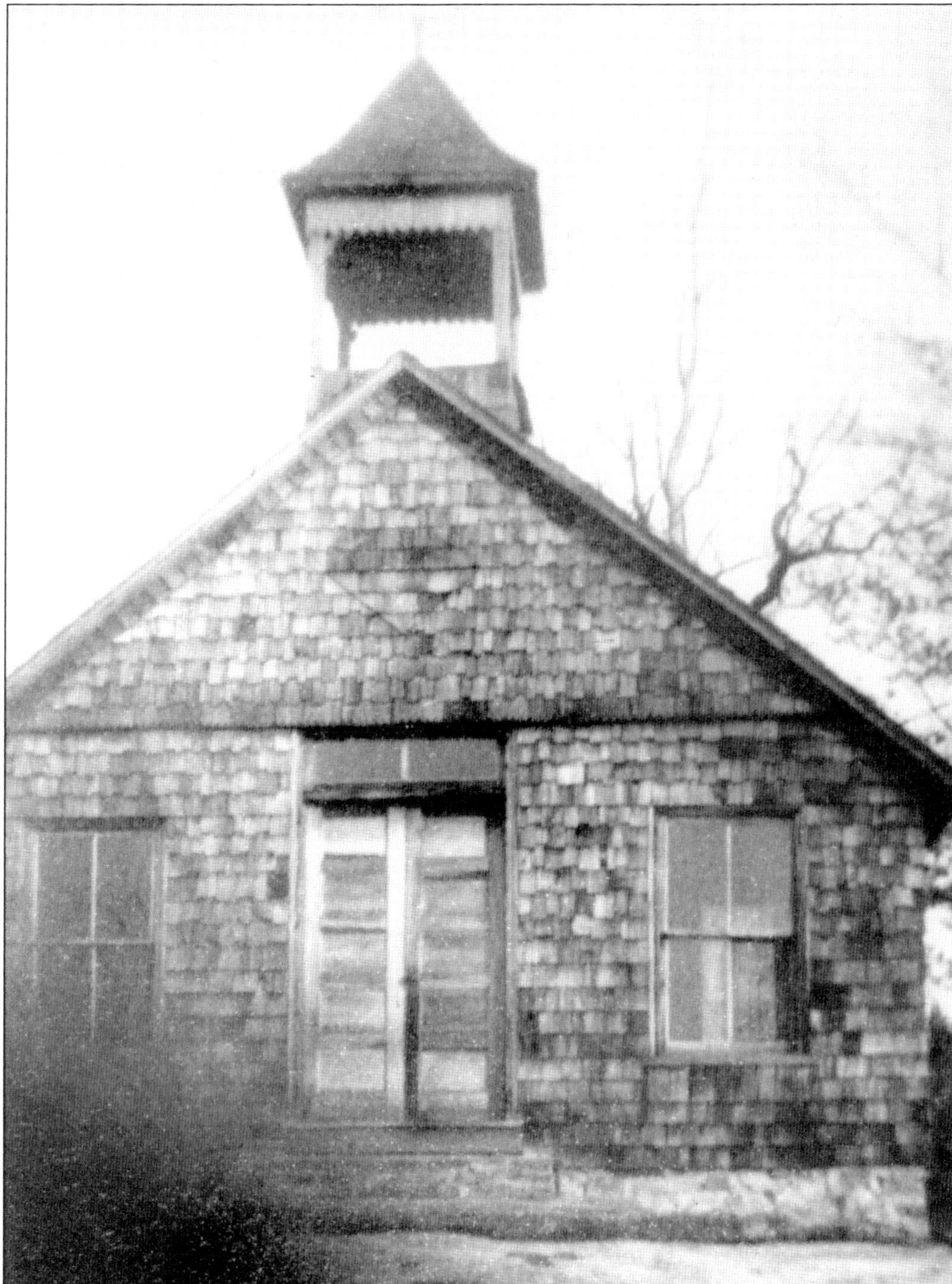

Early in the 19th century, John Waterhouse, a follower of John Rogers of New London, built a house on Pumpkin Hill Road. Rogers's flock, known as the Rogerene Quakers, formed a "peaceable and prosperous" community in the area now known as Quakertown. This building on Colonel Ledyard Highway served as their meetinghouse, and it remains a place of worship today.

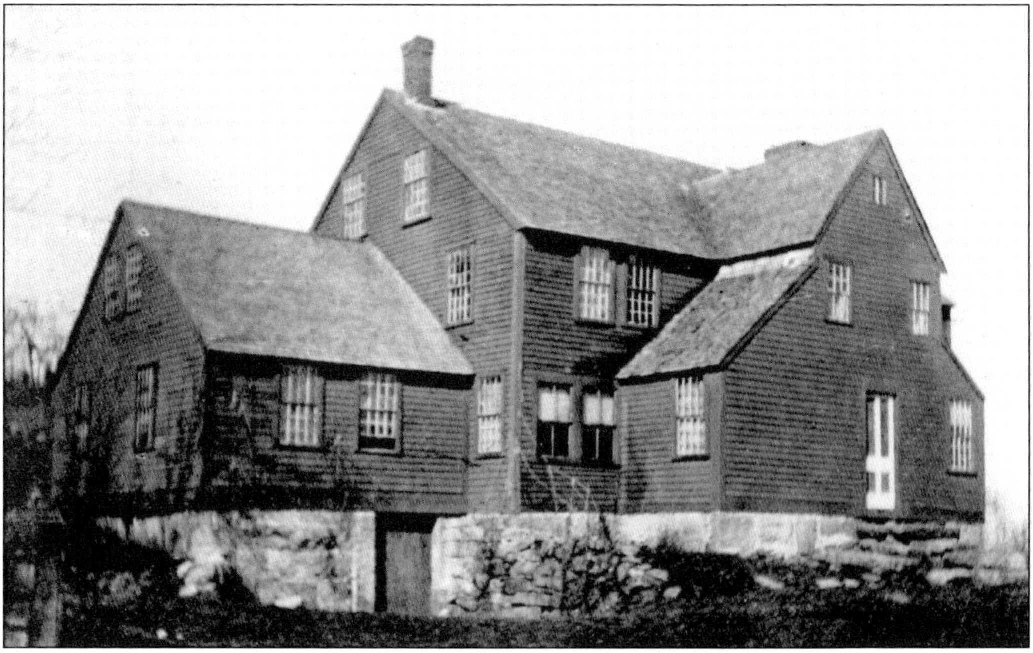

The earliest meetings of the Rogerene Quakers are said to have taken place in this house, which later burned.

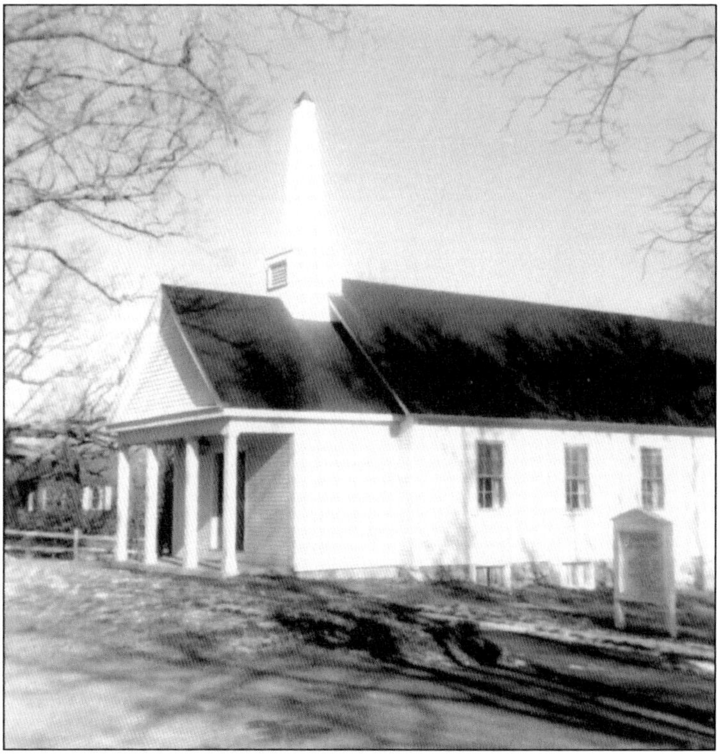

The Quakertown Chapel has had a long and fruitful ministry. Home to the Quakertown Full Gospel Church in the early 1960s, it is today the Ledyard First Assembly of God.

Eight

Lessons Learned

A longstanding Connecticut principle is the universal right to free public education. This has been true since before the American Revolution. By 1706, Groton had organized a plan whereby school would be kept in "severall houses." Two of these, the homes of Lt. John Morgan and Robert Allyn, were in what is now Ledyard.

In 1742, the North Groton Ecclesiastical Society formed its first school committee. This was probably influenced by the previous year's Act for the Encouragement of Better Supporting the Schools, enacted by the Connecticut General Assembly. The act made available money from the sales of so-called "western lands," the unclaimed king's lands in northwestern Connecticut. The committee was to "affix places for three schools"—one in the north, one in the east, and one in the west. The exact locations of these early schools are not known but are believed to have been near the present Geer Hill School (the north), Gallup Hill (the east), and the Nathan Lester House on Vinegar Hill (the west).

By 1770, the North Parish, what is now the town of Ledyard, was divided into 12 permanent school districts based on population and geography. Buildings were erected in each of the districts; those that remain date from the middle part of the 19th century. Two—Gales Ferry and Geer Hill—are preserved as exhibits of the education system of that time. The others have either been demolished or converted to dwellings and offices. A 13th district, in the extreme northeast corner of town, appears on the 1868 map without a number. Apparently, the sparse population of the district never required the construction of a school.

In 1949, the town of Ledyard voted to build its first consolidated elementary school, at Ledyard Center. The district schools were closed, and as the town grew, three more elementary schools were constructed. Until the 1960s, secondary students traveled to Norwich. Ledyard High School was built in 1963 and graduated its first class in 1967. Initially, it encompassed grades 7 through 12. A junior high school, now Ledyard Middle School, was built in 1971 to serve grades 7 and 8.

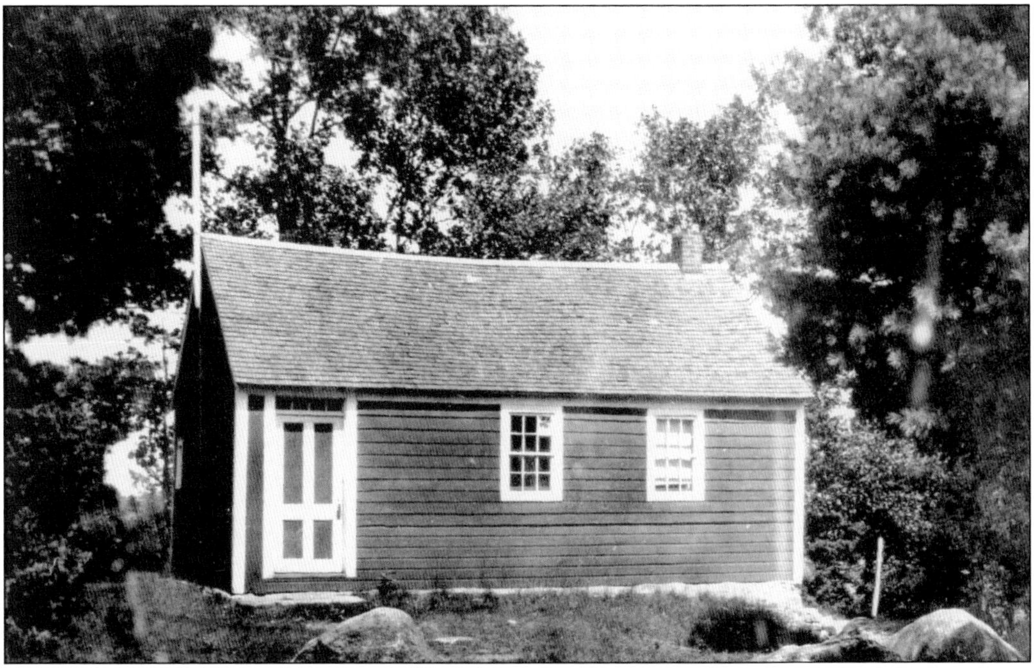

The Unionville School, District 9, was located at the corner of Stoddard's Wharf and Whalehead Roads. This photograph was taken for the Ledyard Board of Education in 1949, after the district schools had closed.

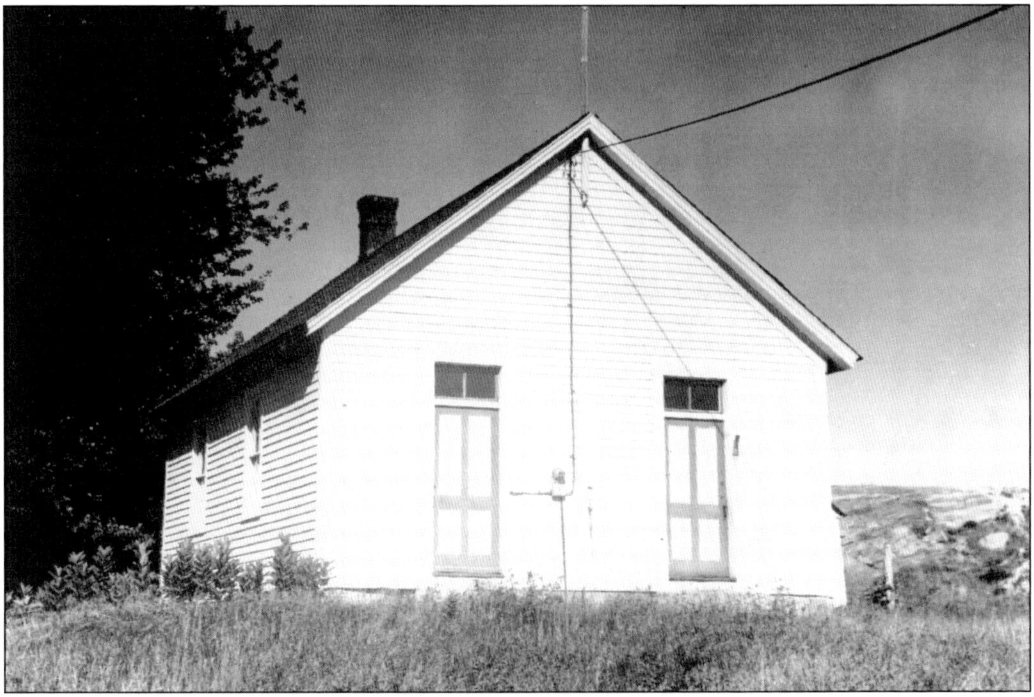

The Long Cove School, District 1, was at the corner of Long Cove Road and Route 12. Following school consolidation in 1949, it became a private home. Now, significantly enlarged, it holds several professional offices.

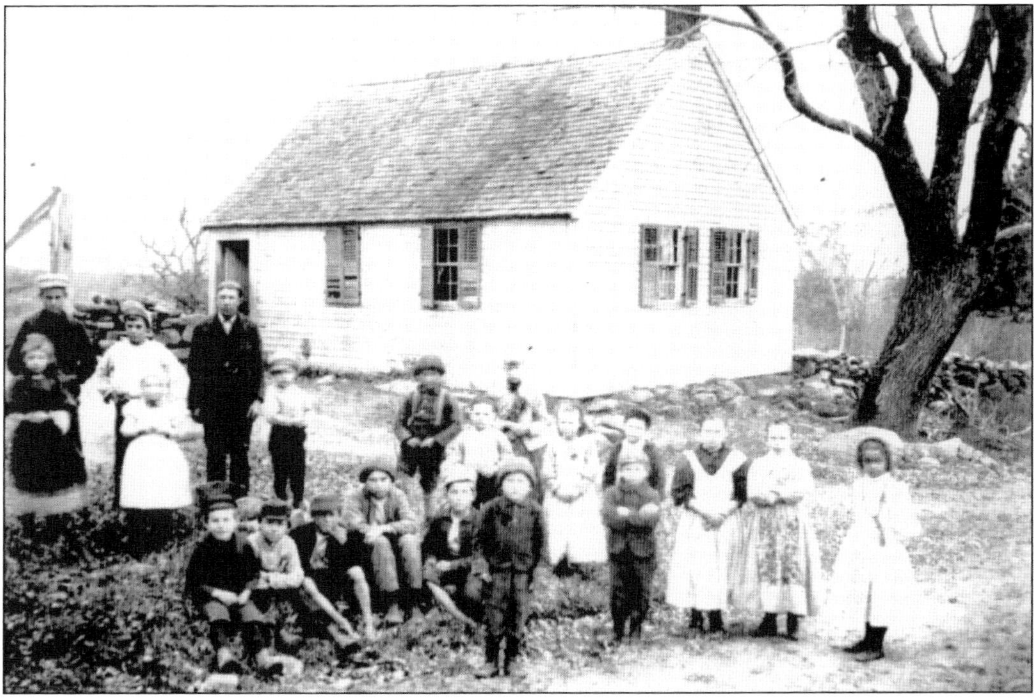

The Unionville School class, with teacher W. S. Allyn, poses for a photograph in 1894. The school survives in its original location as part of a private home.

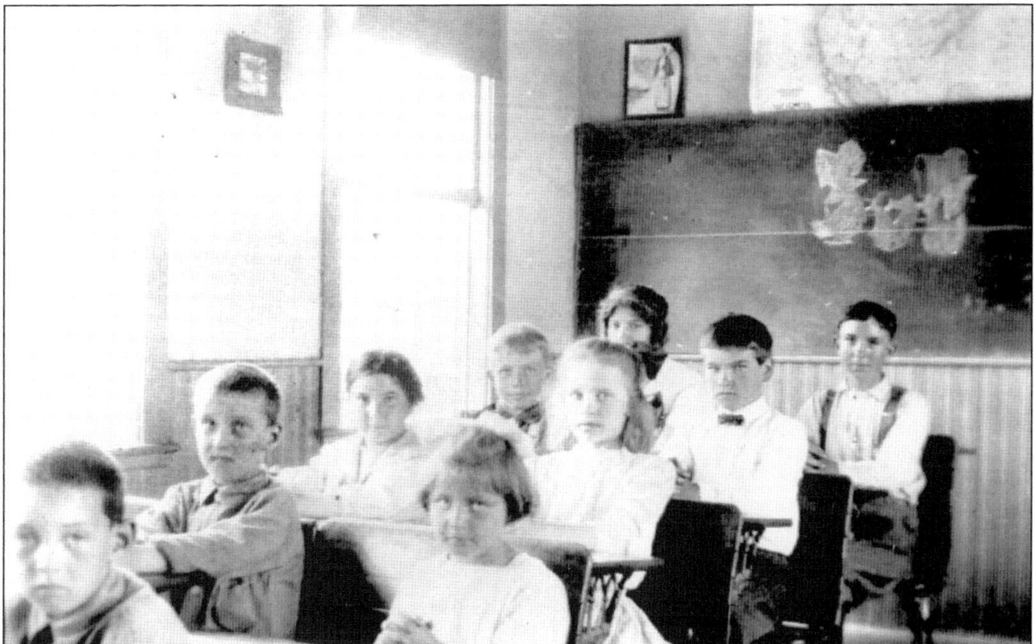

This interior view of the Unionville School demonstrates that, at least on sunny days, the classrooms were well lit. The boy with the bow tie, second from the right, is Amos G. Avery.

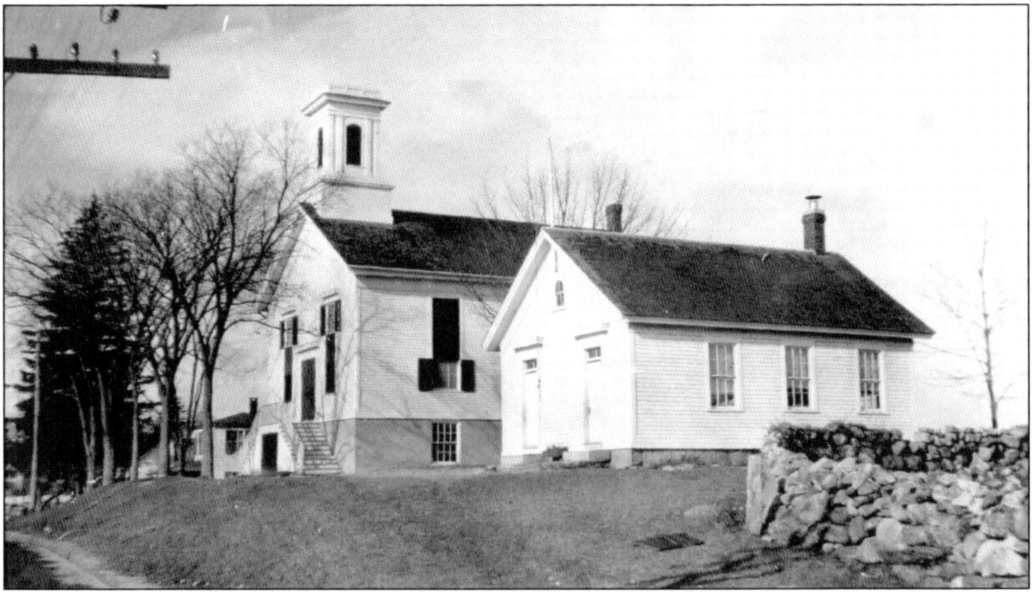

The Gales Ferry School, District 2, was constructed in 1868 on land next to the Methodist church. Now owned by the Ledyard Historical Society, it is one of two district schools in Ledyard maintained in its original configuration. This photograph was taken in September 1922.

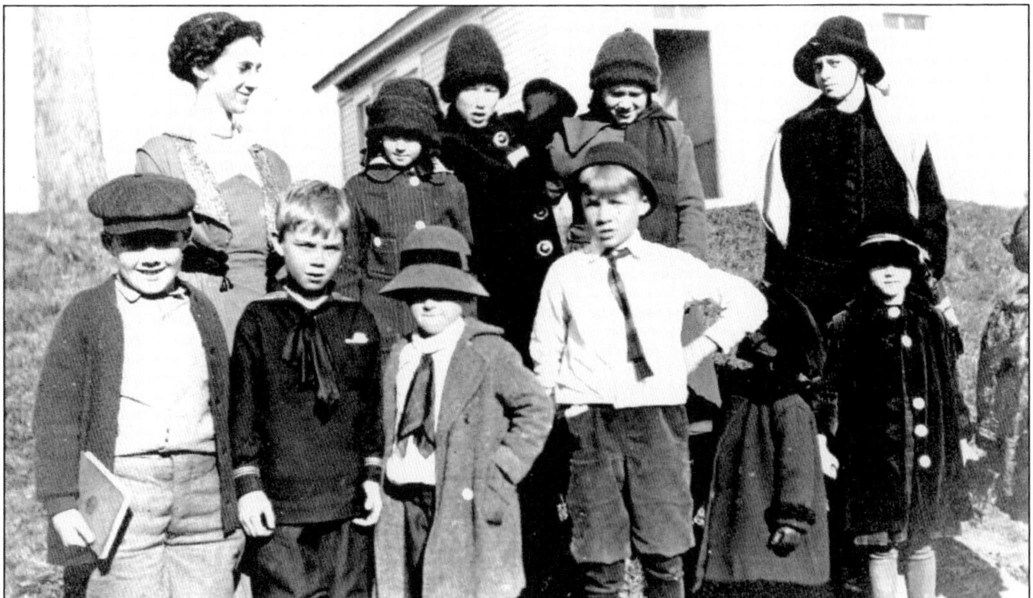

Students of the Gales Ferry class of 1917–1918 pose for a school photograph. From left to right are the following: (first row) Gordon Maniere, Paul Miller, Warren Norcross, Donald Potter, Rose Norcross, EmBeth Bennett, and Dorothy Birch; (second row) teacher Grace Chapman, Madeline Birch, Laura McGuire, Elizabeth Hines, and Gertrude Allen.

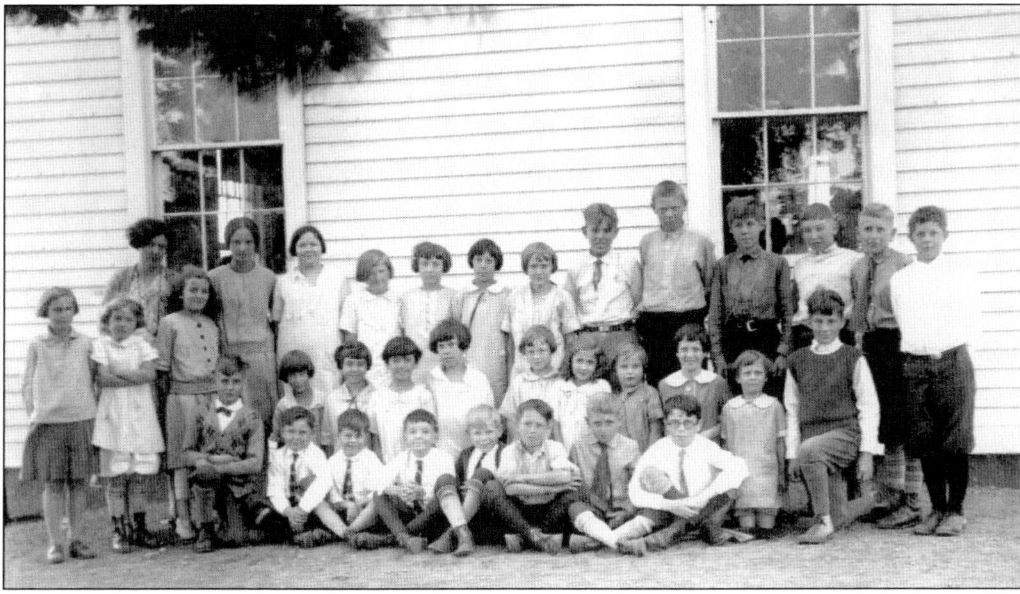

The members of Gales Ferry's 1927 class pose for their photograph. From left to right are the following: (first row) Carl Norcross, Elvin Hartung, Billy Davidson, Robert Hamilton, Herbert Lewis, Frank Jennings, and Joseph DeRusha; (second row, kneeling) Jay Pierce, Barbara Hamilton, Edith Hartung, Elizabeth Main, Frances Maynard, Enid Latimer, May Crandall, Dorothy Hamilton, Bernice Coman, Doris Coman, and Richard Latimer; (fourth row) Louise Howard, Ruth Hurlbutt, teacher Evelyn Whipple, Marilyn Rogers, Helen DeRusha, Ruth Main, Peggy Parker, Carol Norman, Christine Miller, Ruth Allyn, Howard Nye, Harry Whipple, Edmund Norman, John Buckman, Louis Jennings, and Earl Coman.

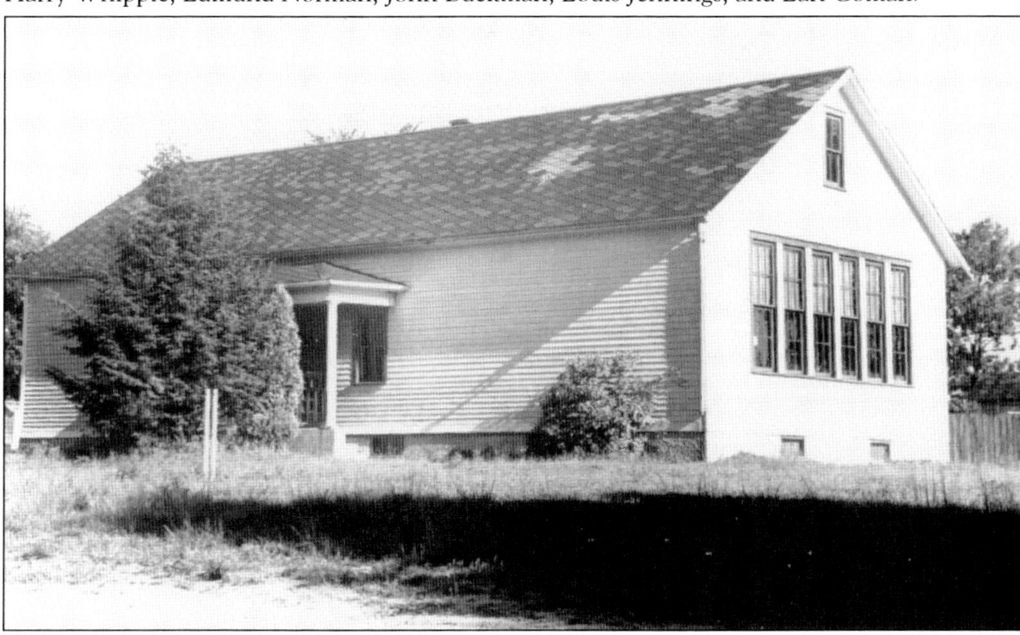

Successively larger classes led to the construction on Hurlbutt Road of a two-room school, which opened in January 1929. This photograph was taken after the school closed in 1949 but before the building became the Gales Ferry Community Center.

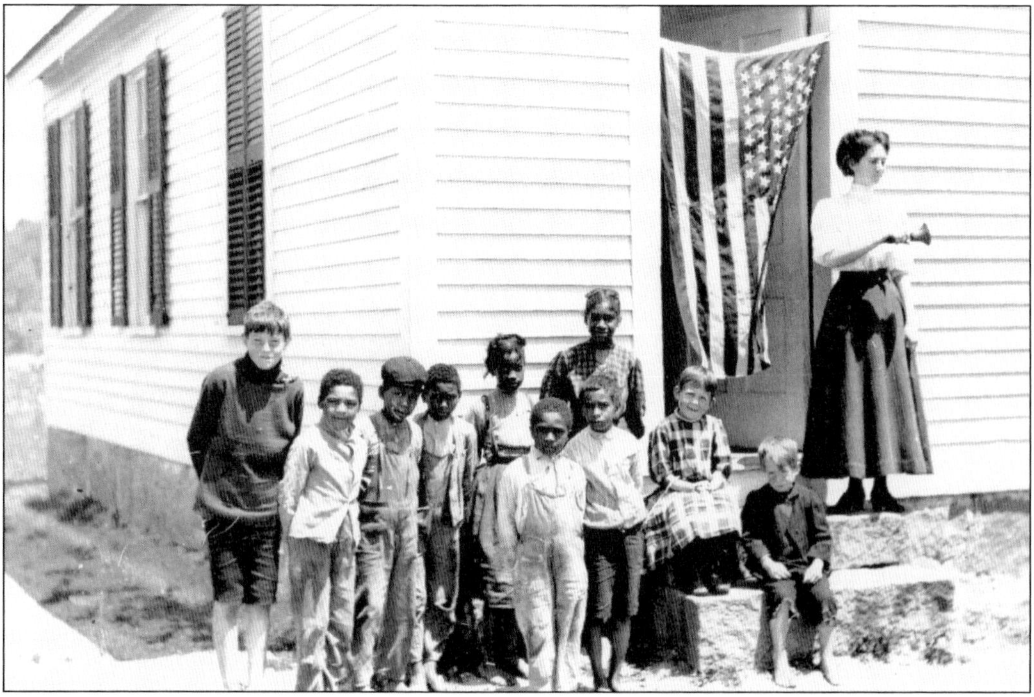

The Stoddard District School, No. 13, was located on Whalehead Road. Its integrated student body stemmed from a community of Cape Verde Islanders who came to Allyn's Point to work on the railroad. Teacher Grace Chapman rings the bell for class during the 1908–1909 year.

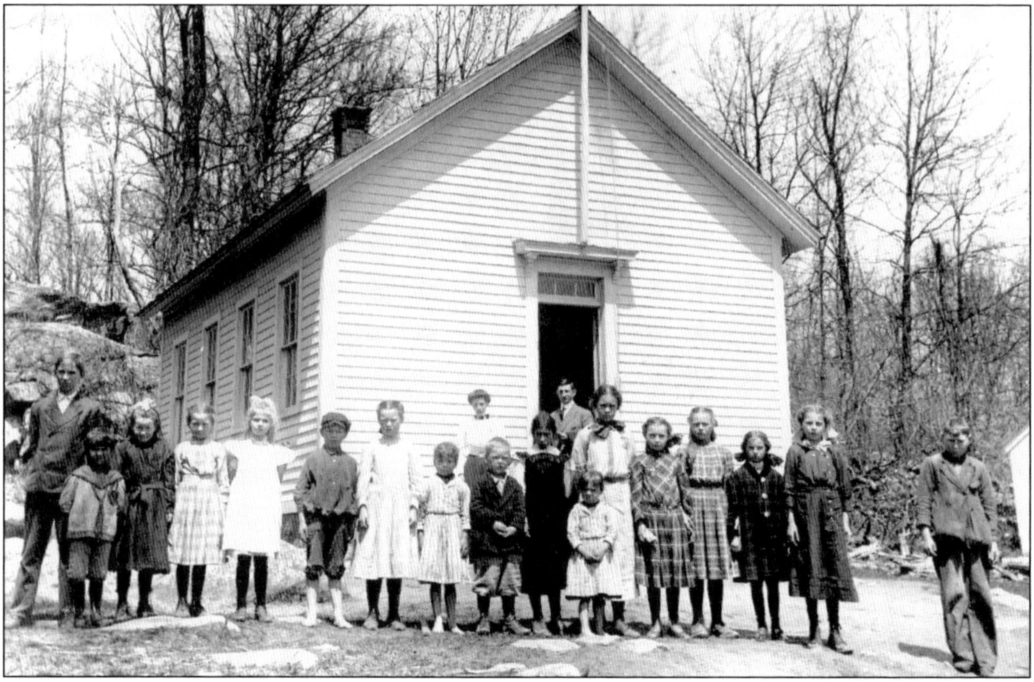

The Cider Hill School, District 7, was located on Shewville Road, near the present intersection with Town Farm Road. It is now a private residence.

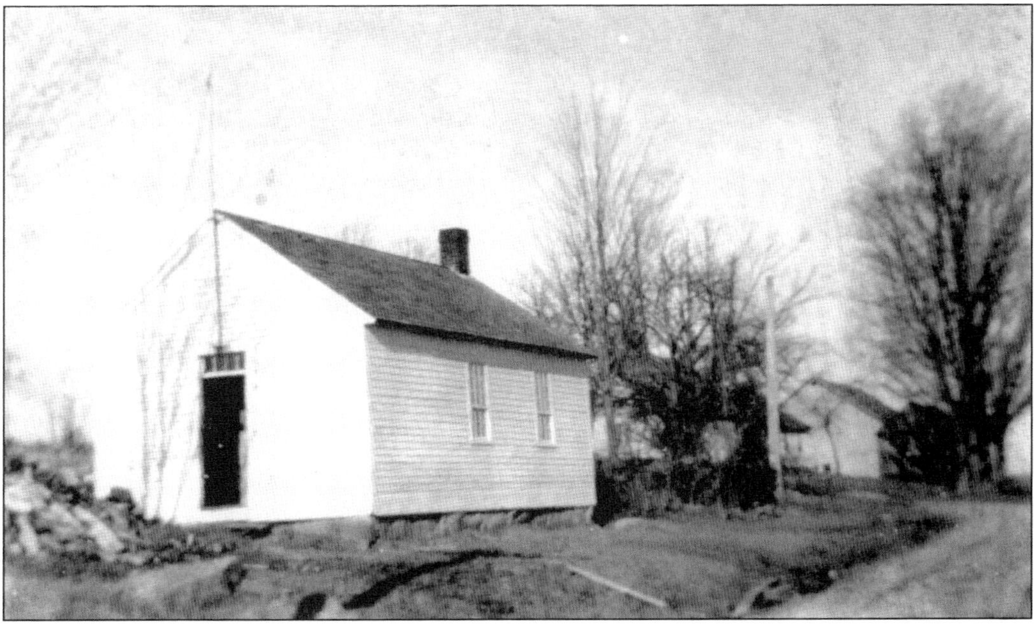

The Gallup District School, No. 8, stood on the corner of Gallup Hill and Spicer Hill Roads. Athletic fields for the new Ledyard High School now occupy this site.

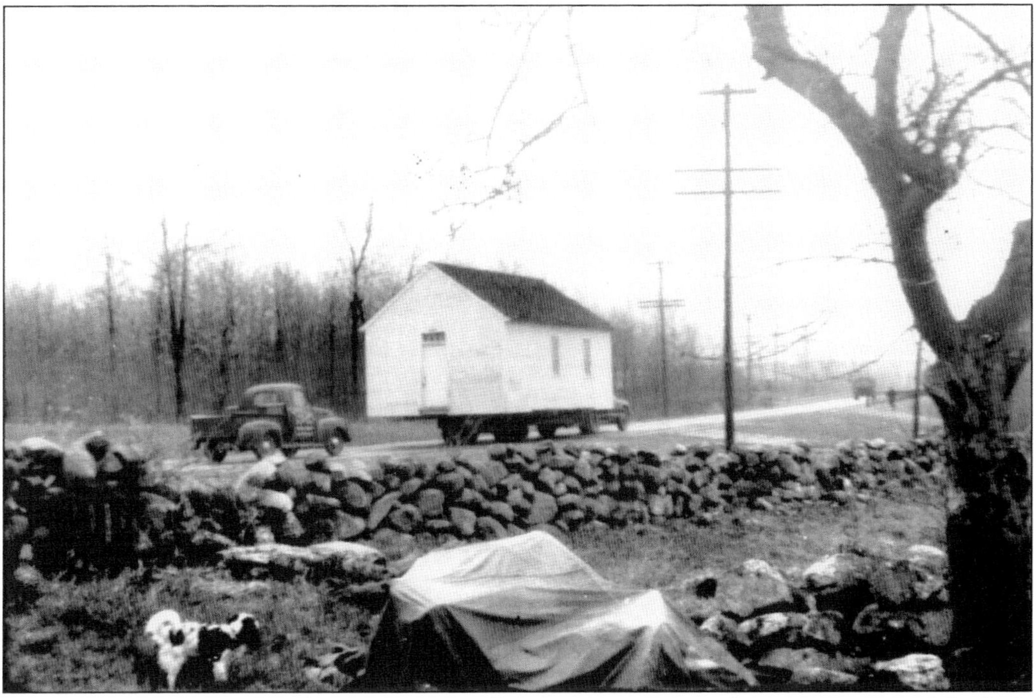

The Gallup District Schoolhouse was moved to Groton prior to the construction of the high school. It is now a private residence on Route 184.

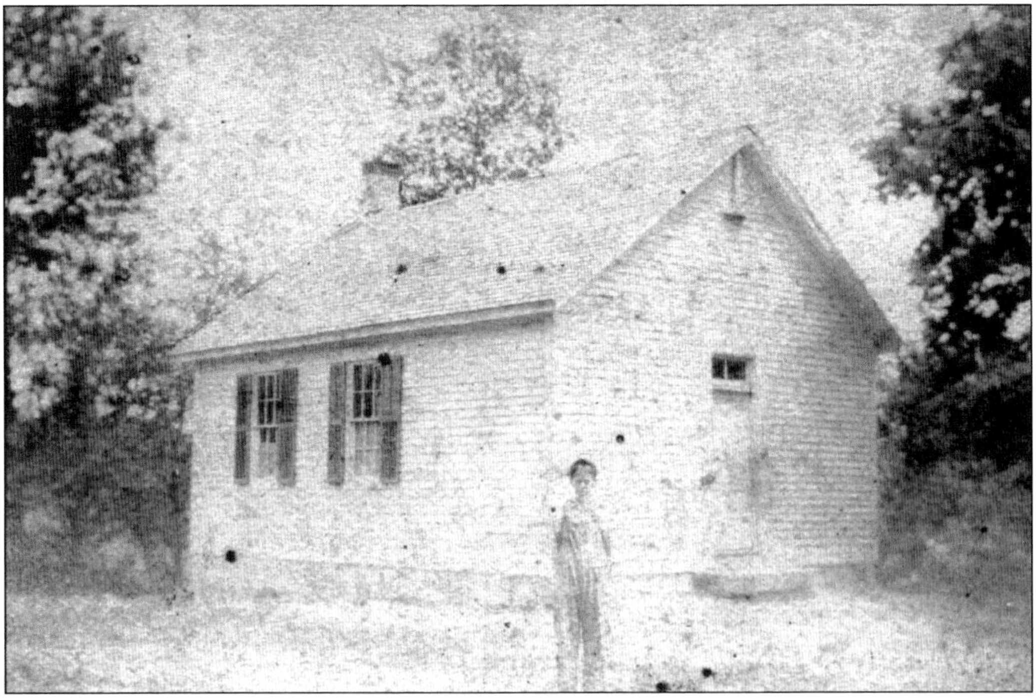

The Lester District School, No. 10, was located on Long Cove Road, just south of the Nathan Lester property. This is the only known photograph of it.

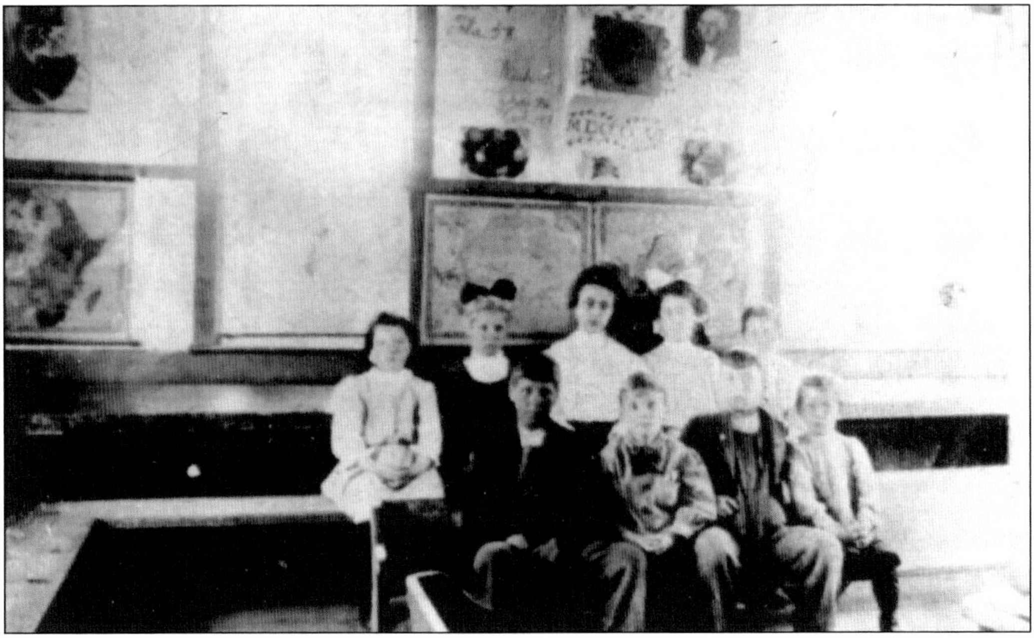

The earliest furniture in the district schools consisted of fixed benches around the perimeter facing a desk ledge below the window sills. This took advantage of the natural light. Shown here *c*. 1910 are, from left to right, the following: (first row) Everett Thompson, Walter Mather, Harold McGuire, and Carl Thompson; (second row) Evelyn Whipple, Annie Thompson, teacher Maude Hauck, Elsie McGuire, and Nellie Hoffman.

This photograph bears the inscription "Quakertown School or Hall, 1867." Although it is larger than any of the town's other schools, it is of similar design. No trace of it remains.

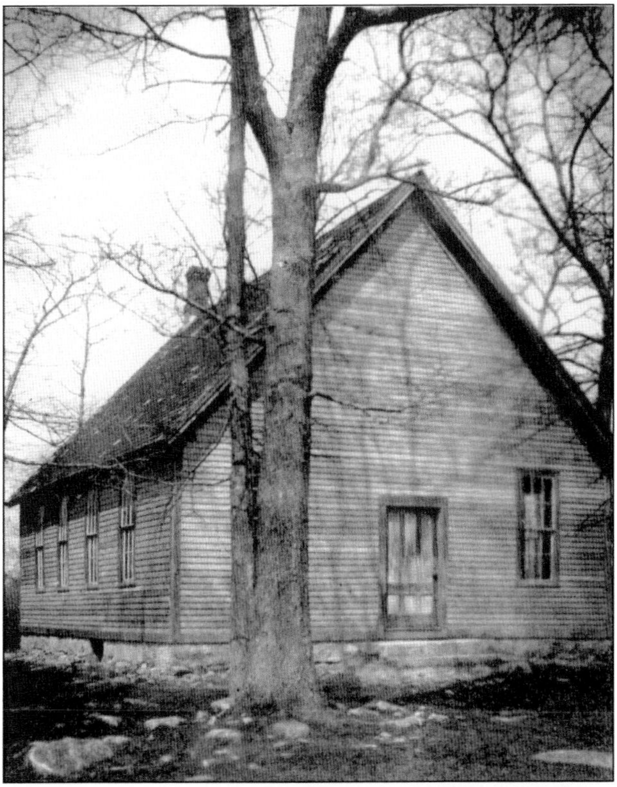

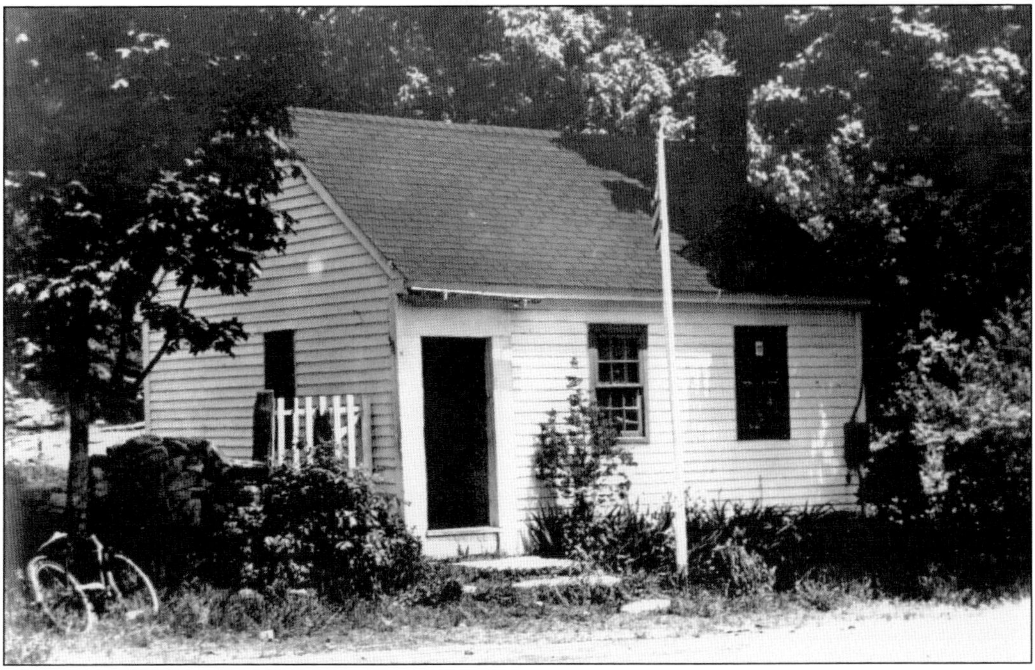

The second preserved district school in Ledyard is the Geer Hill School, on Colonel Ledyard Highway. Owned and maintained by the Geer School Association, it served District 4. This photograph dates from 1949.

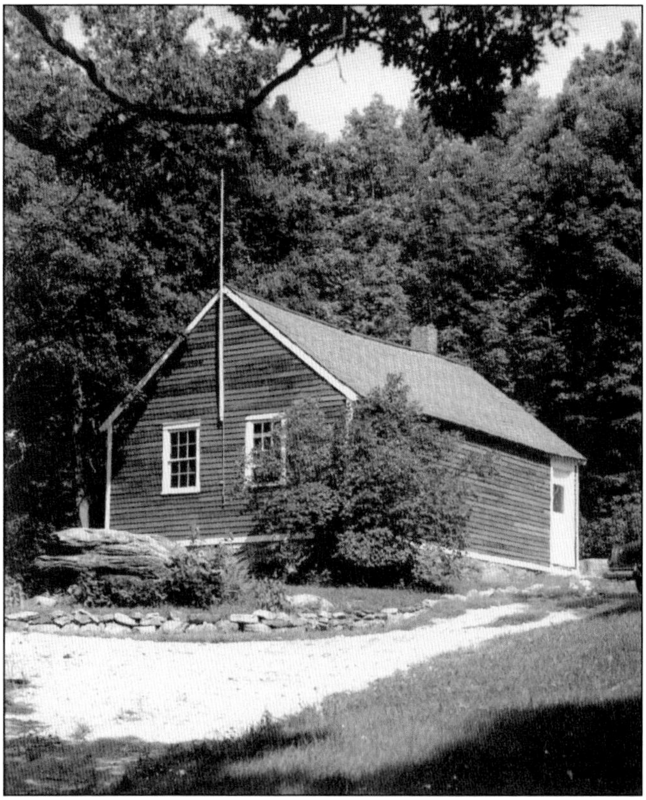

The Lambtown School, District 11, was located on the western portion of Lambtown Road. Recently closed when this photograph was taken in 1949, it was demolished in the 1960s.

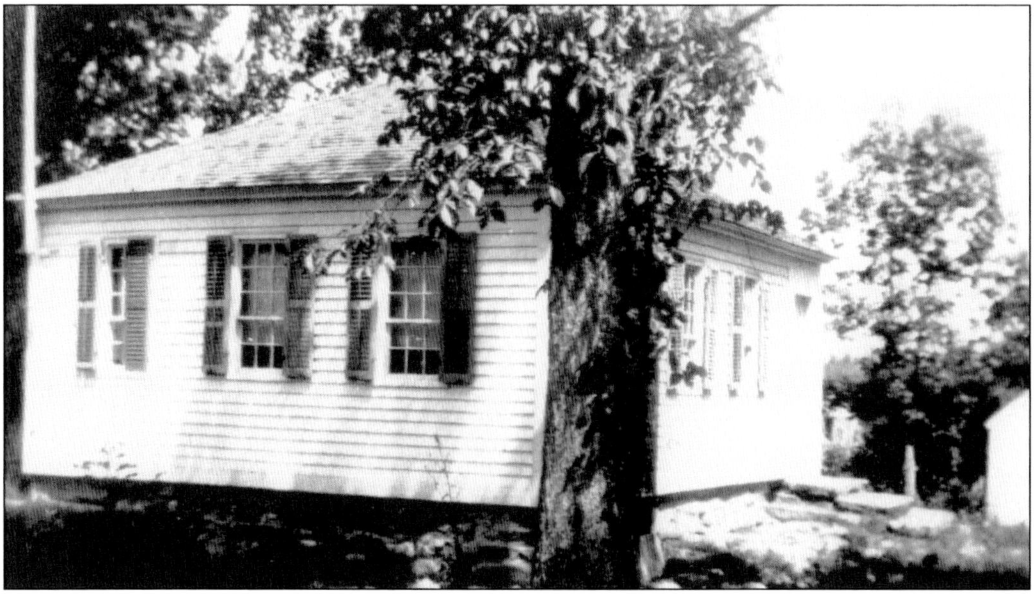

Ledyard Center had a district school located behind the Bill Library. Of unusual design, it was constructed by a master builder who worked from his own plans.

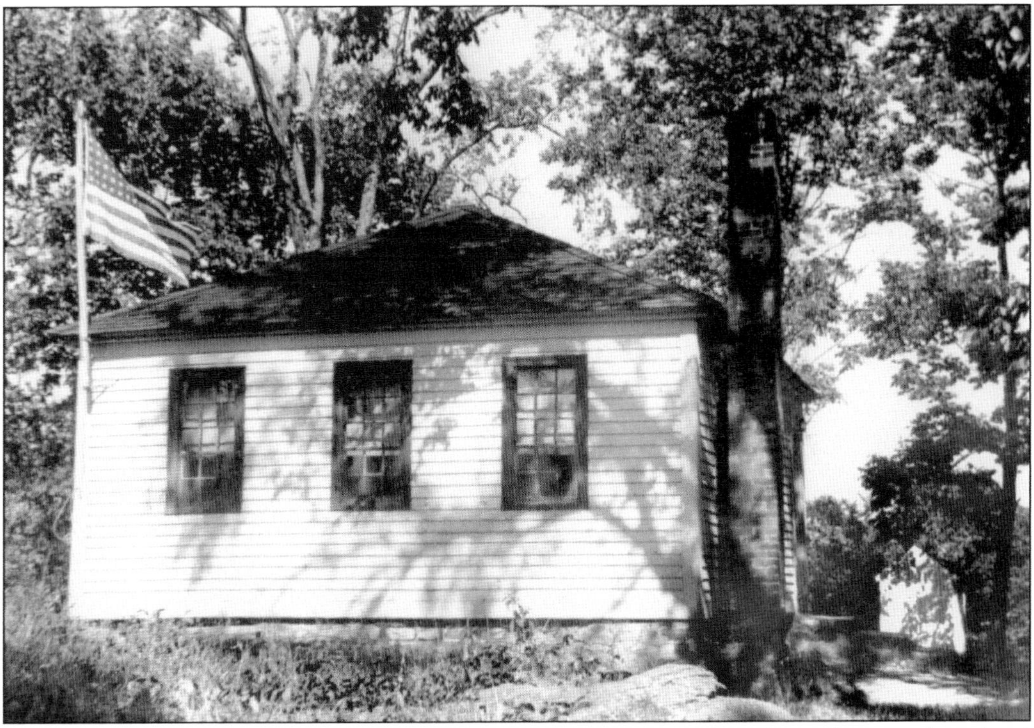

This photograph of the Ledyard Center School, District 5, was taken about the time the school closed in 1949. The building was later used as a meeting place for several groups. Moved onto the Ledyard Fairgrounds at the time of the library expansion in 1983, it is now being restored.

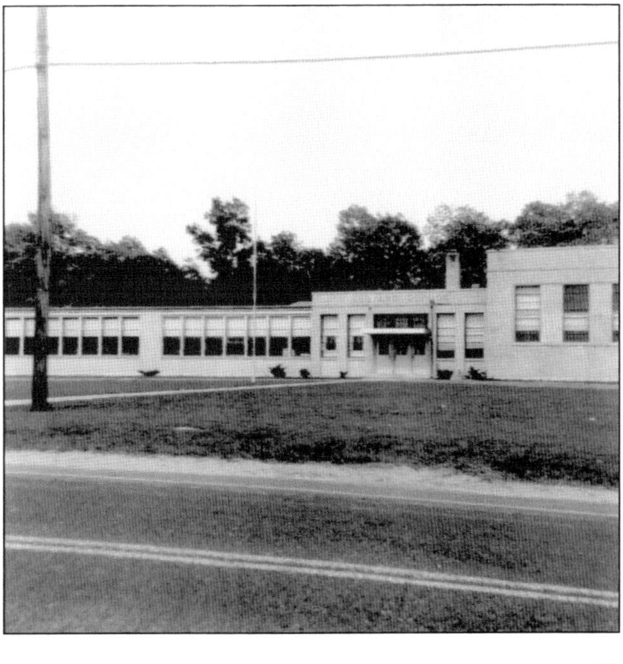

Ledyard's first central school, then named Ledyard Consolidated School, opened in 1949. When this photograph was taken in 1957, the circular driveways in front had not yet been created.

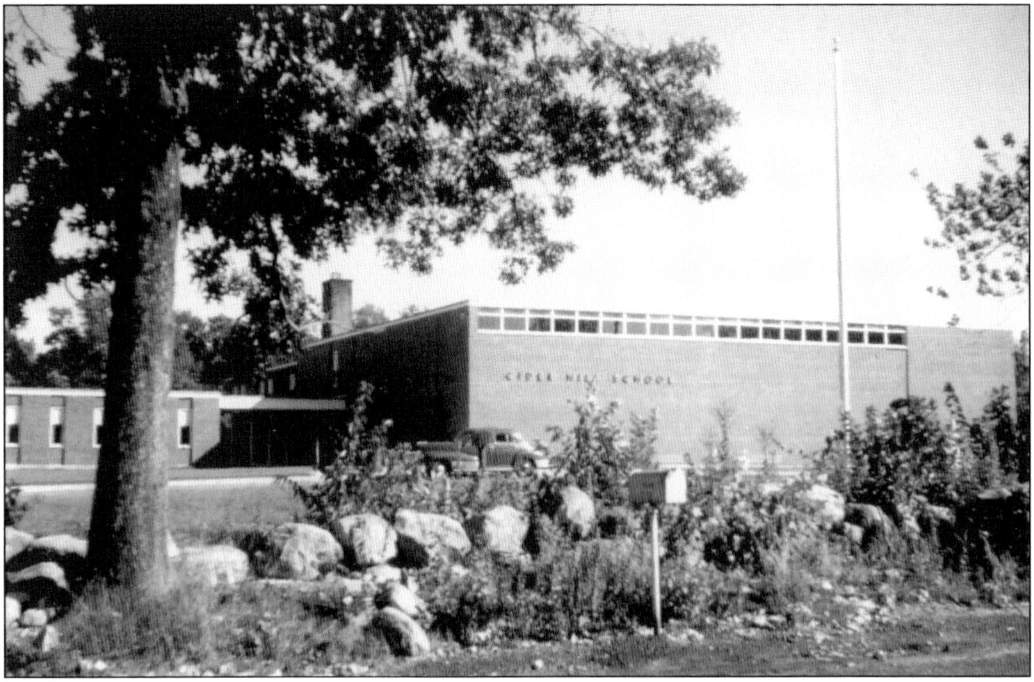

The present Gallup Hill School, at Town Farm and Gallup Hill Roads, was called Cider Hill School when it was built in 1965. It was renamed upon opening to reflect its proximity to Gallup Hill.

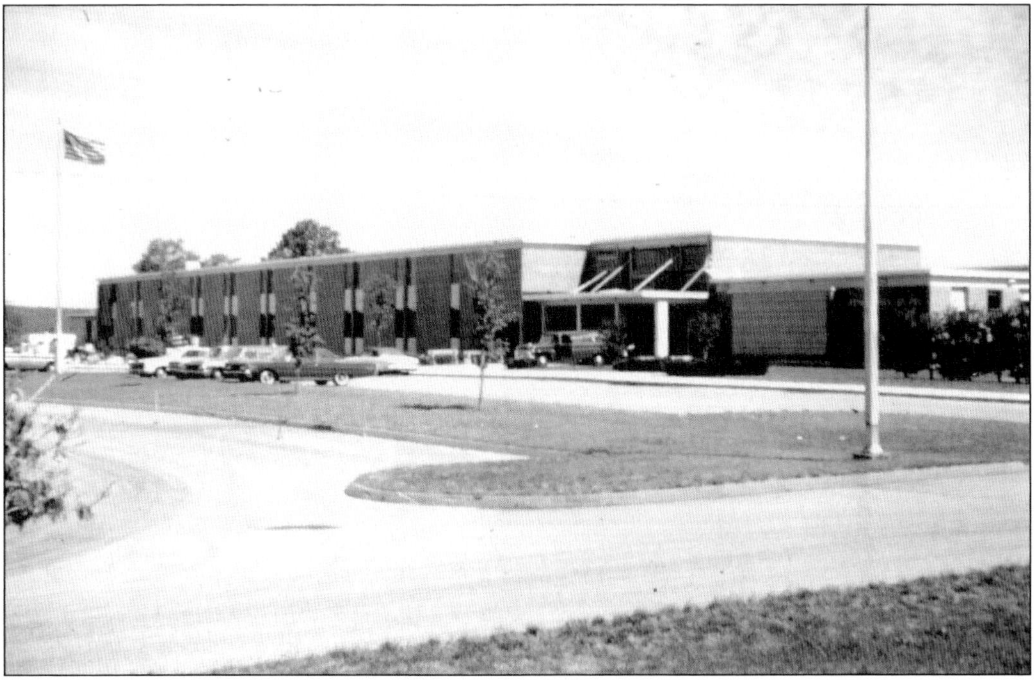

Ledyard High School, at the corner of Colonel Ledyard Highway and Gallup Hill Road, opened in 1963 and graduated its first class in 1967. Several additions have been made since this 1965 photograph.

Nine

Living Off the Land

Early Ledyard is correctly described as an agrarian community. "Farming" or "agricultural" community would be apt descriptions as well, but country life in the 18th, 19th, and early 20th centuries involved more than milking cows and cutting hay. Virtually everything needed for life evolved in some way from the land: food, drink, clothing, and materials for shelter.

Trees harvested from the forests provided the building materials, and Ledyard had several sawmills powered by the water in the streams. Stone was cut from the earth, much of Ledyard's granite coming from a quarry at what is now the naval submarine base. A witch hazel mill once stood off Stoddard's Wharf Road, and bayberries were harvested and processed for their wax.

As late as the mid-19th century, farms operated in the heart of Gales Ferry Village, and all of the major hills in town—Geer Hill, Church Hill, and Gallup Hill—were home to large family farms. Much of the land that is now wooded was cleared for crops and the grazing of animals. The stone walls one now sees in the woods are shadowy reminders of the once open space.

As recently as 30 years ago, there were several dairy farms in the town of Ledyard. Today there is but one. The town's agrarian roots are not forgotten, though. When Ledyard High School was founded in the 1960s, its planners recognized the value in the rural heritage and established a regional vocational agriculture program, now called Agriscience and Technology. One of 19 such regional centers in the state, it educates students from a number of surrounding towns.

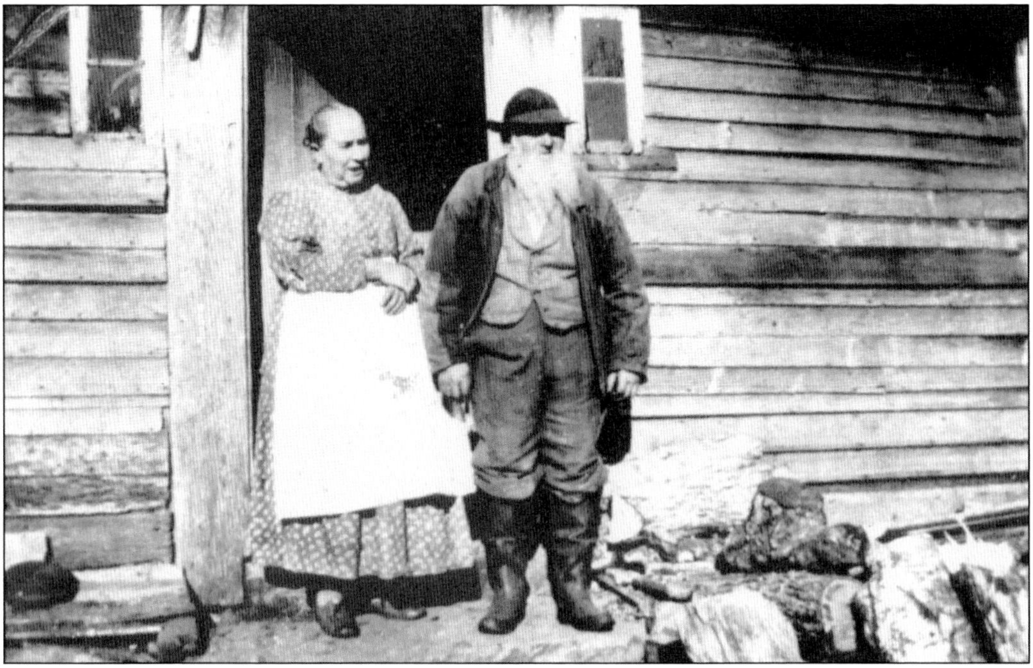

The Allyns personify the hardworking farm family. Elisha Allyn (1822–1900) and Maria (1841–1909), his second wife, are buried in the Allen-Satterlee Cemetery on Sandy Hollow Road.

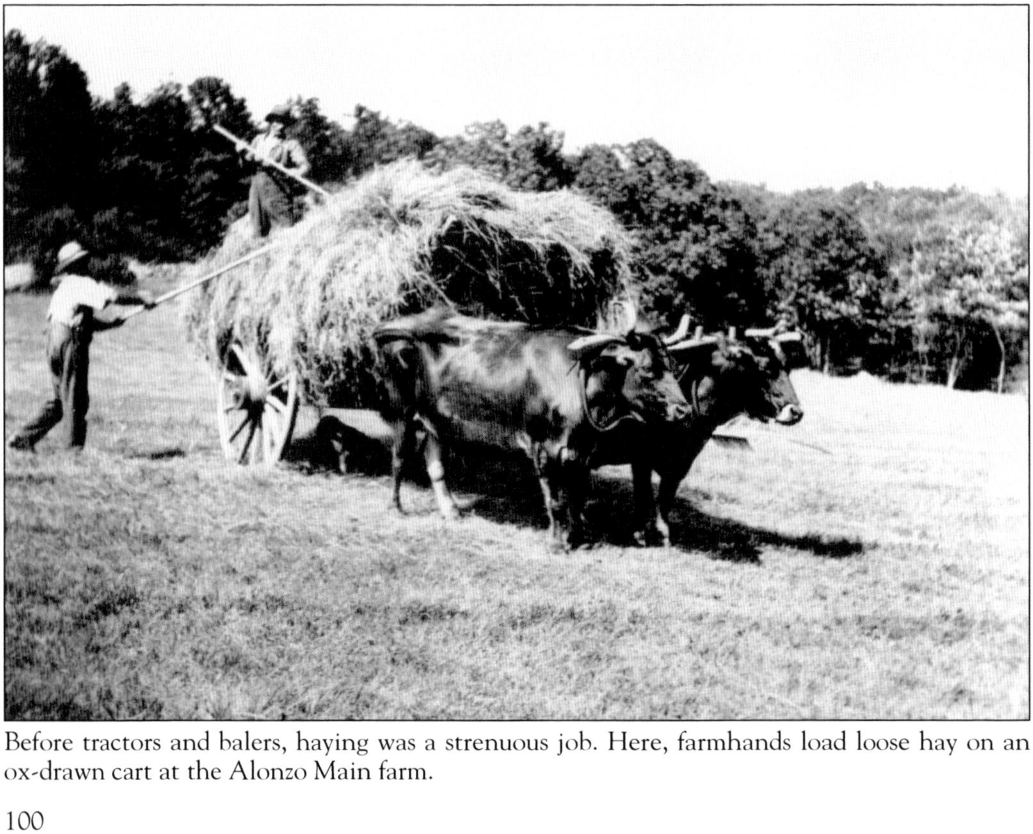

Before tractors and balers, haying was a strenuous job. Here, farmhands load loose hay on an ox-drawn cart at the Alonzo Main farm.

Alonzo Main (b. 1856) was a descendant of Christopher Avery. He farmed near Long Pond.

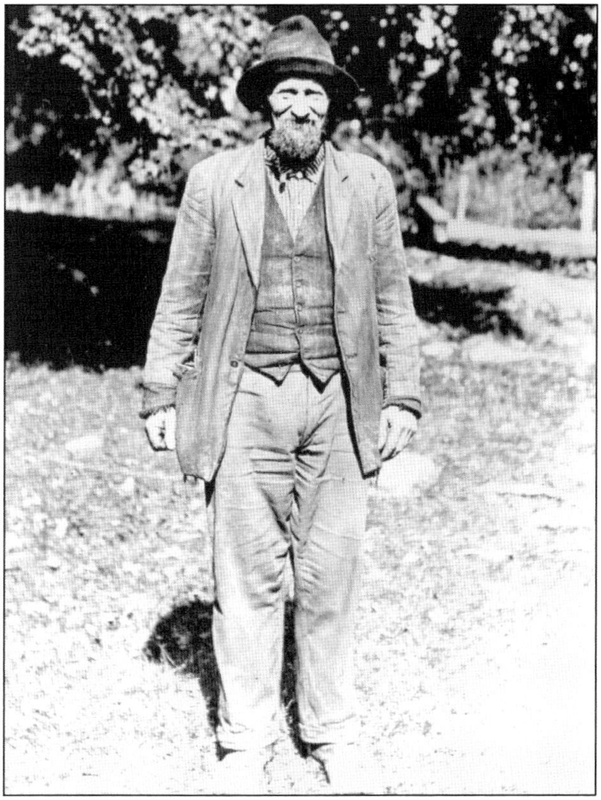

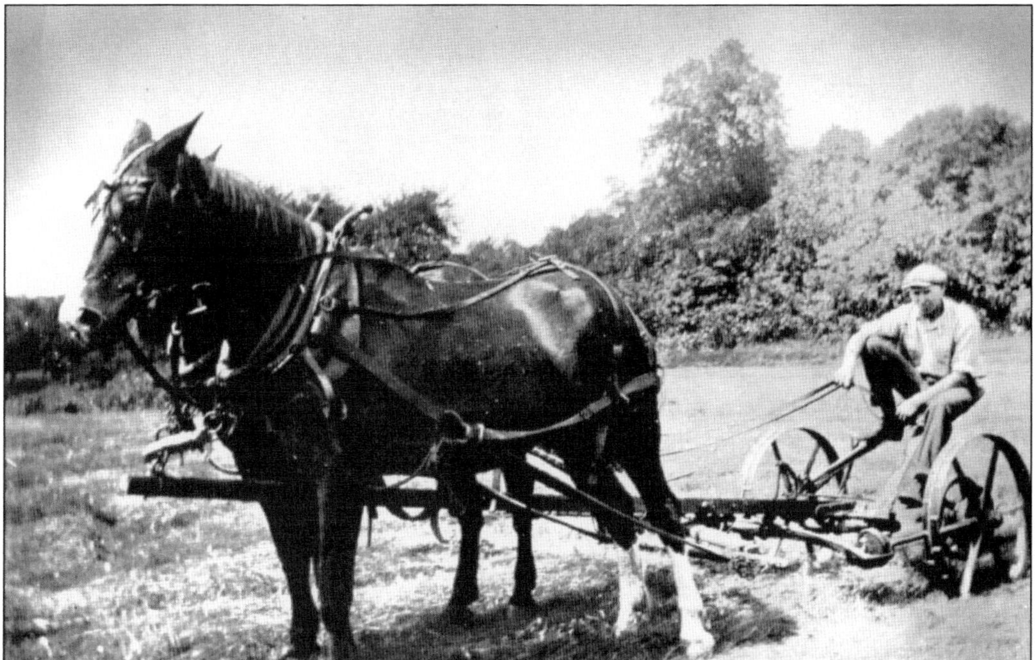

Hay was cut with horse-drawn mowing machines and was then left to dry before being stored loose in the barn. Here, Alonzo Main's son Jim and his horse rest from their mowing.

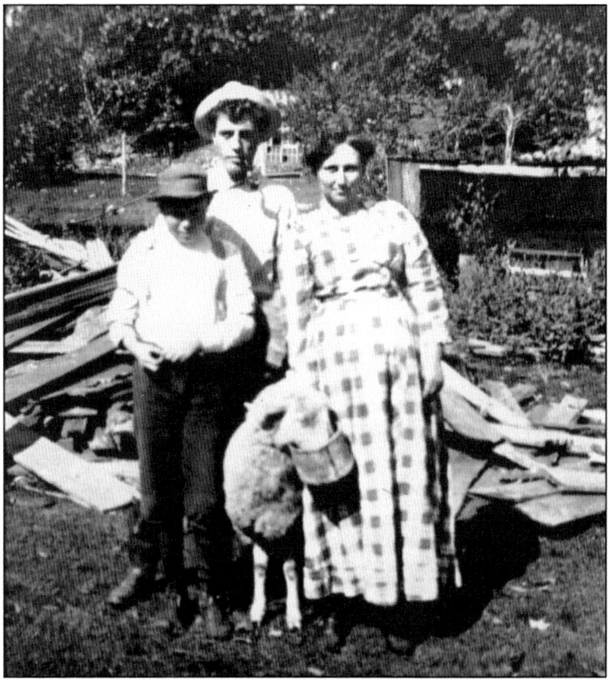

Clifford Stimpson (left) and his mother, Mabel, feed the sheep. The Stimpsons lived on Center Groton Road, south of Ledyard Center. Clifford (b. 1899) was Alonzo Main's grandson. The other person is unidentified.

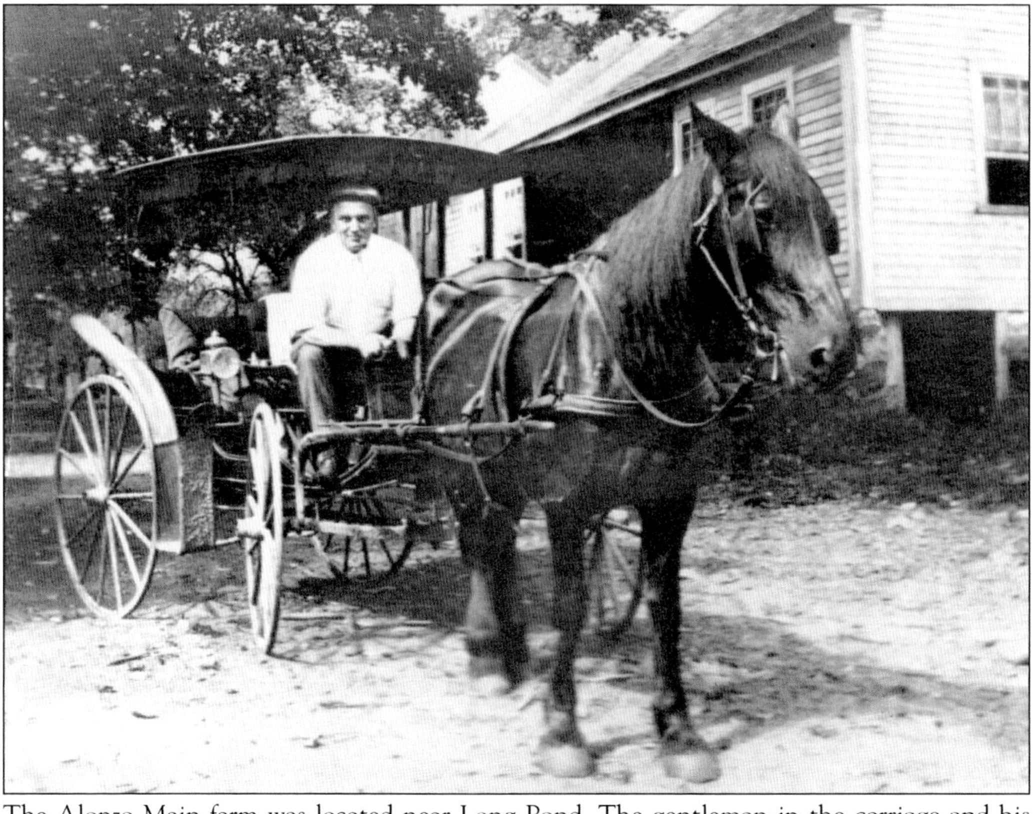

The Alonzo Main farm was located near Long Pond. The gentleman in the carriage and his horse are both unidentified.

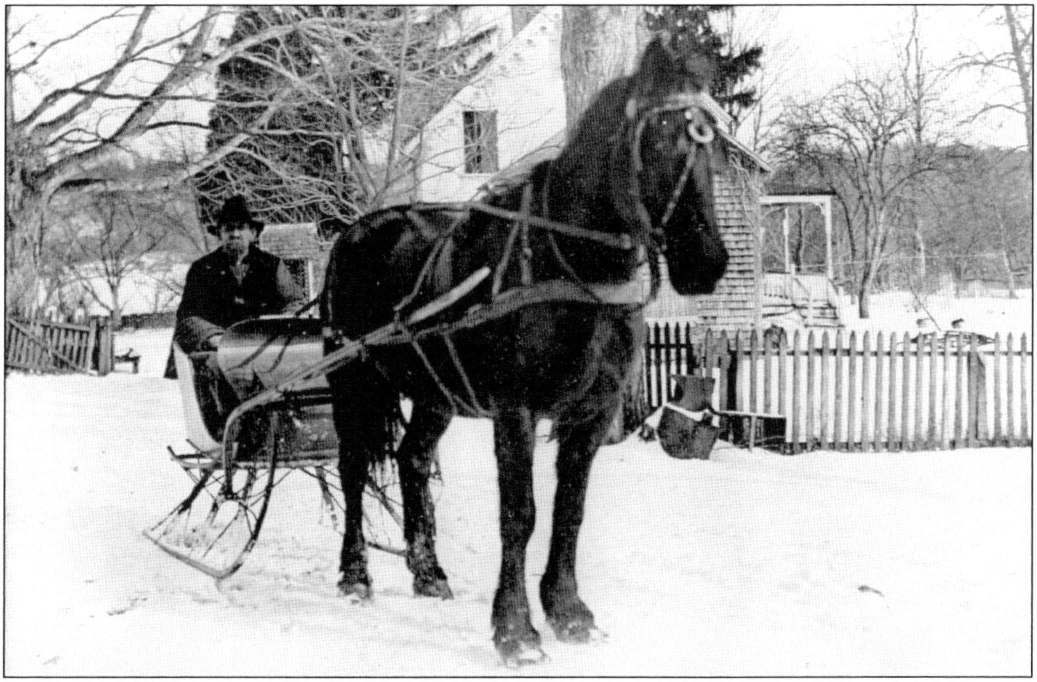

Alonzo Main sets out for town by horse and sleigh. Alonzo's twin sister, Melissa, married Joseph Holdridge. The Holdridges are buried in the Ledyard Center Cemetery.

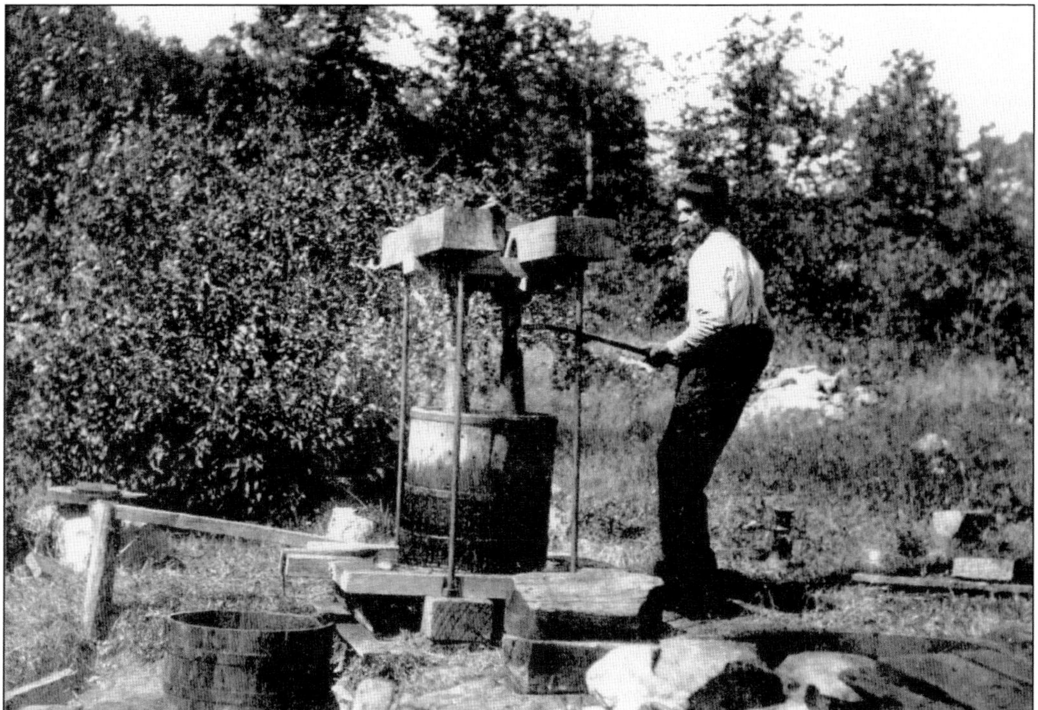

Cash crops were varied in stony Ledyard. In this photograph, "Martha Langevin's French father" presses bayberries for wax in the area known as Mashantucket.

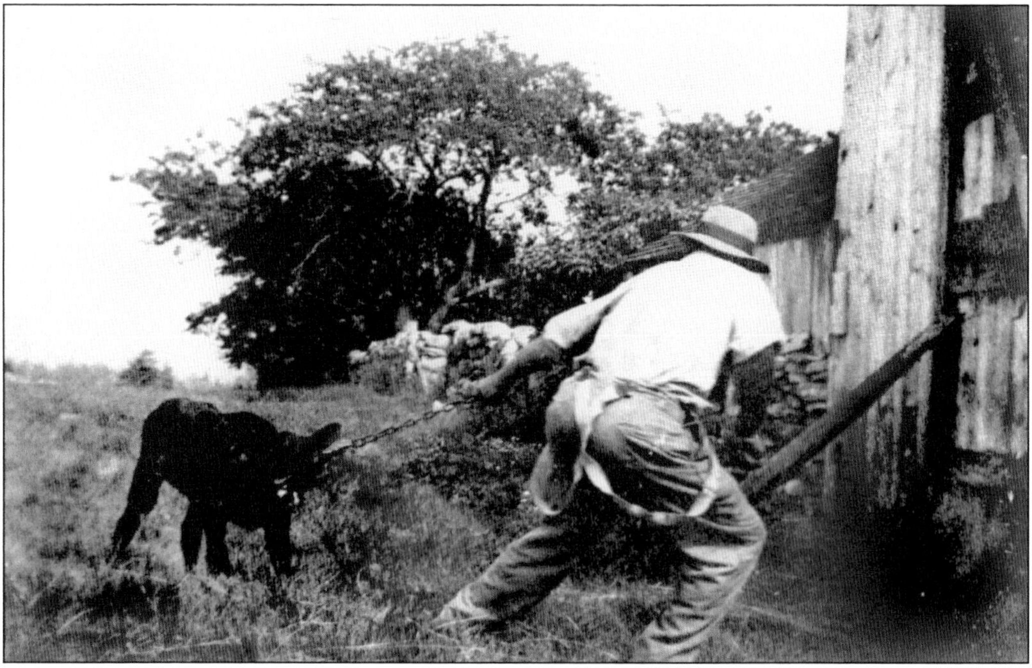

Augustus Ackley (1839–1926) farmed at Quakertown near the Groton town line. Here, he struggles to get a calf into the barn.

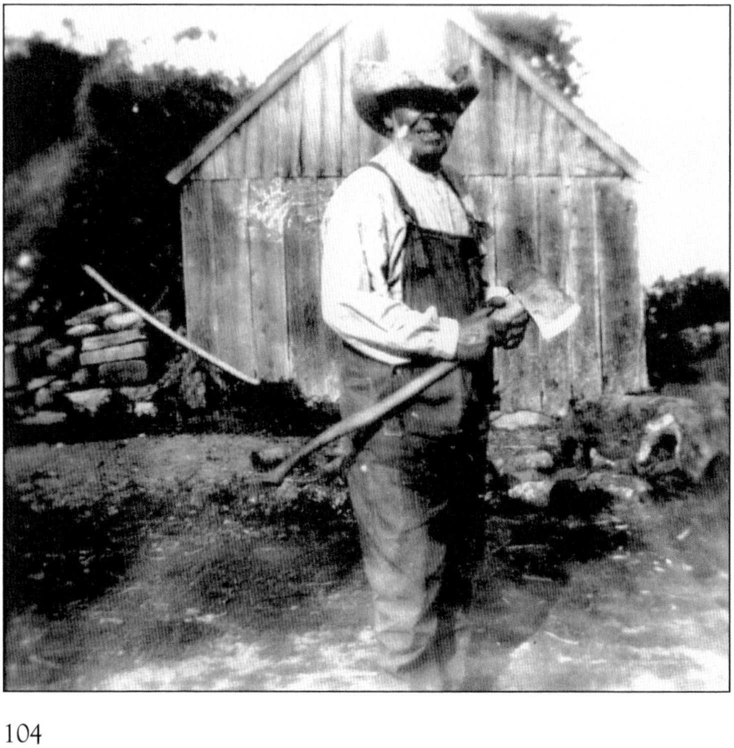

Augustus Ackley prepares to chop wood. The clean-shaven Ackley pictured here is perhaps younger than the bearded one in other photographs.

Augustus Ackley brings the feed pail to his livestock. A native of Maine, he lived in Quakertown and is buried there in the Union Cemetery.

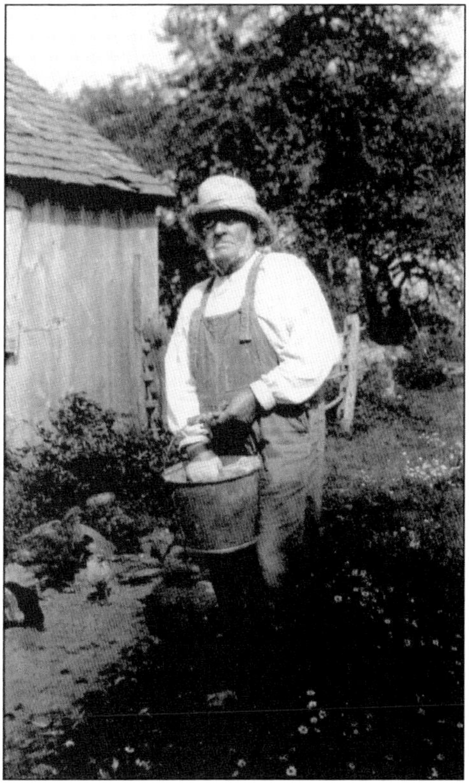

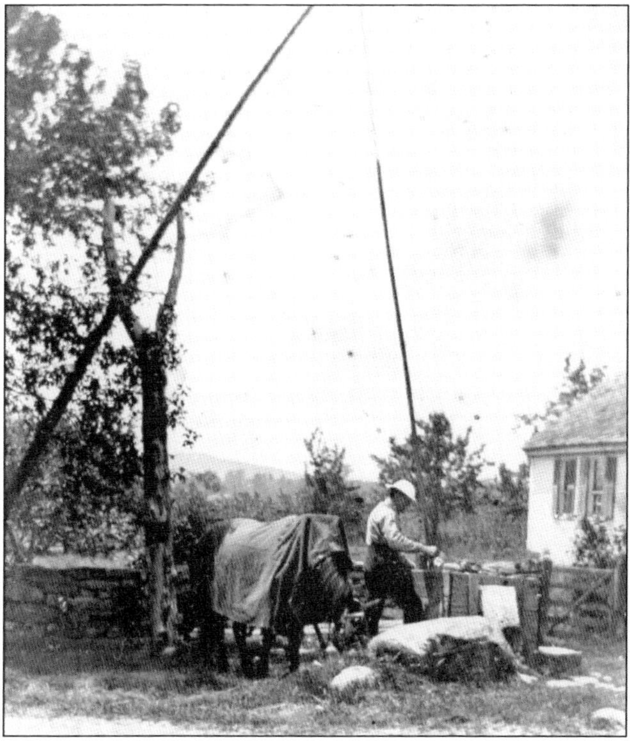

Farming continued at the Thomas Allyn place on Allyn's Point long after the railroad and coaling ships arrived. Thomas's son Cyrus waters his horse at the magnificent well sweep c. 1910.

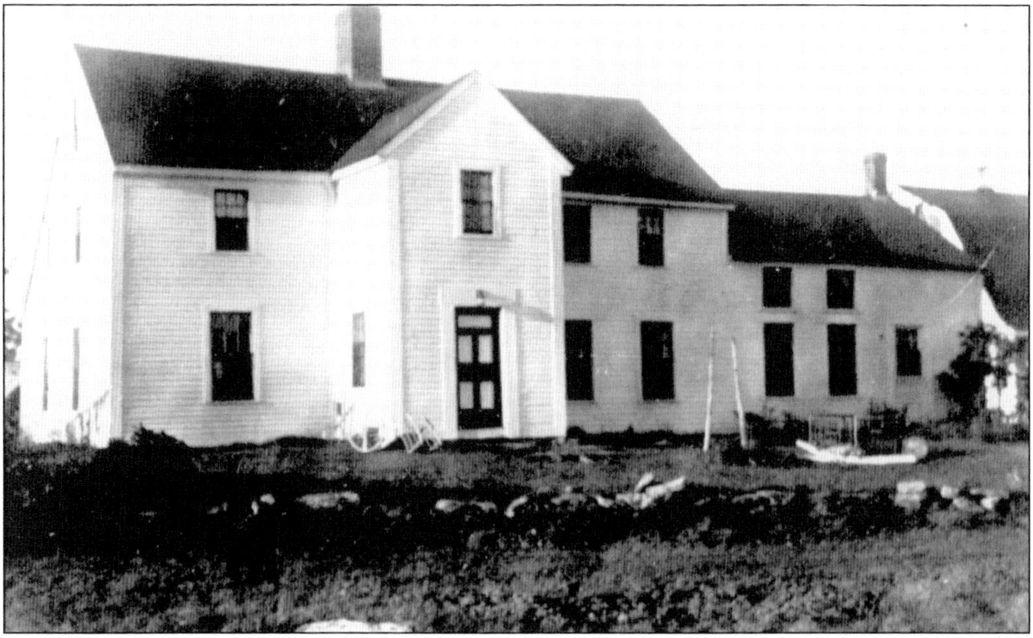

Most towns had a "poor farm," where the indigent were housed and cared for, and where they worked if they were able. Ledyard owned its own "town farm" on what is now Town Farm Road. This photograph shows the farmhouse in the early part of the 20th century.

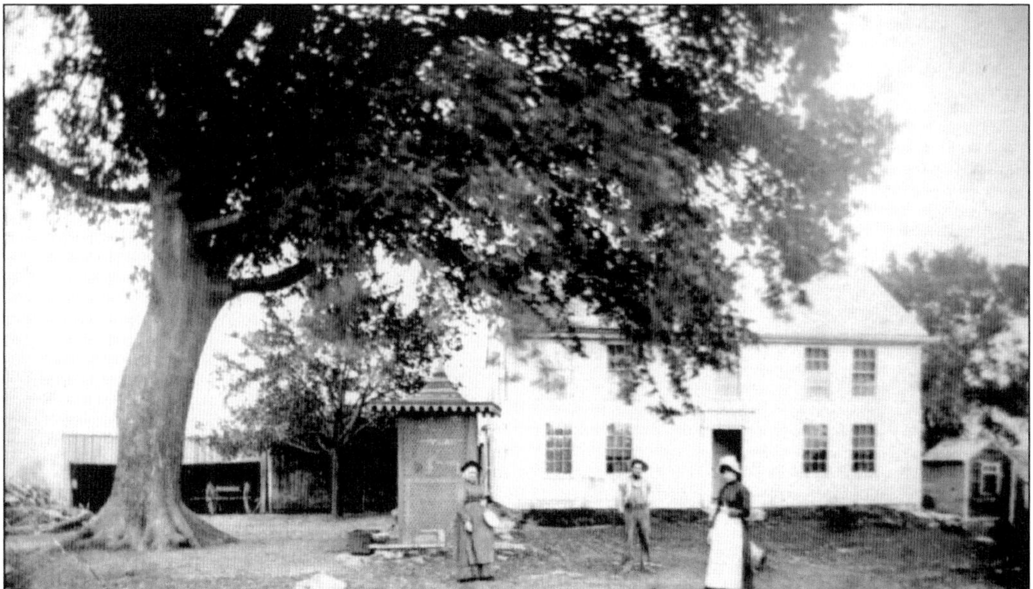

A farm family stands in the dooryard at what is now the Wiemann farm on Avery Hill Road. The well house is an attractive piece of Victorian farm furniture.

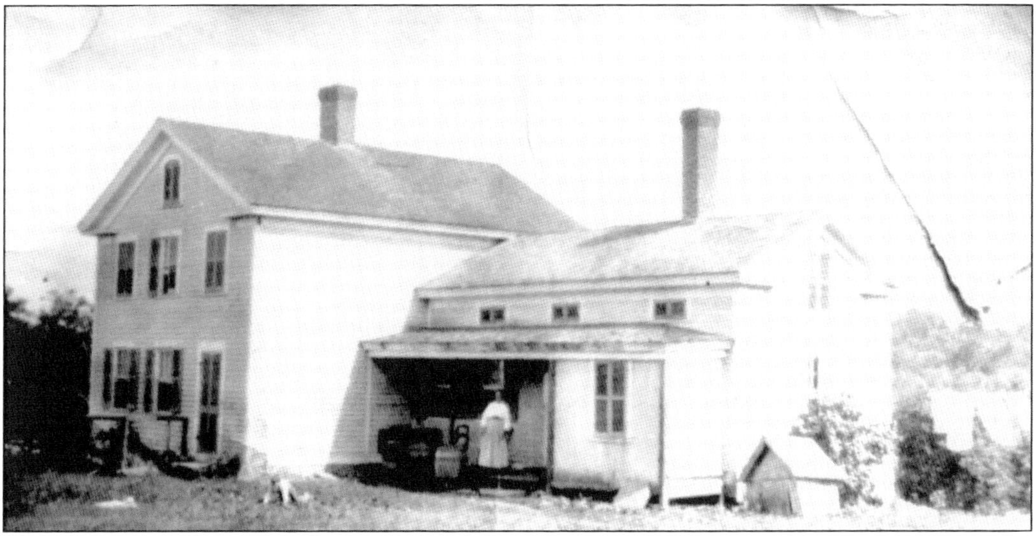

The Enos Gray farm on Iron Street operated well into the 1970s. The farmhouse is still standing, but most of the farmland has been put down to housing developments.

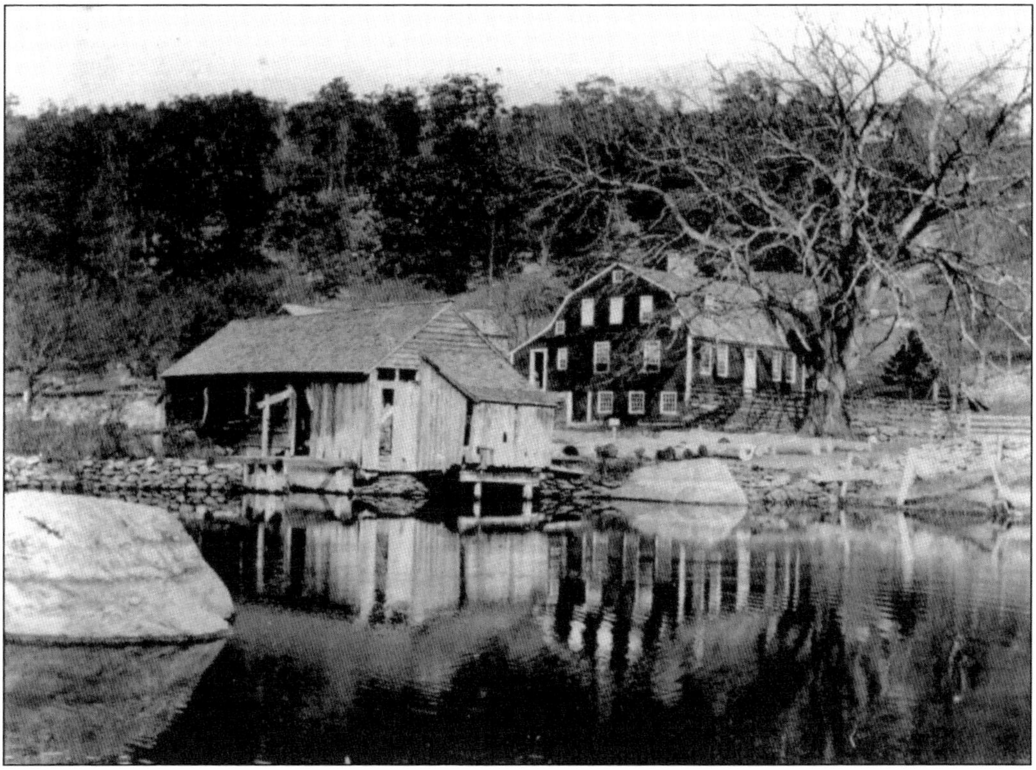

The land produced not just hay, grains, and berries. Wood was a cash crop, and several sawmills provided materials for building. This is the sawmill on Flat Brook, upstream from Long Cove. It was in operation as early as 1783, when Benjamin Bill bought it. The house in the background is often called the Richards House, after the owners during the latter part of the 19th century.

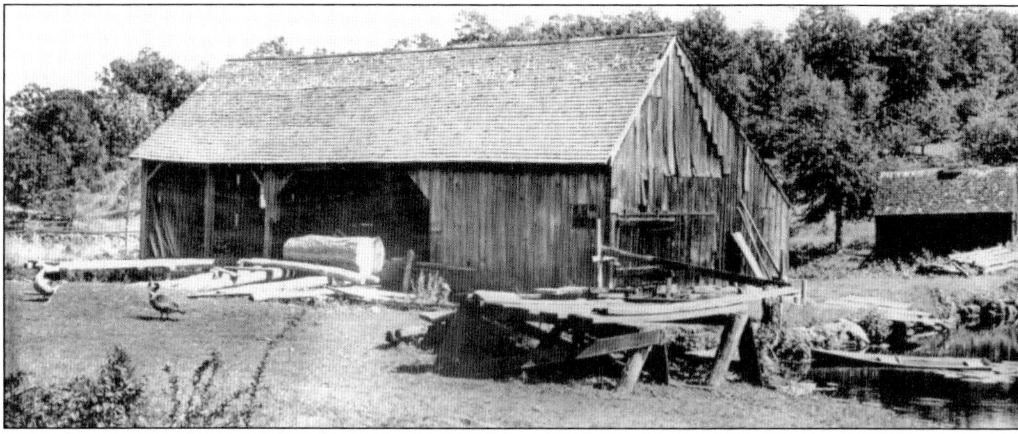

The Harry Main Sawmill on Iron Street was remarkable in retaining its up-down saw mechanism long after most mills had converted to circular saws. Main was still operating it when this photograph was taken *c.* 1935.

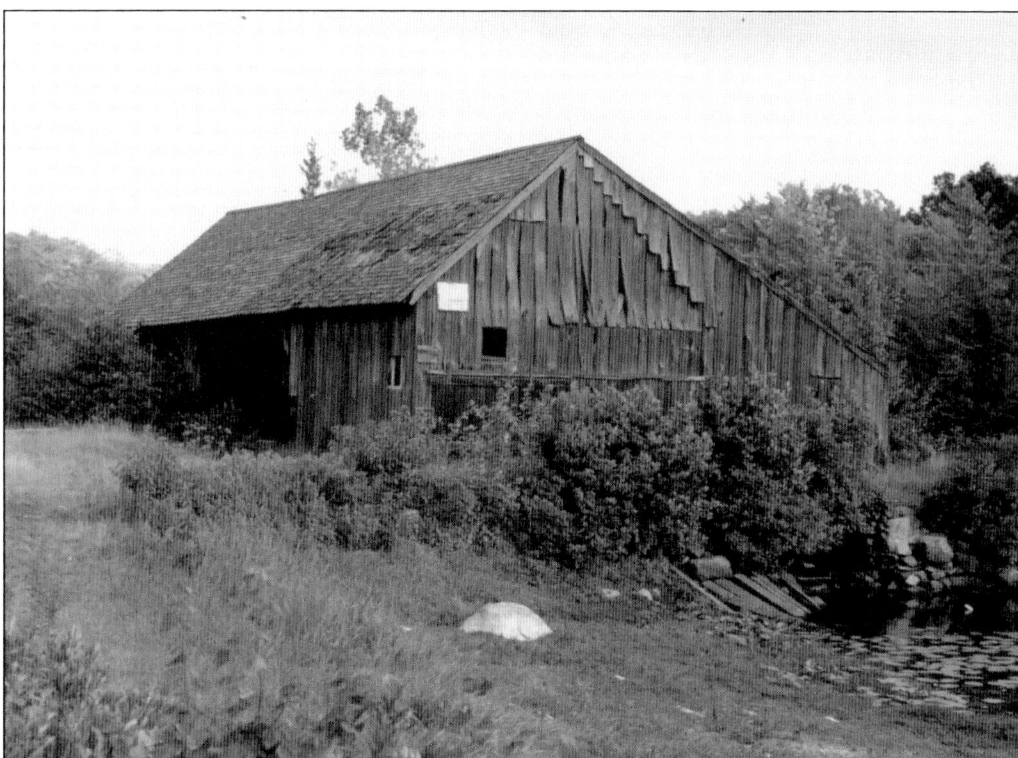

By the 1960s, the Main Sawmill had been inoperative and derelict for nearly 30 years. It was in this condition when the town acquired the property.

Wendell Comrie, who restored the mill and put it back in operation, watches one of the first logs to be cut into lumber.

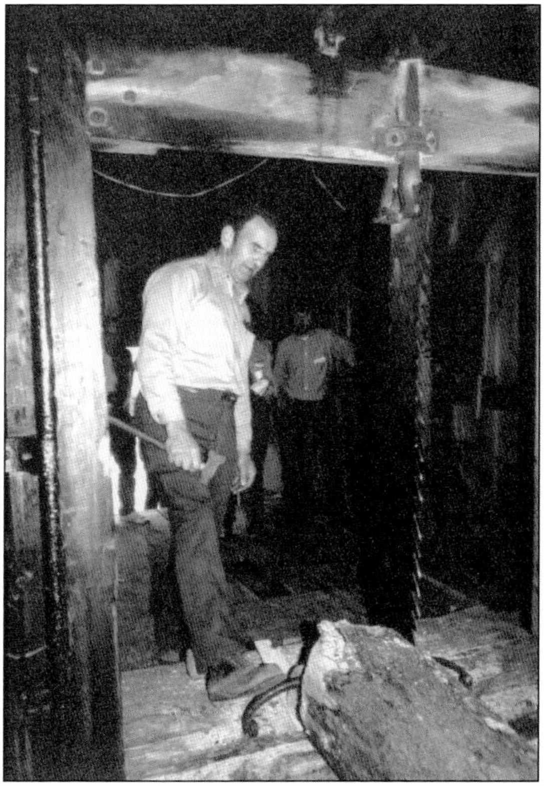

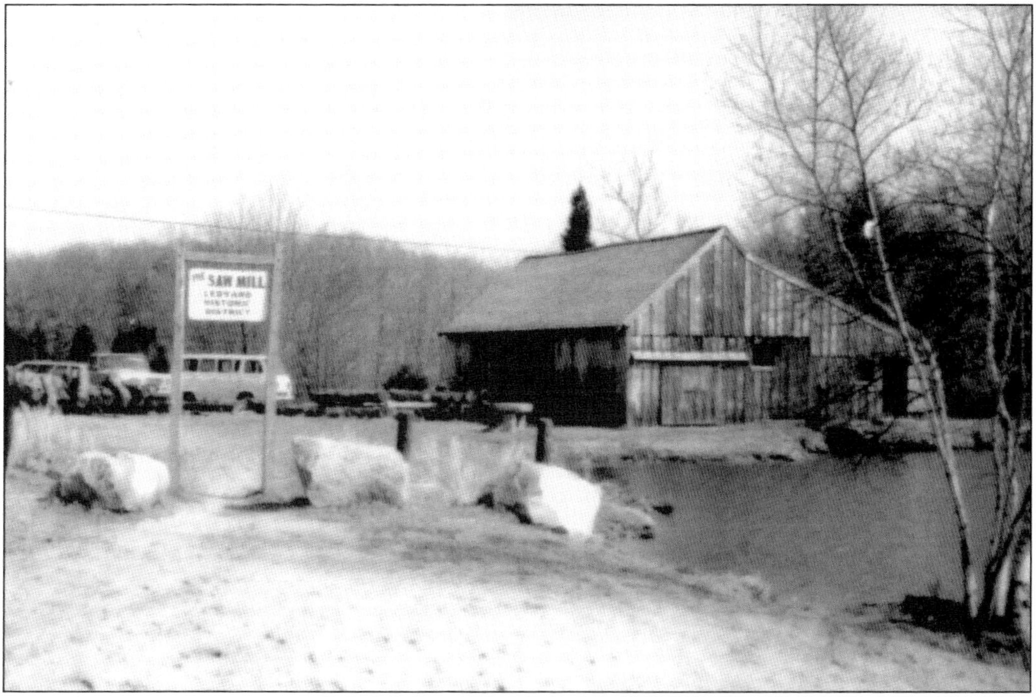

The Main Sawmill was acquired by the town of Ledyard and restored in the early 1970s. It is now part of a town historic district.

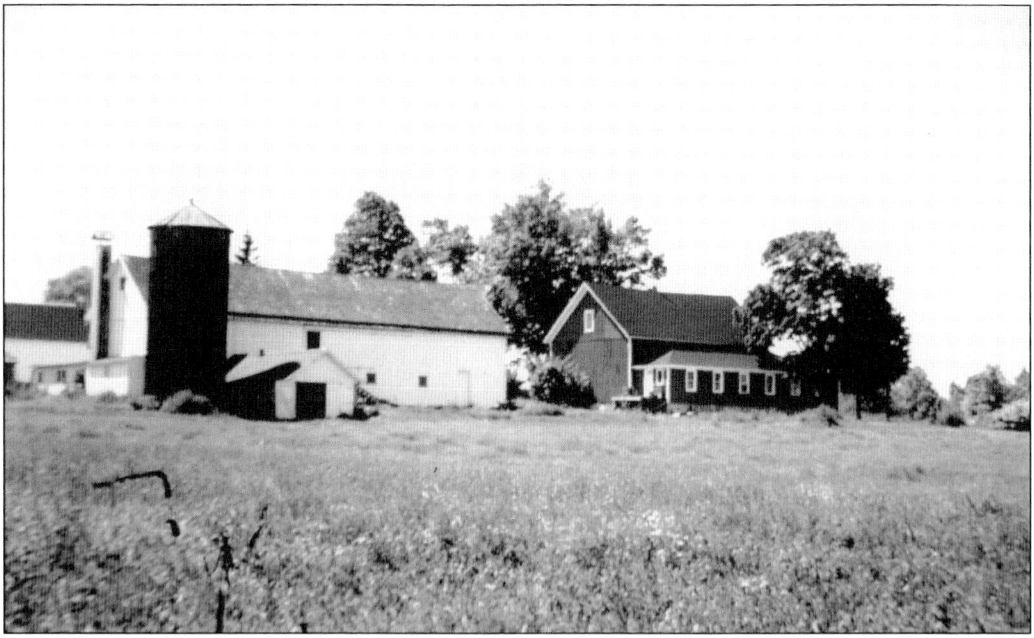

The Fred Allyn farm, on Colonel Ledyard Highway, is owned by descendants of Israel Allyn and is the property from which Israel's son William I. Allyn conducted his business as Ledyard town clerk. This 1964 photograph depicts a scene that has nearly vanished from the Ledyard landscape. The farm, which grows hay and apples, is still in the Allyn family.

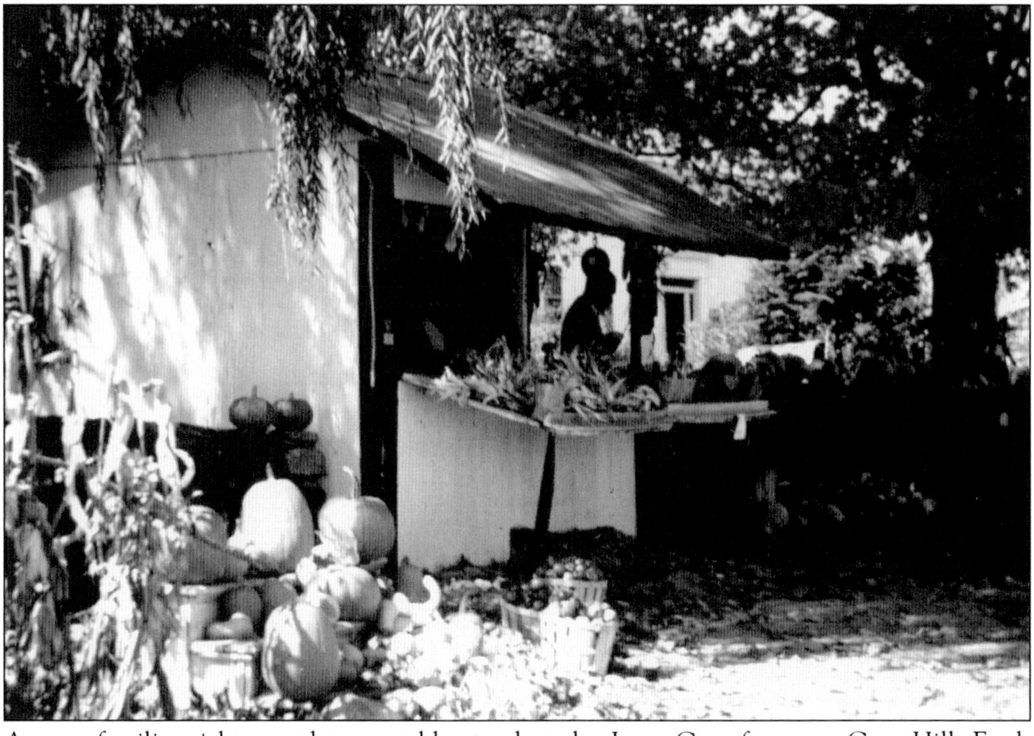

A once familiar sight was the vegetable stand at the Isaac Geer farm, on Geer Hill. Fresh produce is still available at roadside but not on Geer Hill. This photograph is from 1964.

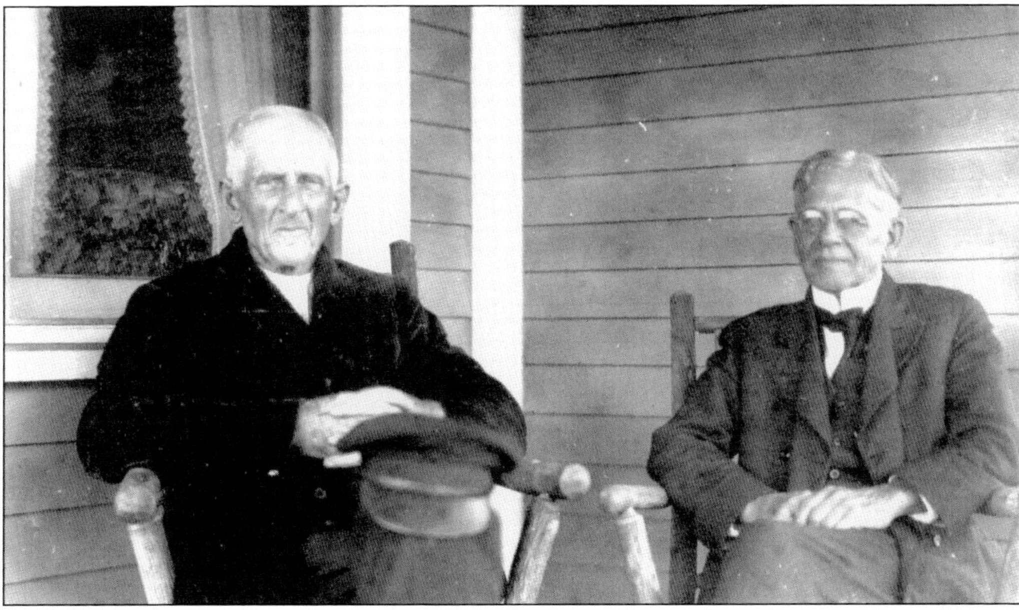

Noyes Billings Allyn was the son of a whaling captain, a man of some wealth, and an influential force in village affairs. His property, inherited from his father, encompassed a large tract near the river on Hurlbutt Road. Here, Allyn (left) chats with his neighbor, Rev. Allen Shaw Bush, on Bush's porch at Gales Ferry in 1918.

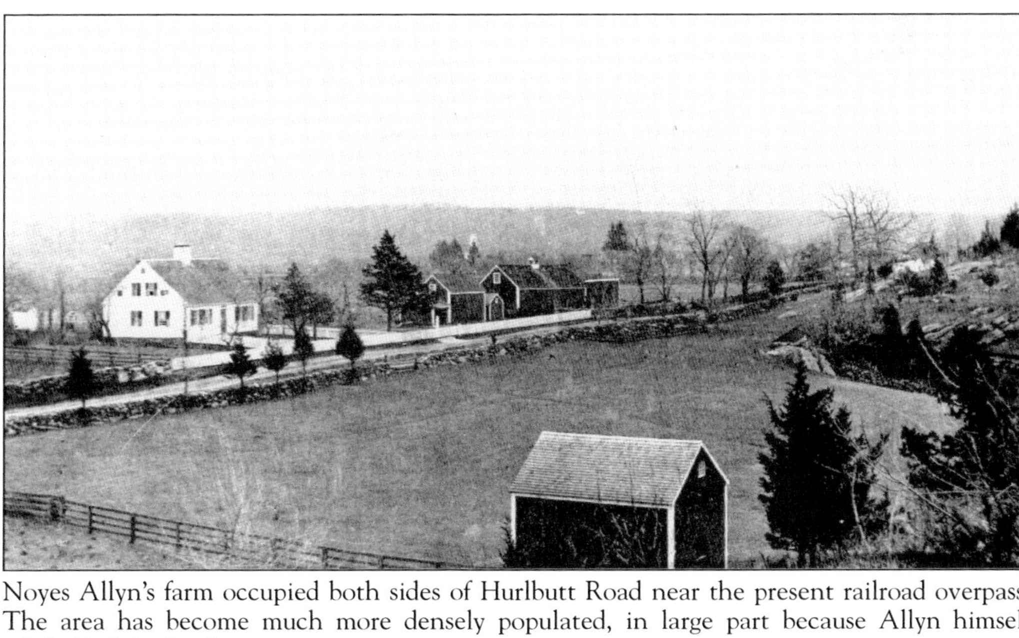

Noyes Allyn's farm occupied both sides of Hurlbutt Road near the present railroad overpass. The area has become much more densely populated, in large part because Allyn himself subdivided the land.

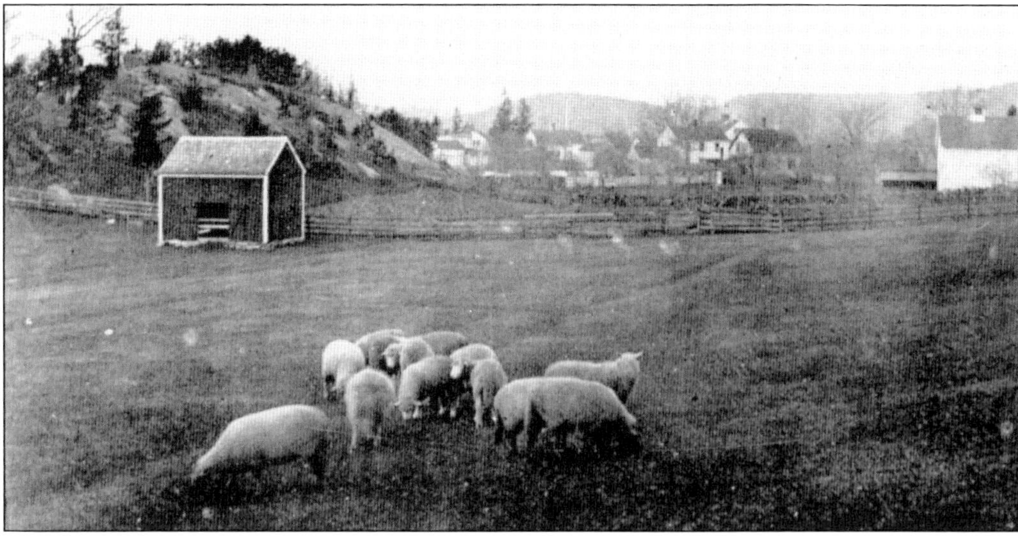

A gentleman farmer, Noyes Allyn kept a herd of sheep at his Hurlbutt Road property. This view is looking west toward the river.

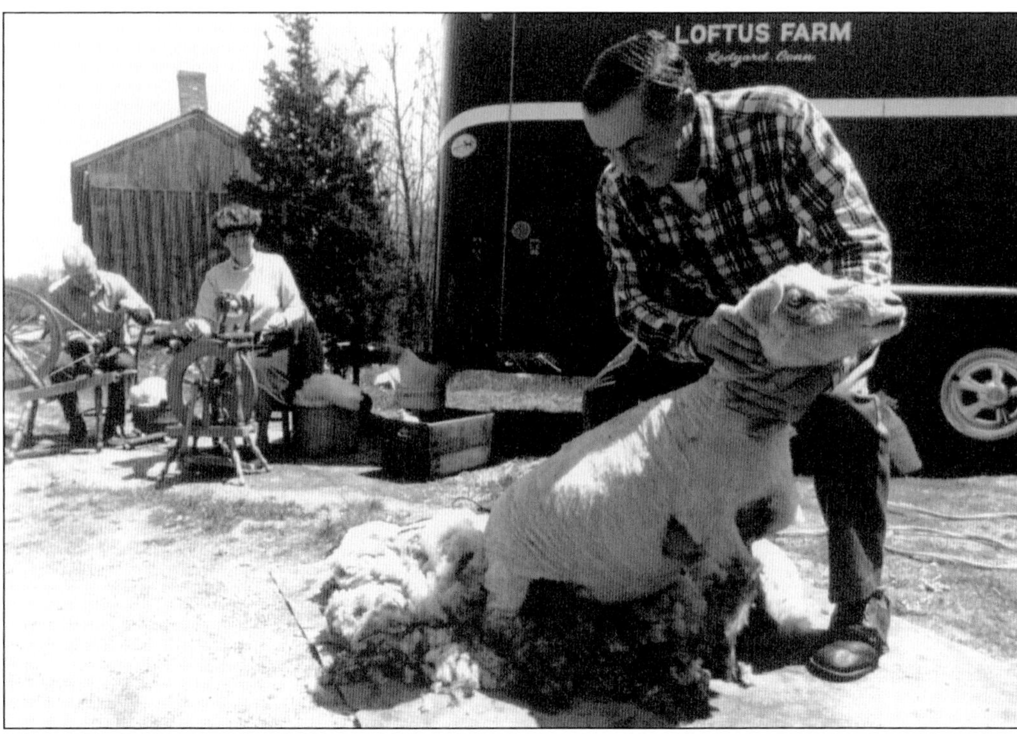

Although few Ledyard residents still live off the land, a few practitioners of ancient arts keep the crafts alive. Here, Gilbert "Gib" Hagen (right) finishes shearing a sheep while spinners make the wool into yarn.

Ten

Getting from Here to There

The development of towns invariably follows transportation, and so it has been with Ledyard. Road, river, and, more recently, rail have shaped the way the town has grown. The earliest settlements arose at the intersections of major roads and where the roads met the ferry at the river. Thus developed the Crossroads, the Center, and the Ferry.

The Norwich and Worcester Railroad reached Allyn's Point in 1844, and from that time, passenger steamers on the river met trains there. At that time, the most convenient way to reach Gales Ferry by rail was to disembark the train at Uncasville, on the west side of the Thames, and take the ferry across the river. In 1899, the New York, New Haven and Hartford Railroad, which had taken over the Norwich and Worcester, extended the line southward through Gales Ferry to Groton. Fifteen trains stopped daily at the Gales Ferry station. The extension of the railroad made redundant the steamer traffic on the Thames. In a like manner, the automobile gradually supplanted the train for local travel, and the station was closed in 1927. Passenger service on the line survived until the 1970s, and today the Providence and Worcester Railroad runs frequent freight service on the line.

The north-south road on the western side of town was Military Highway, from "the Drawbridge" at Poquetanuck Cove to what is now the naval submarine base in Groton. During World War II, in response to rapid expansion of the base, a new highway was built from Gales Ferry southward, farther to the east. This is present Connecticut Route 12, at one point designated the busiest two-lane road in Connecticut. Increased development has changed what was once an open rural highway, on which one could traverse the town without stopping, to a congested route with turning lanes and traffic lights.

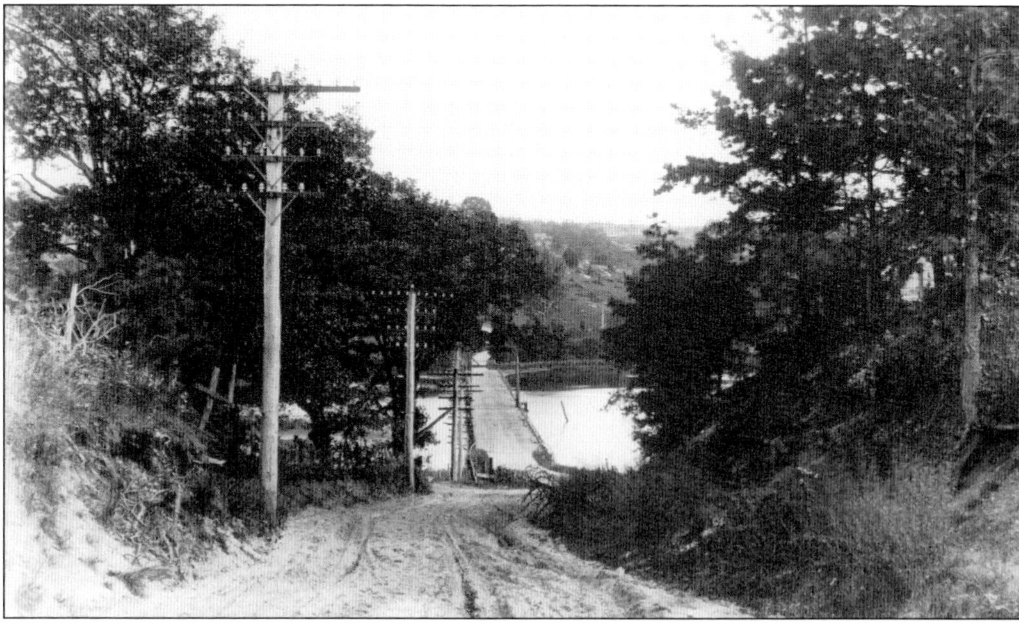

The northern approach to Gales Ferry crosses Poquetanuck Cove at the Drawbridge. Although the bridge has not "drawn" in recent memory, the name lives on. In 1871, the boundary between Ledyard and Preston was moved southward to the middle of the cove, making the neighboring town responsible for upkeep of half the bridge.

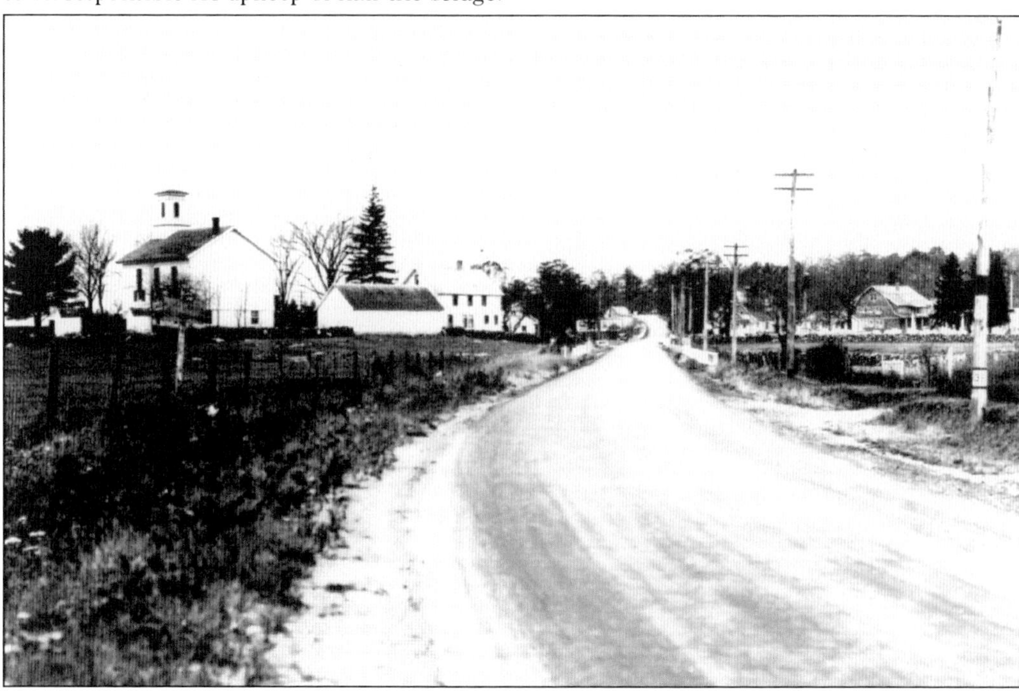

Now the hub of commercial Gales Ferry, the intersection of Military Highway and Hurlbutt Road was high, wide, and lonesome when this photograph was taken. The old Methodist church is prominent, with carriage shed behind and the 1928 parsonage next door. The present Gales Ferry Post Office is located in the area in the right foreground.

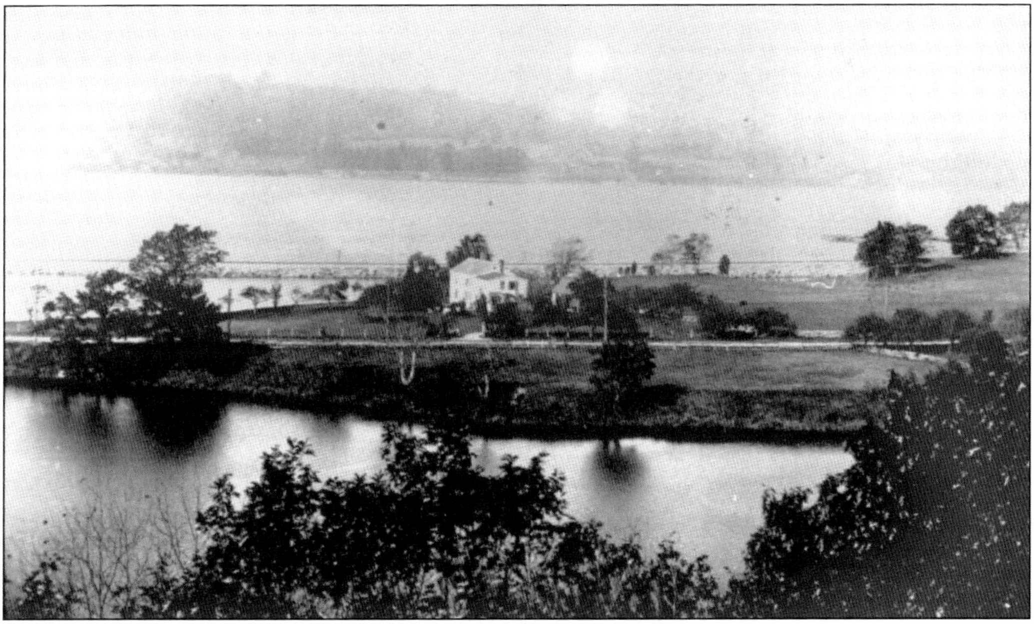

Looking due west from the ledge on what is now Inchcliffe Drive *c.* 1910, one sees the site of the icehouse, which later became the Riverbend Casino and later still Erickson's Store. The property is now a municipal waterfront park.

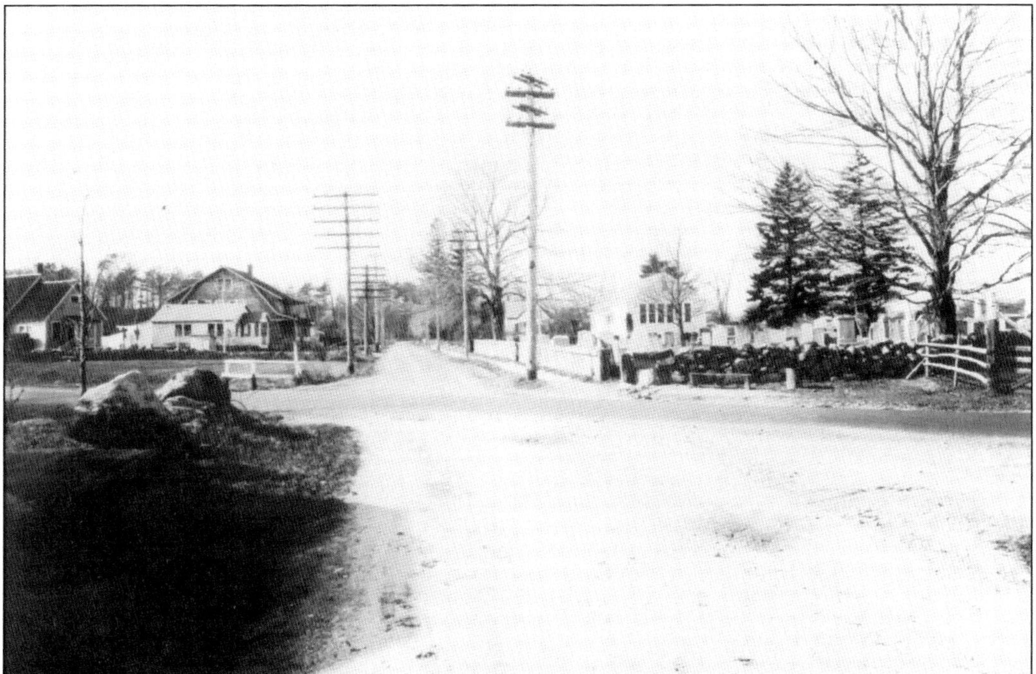

Approaching the Military-Hurlbutt intersection from the east, one sees the two-room school behind the cemetery to the right. Today, the memorial parklet is located at the far left corner of this photograph.

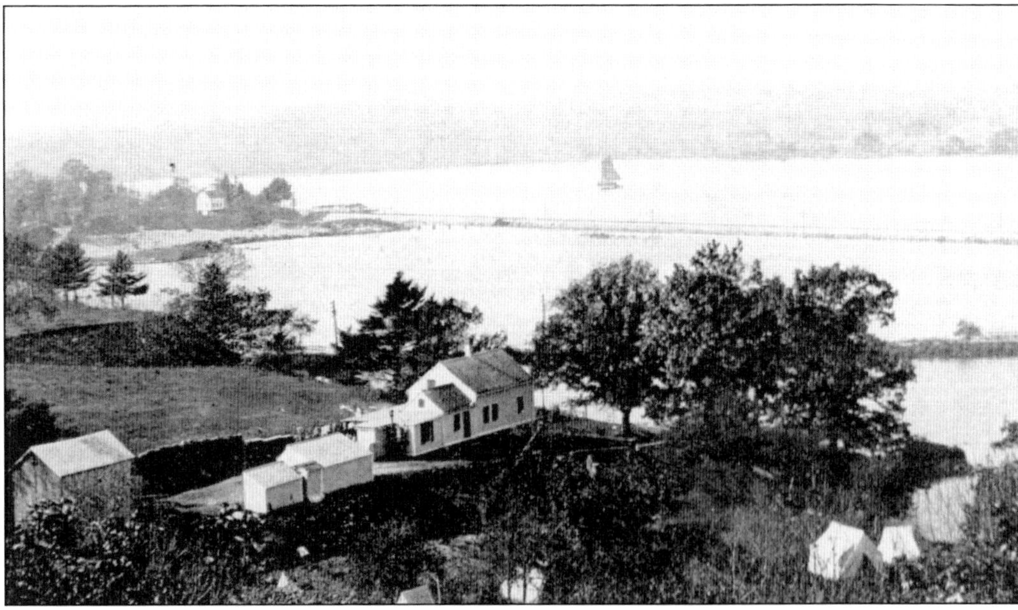

Long Cove is one of several Ledyard locations where road meets rail, which in turn meets river. The far causeway is the rail line; the road causeway for Military Highway can just be seen through the trees. A lone sailboat heads south toward the sea.

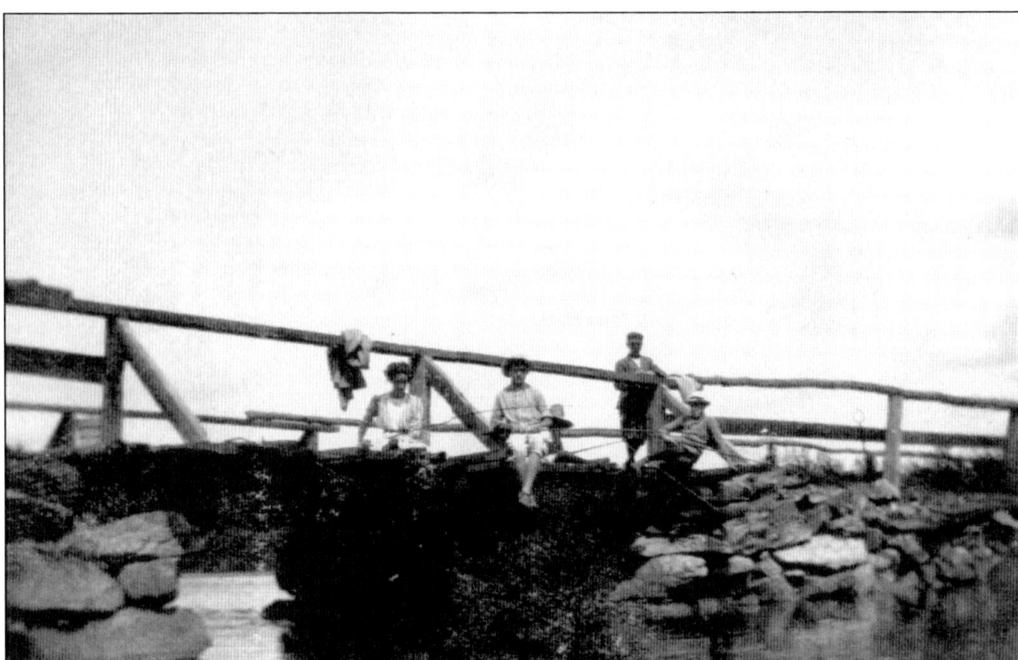

The Wulf children and their friends fish for "young blues" at the Long Cove bridge on Military Highway in 1906. Pictured here are, from left to right, Ruth, Oli, Helene, Ed, and Bob.

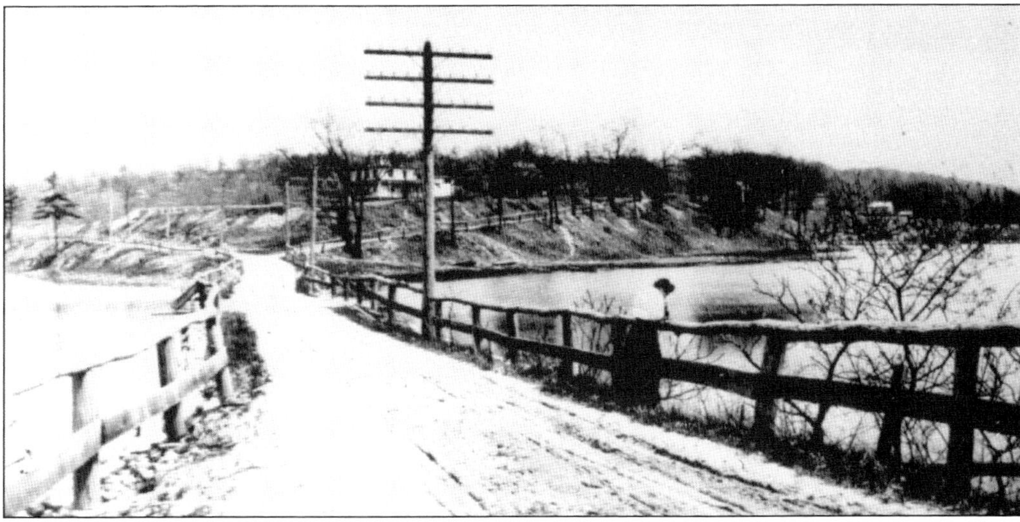

Military Highway crossed Long Cove on a rickety bridge. The Italianate Charles Stoddard house can be seen behind the telegraph pole. The woman may be taking a photograph.

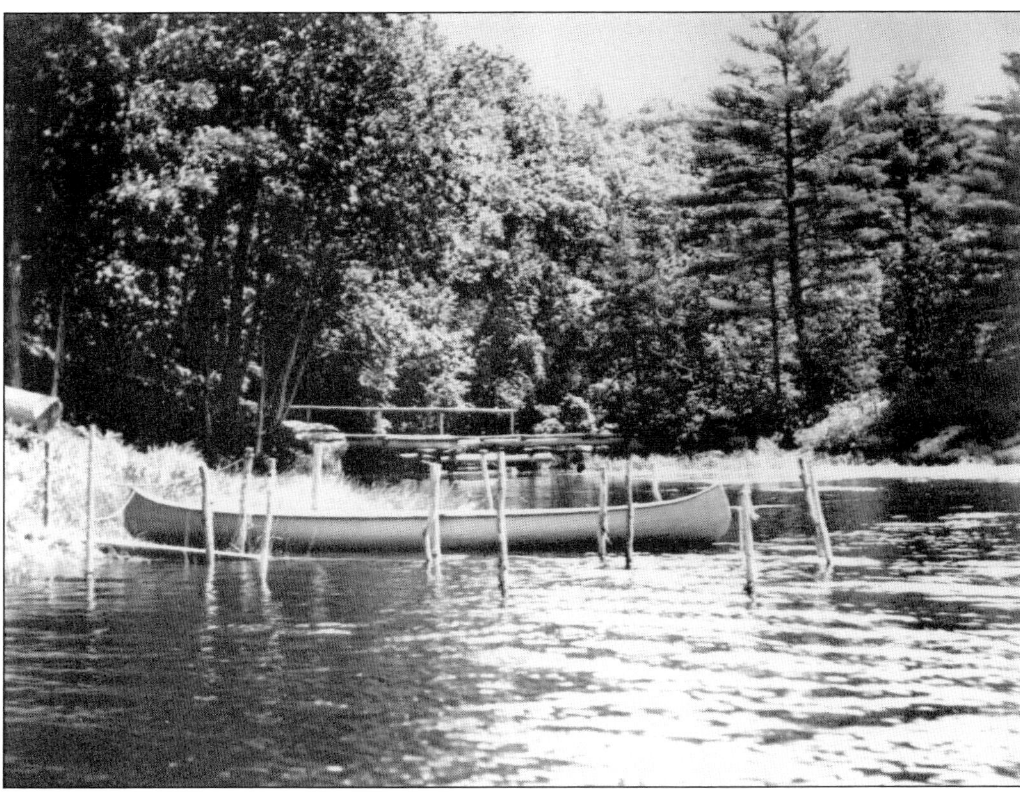

A canoe seems a placid form of transport in the headwaters of Long Cove. The bridge forms the original access to the section now known as Pinelock.

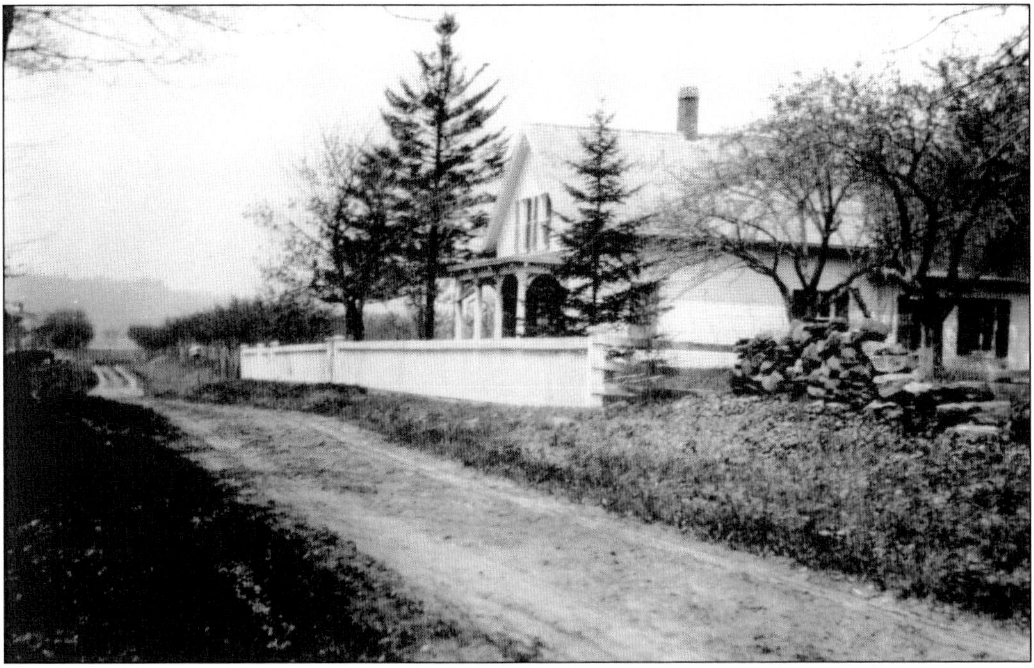

Many of today's improved town roads were once sandy lanes. Long Cove Road was just such a lane when this photograph was taken, although the house, built *c.* 1869 by George Bailey, looked much the same behind its white picket fence as it does today.

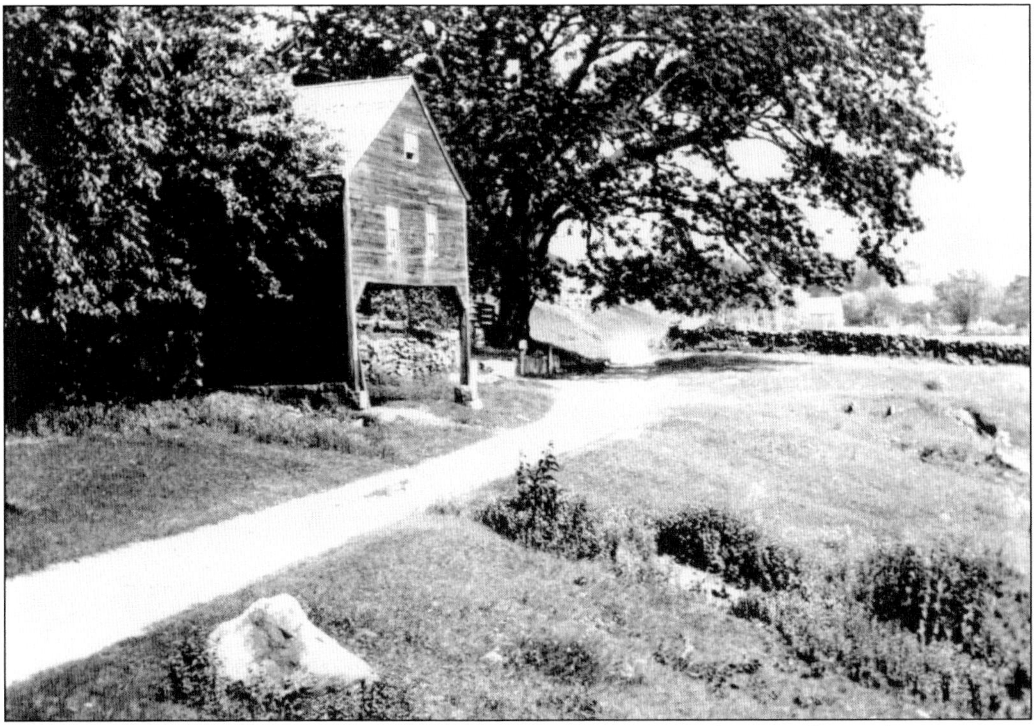

The upper reach of Long Cove Road passes the Richards stable. The spreading oak tree was cut down only in the 1990s.

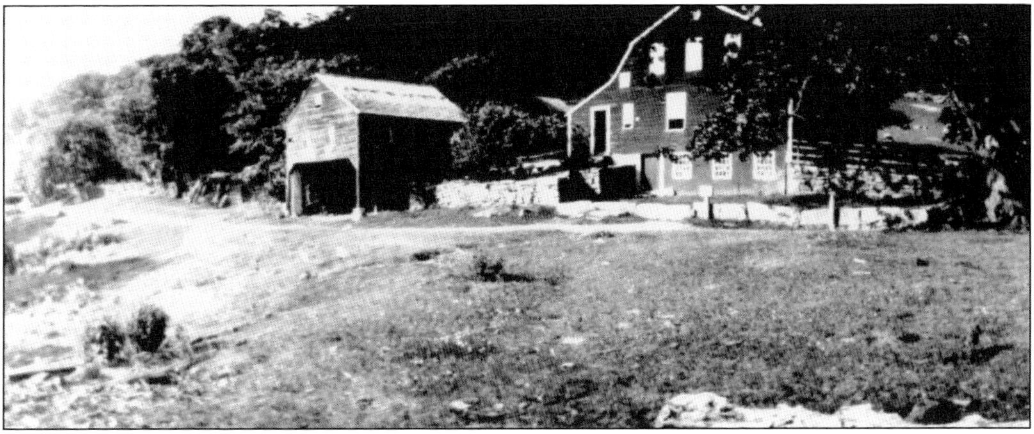

Seen here are the Richards house and stable on Long Cove Road. This house and the adjacent sawmill were owned by Benjamin Bill Jr., a veteran of the Battle of Groton Heights, from 1783 to 1792. The sawmill was later owned by Charles Stoddard and subsequently by George Bailey.

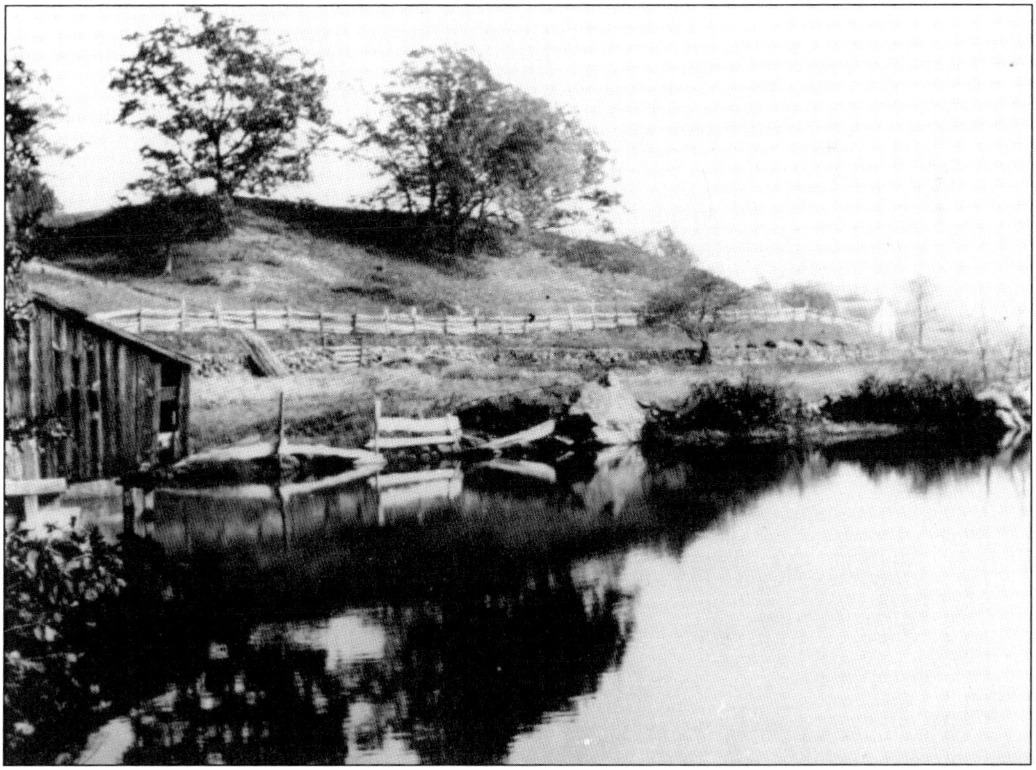

Oak trees overlook the millpond at the Stoddard Sawmill on Long Cove Road. The Long Cove School can just be seen to the right.

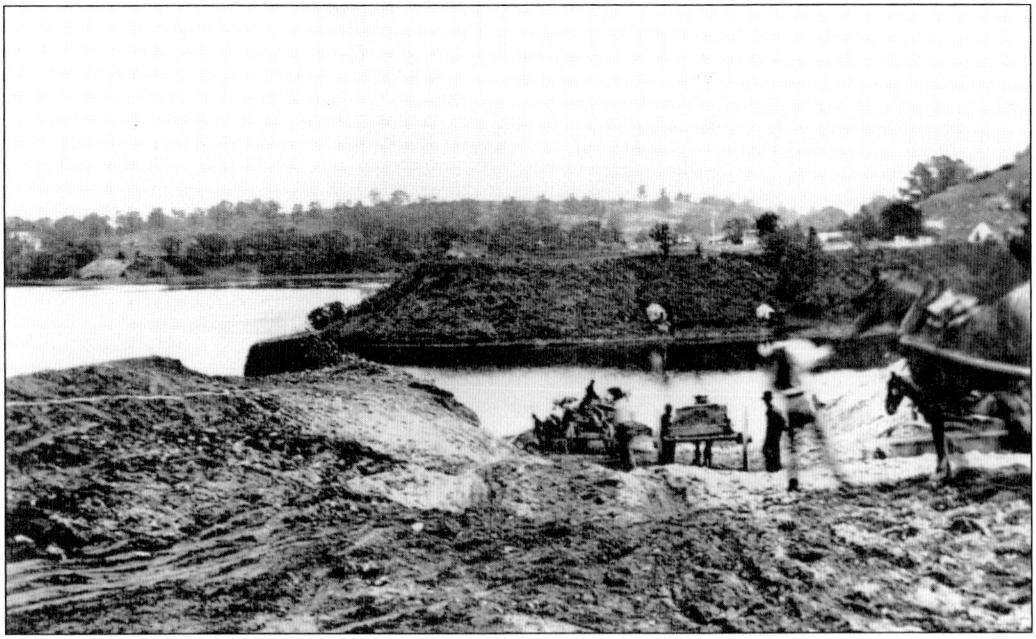

In 1898, the New York, New Haven and Hartford Railroad finally began to extend the rail line from Allyn's Point southward to Groton. Much work by beasts, wagons, and men was required to bridge Clark's Cove just north of the Ferry. The first train passed through the village in 1899.

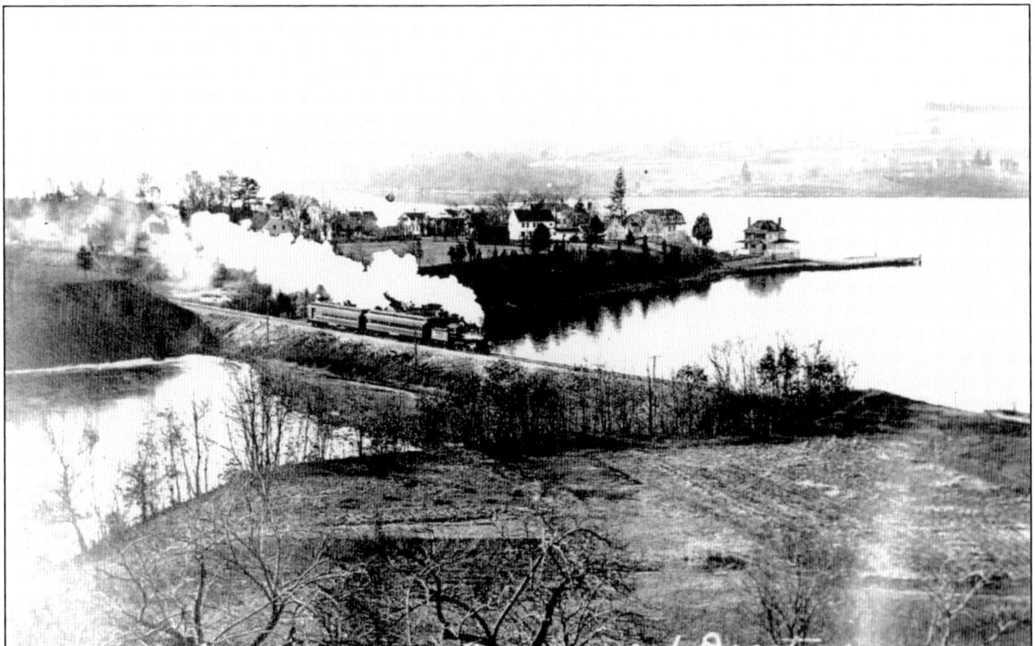

By 1900, 15 trains stopped daily at Gales Ferry. Here, a passenger train crosses the recently completed causeway across the mouth of Clark's Cove on December 17, 1912.

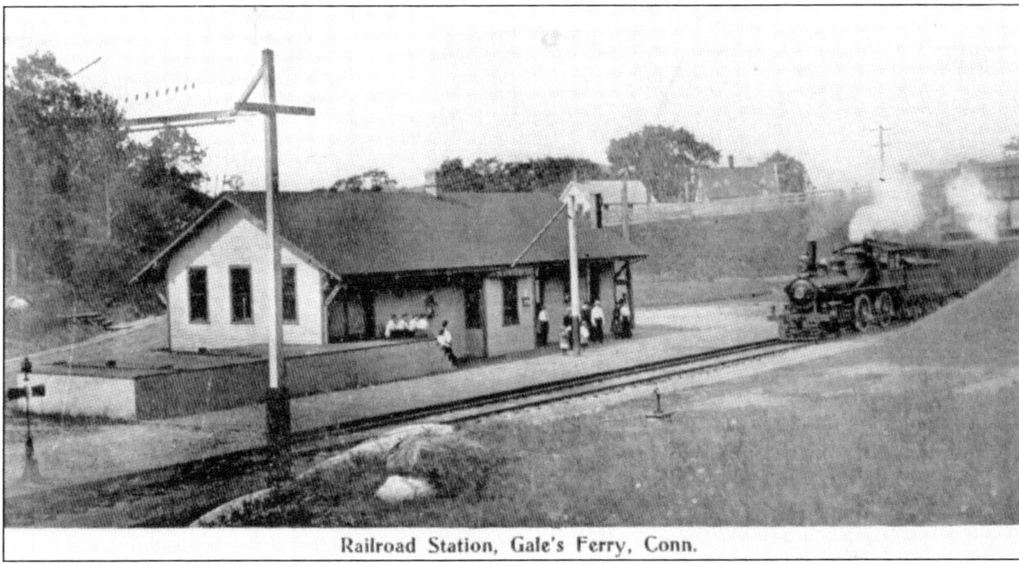

Gales Ferry had the only fully equipped station on the lower end of the Norwich-Groton line. This postcard view shows a train arriving from the north for waiting passengers.

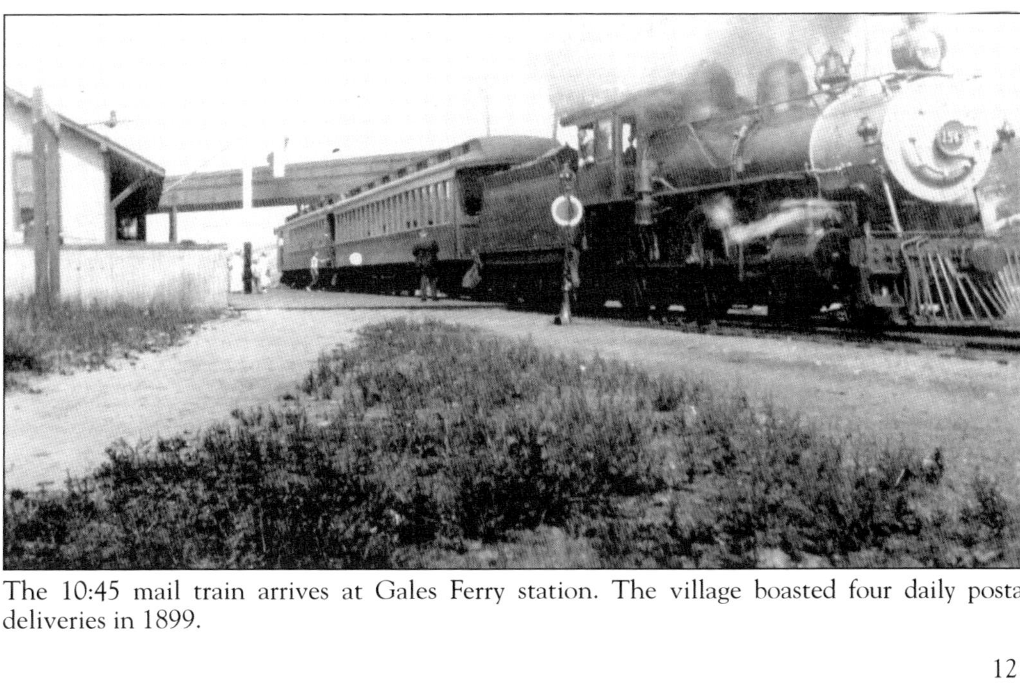

The 10:45 mail train arrives at Gales Ferry station. The village boasted four daily postal deliveries in 1899.

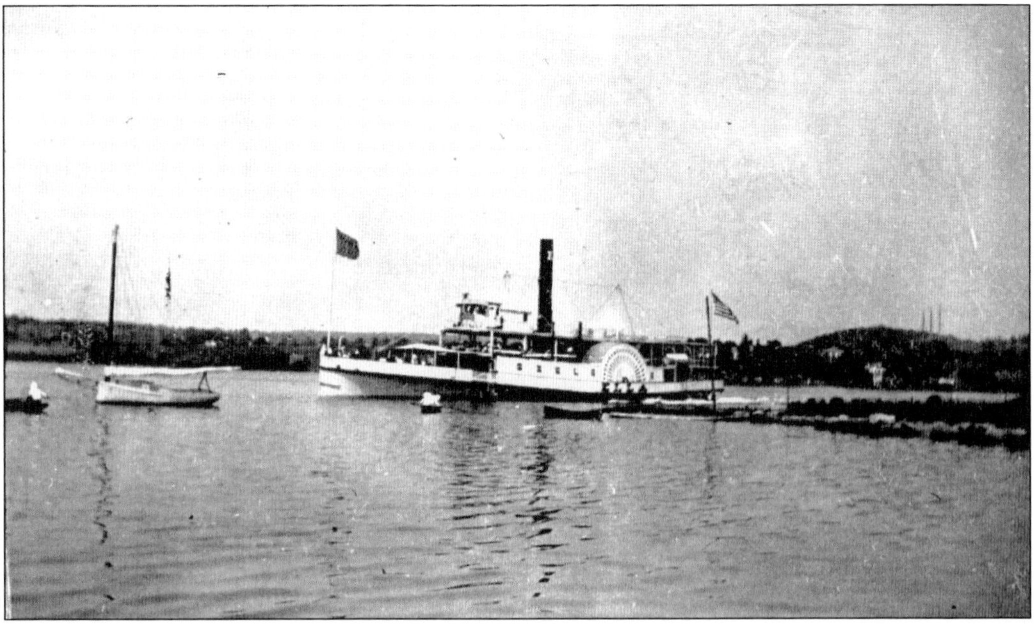

The side-wheeler *Ella* was a popular form of transportation from Norwich southward on the river. Here, it docks at Upper Wharf in Gales Ferry.

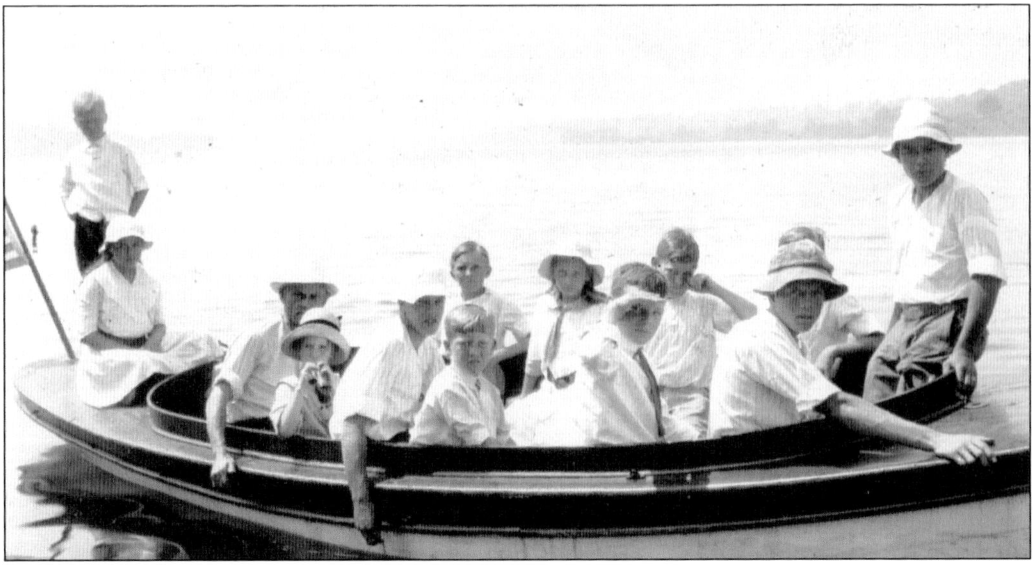

Riverside residents used the waterway for transportation. The *Togo*, a launch belonging to a family on the Bluff, was often used for excursions and for watching the Harvard-Yale Regatta.

Small water craft frequented the Thames, too. This pensive canoeist is Allen DuMont, later a pioneer in the development of television.

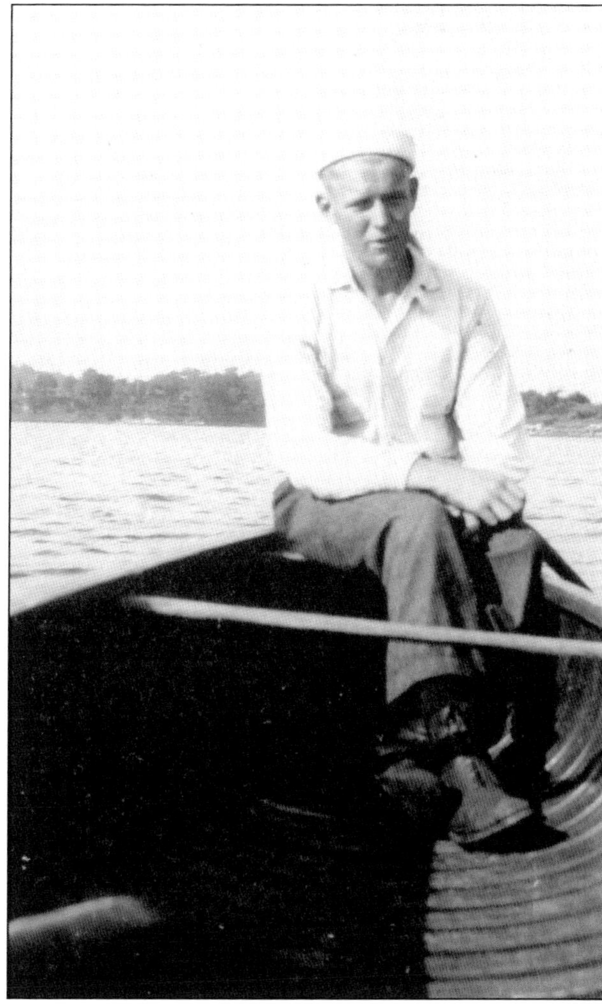

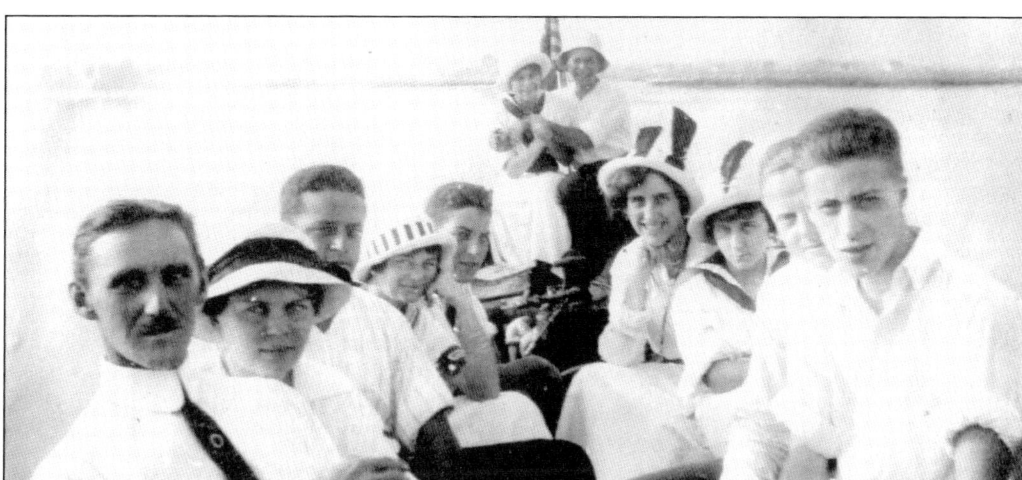

A partying crowd enjoys the return from New London on the *Togo* c. 1918.

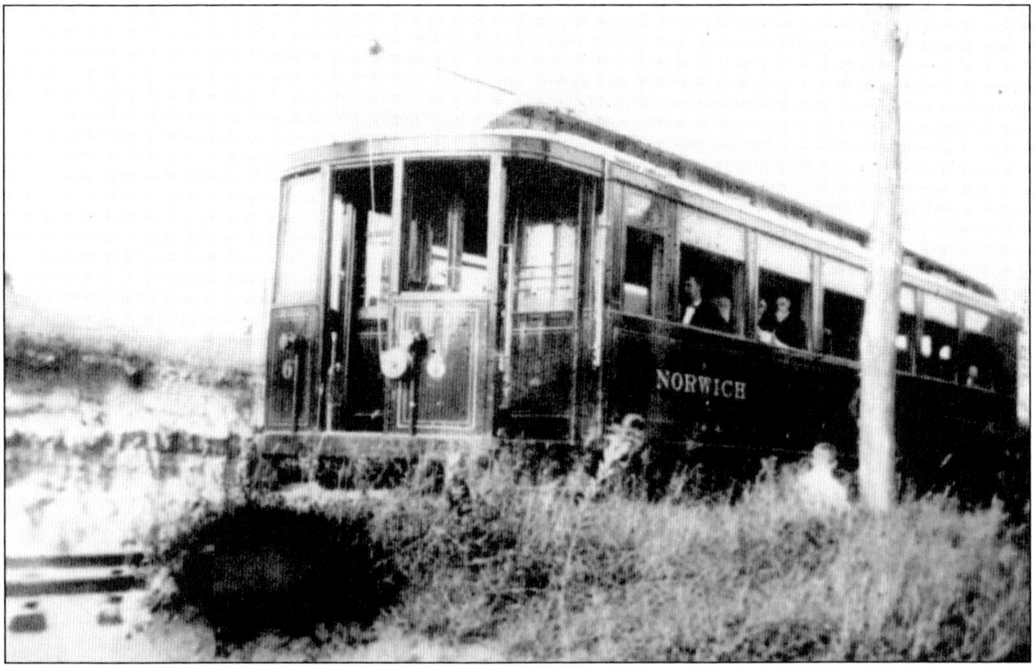

The northeast corner of Ledyard was on the Norwich-Westerly trolley line. Southeastern Connecticut had an extensive, though short-lived, trolley network.

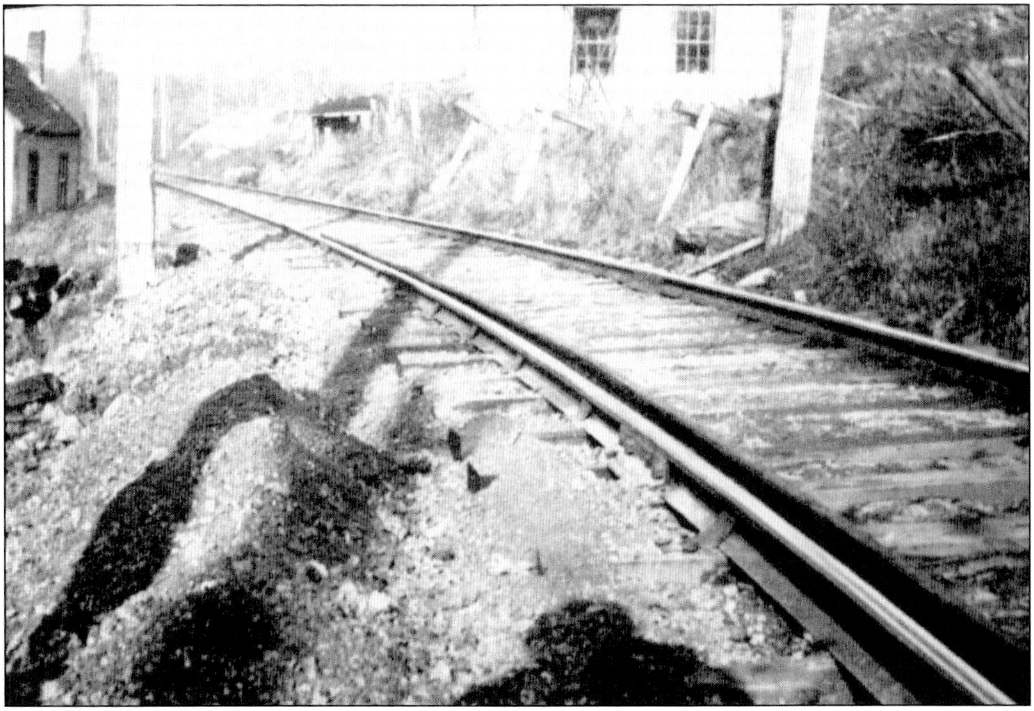

The trolley line through Ledyard ran close to present Route 2.

The tracks from the Norwich-Westerly trolley are long gone, but the roadbed can be seen at several locations near the present Foxwoods Resort Casino.

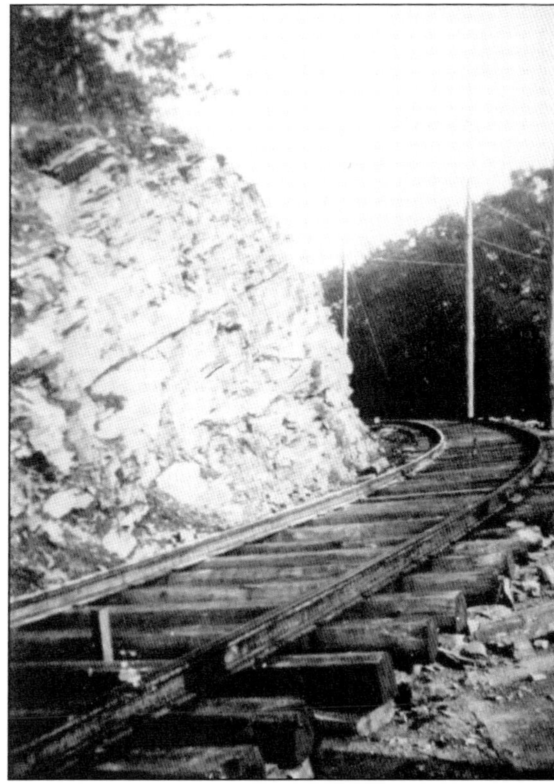

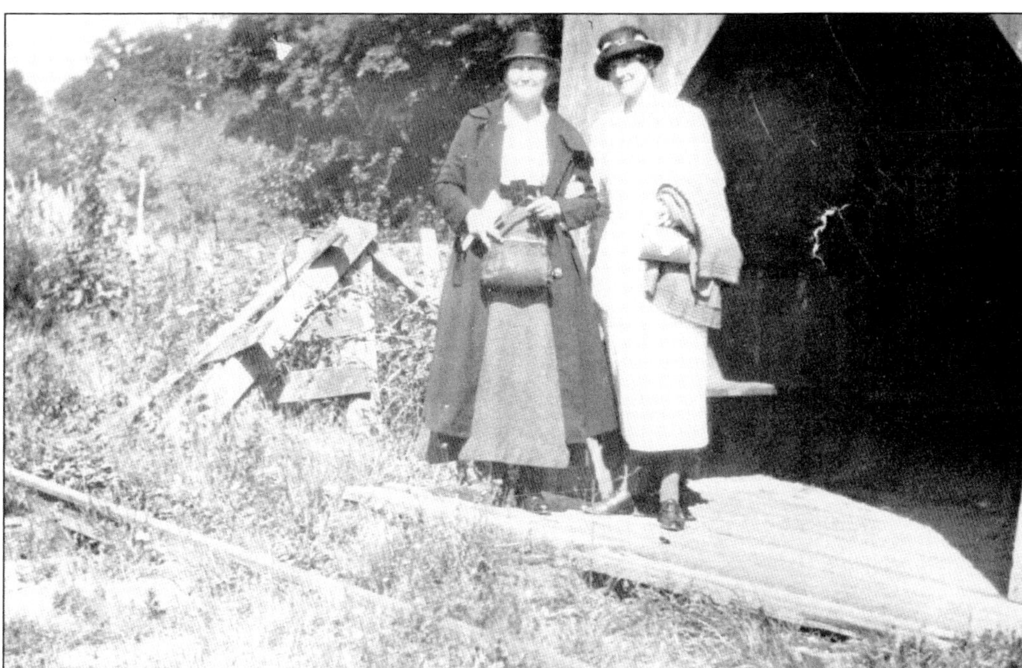

Two ladies are ostensibly waiting at a shelter for the next trolley. The overgrown and rusty rails, however, suggest they are several years too late.

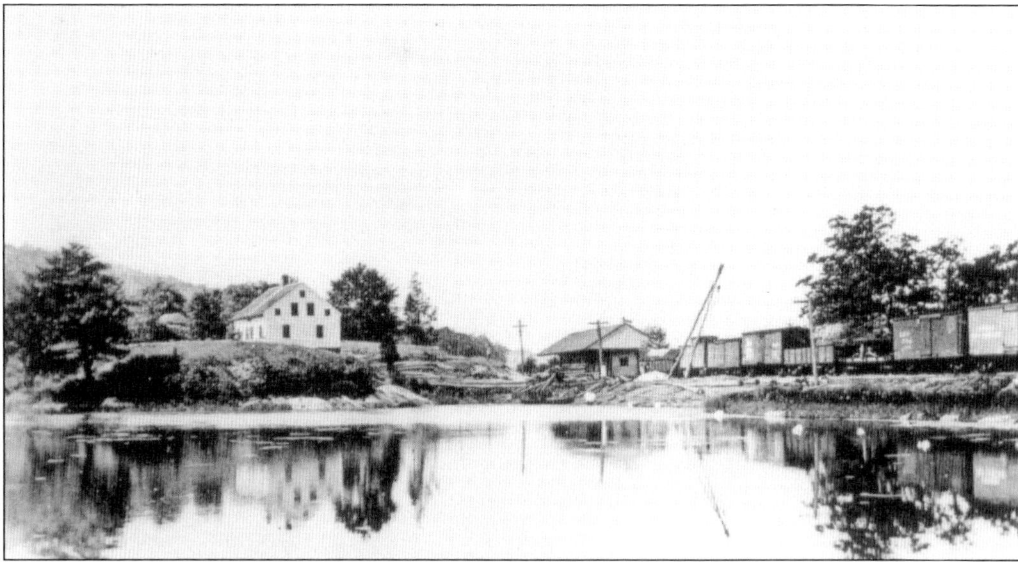

From 1844 to 1899, Allyn's Point was the southern terminus of the rail line. Here, both passenger and coaling met the trains and exchanged their cargo. This view looking south shows the Thomas Allyn house, now relocated to Route 12, and the Allyn's Point station.

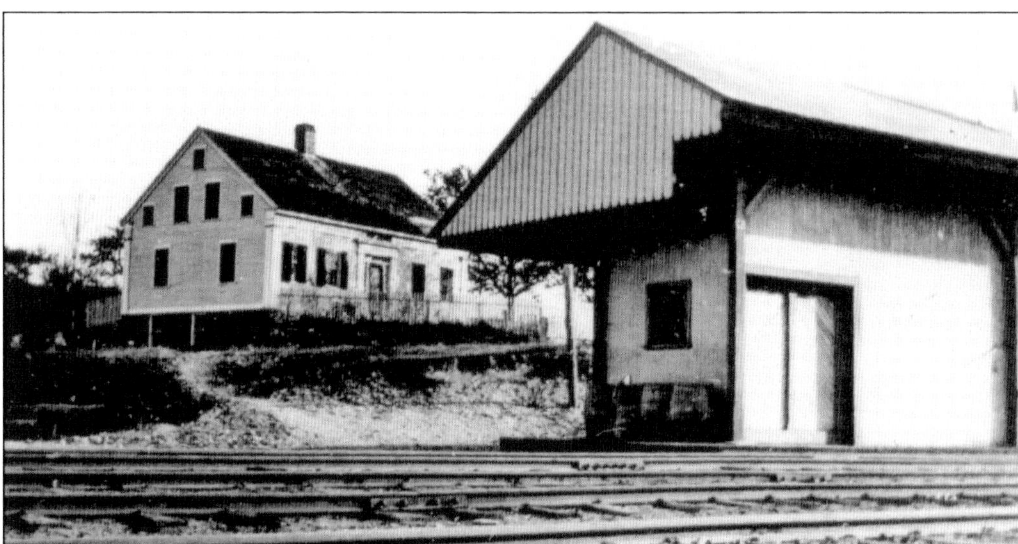

Looking upward past the station, one sees the familiar view of the Thomas Allyn house. The house served as a post office after the coming of the railroad.

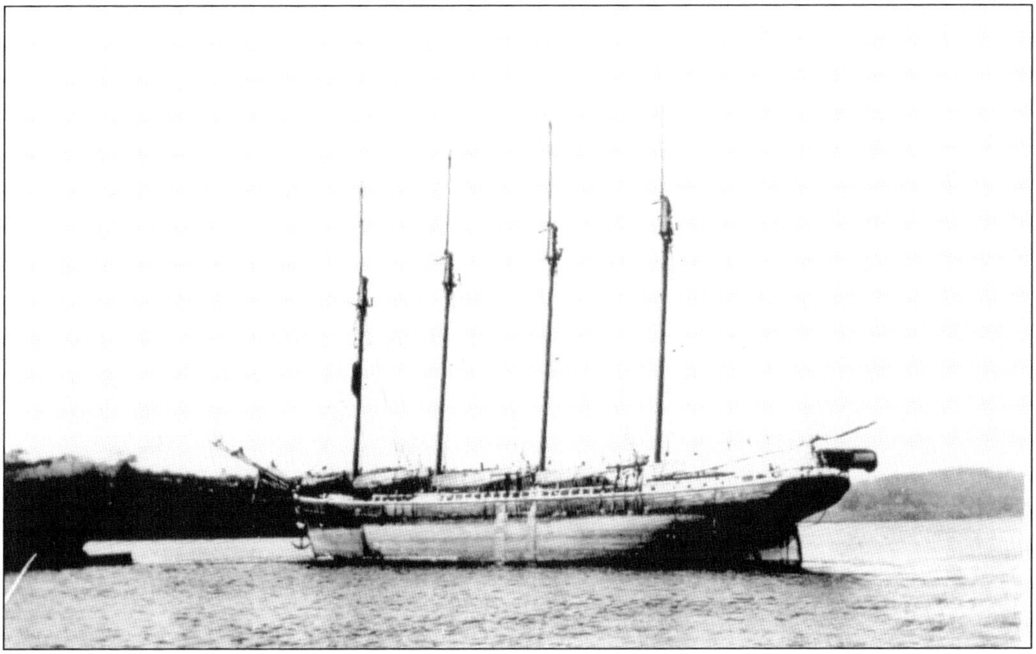

A four-masted coaler lies at anchor off Allyn's Point. The Point was a principal port for offloading coal for shipment north by rail.

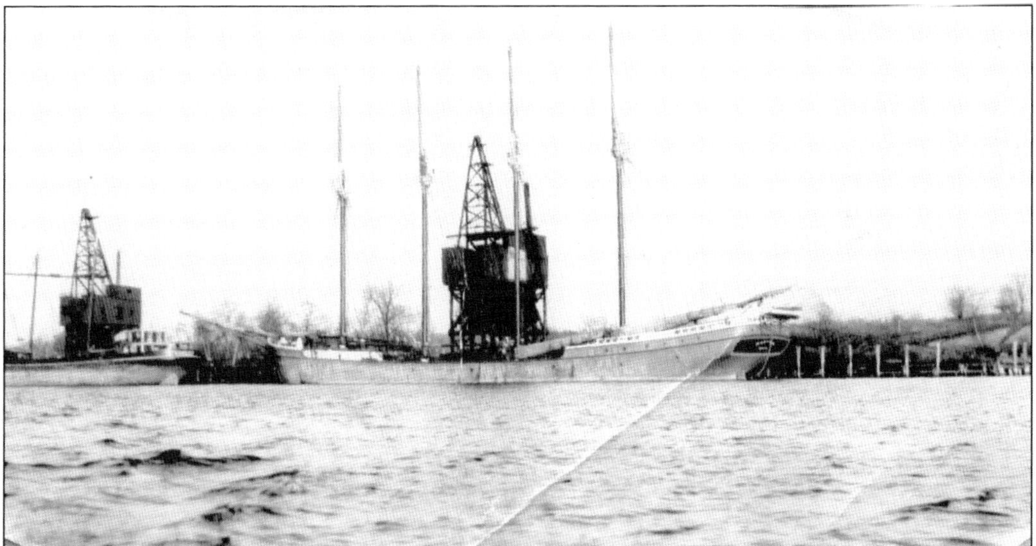

The quay at Allyn's Point was long enough to unload several coalers simultaneously. Huge gantry cranes lifted coal off to waiting rail cars.

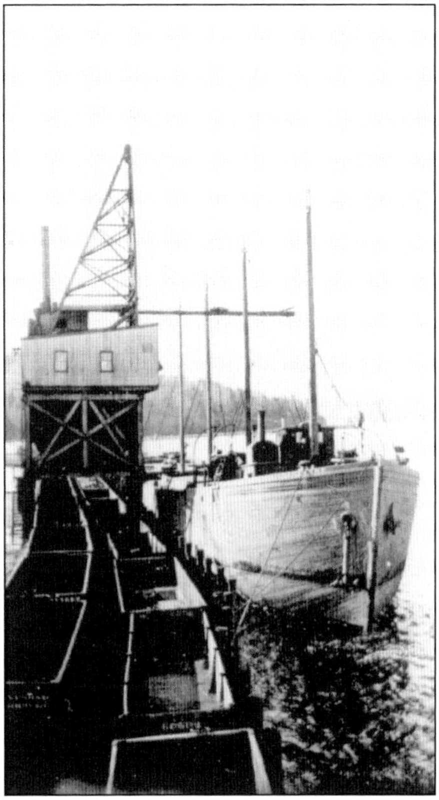

A double-track rail line on the Allyn's Point pier allowed fast unloading of the coal ships. Several could tie up at one time.

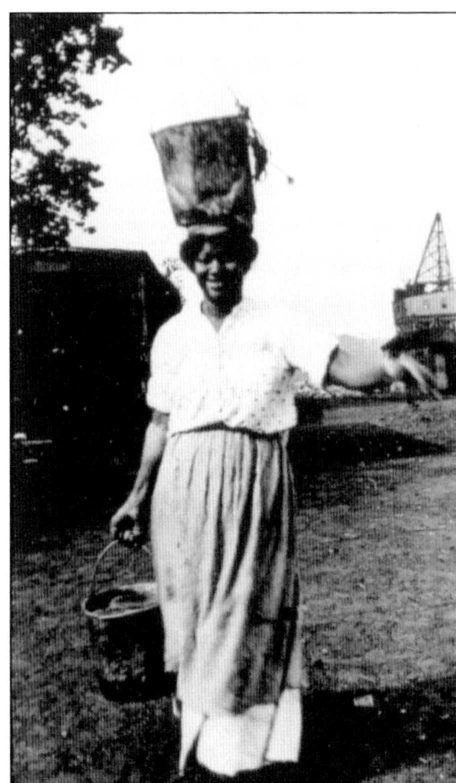

A community of Cape Verdean immigrants made Allyn's Point a cosmopolitan neighborhood in the early part of the 20th century. This woman demonstrates a high degree of balance and coordination.